THE
GRIFTER'S
CLUB

THE GRIFTER'S CLUB

TRUMP, MAR-A-LAGO, AND THE SELLING OF THE PRESIDENCY

Sarah Blaskey, Nicholas Nehamas,
Caitlin Ostroff & Jay Weaver

PublicAffairs
New York

PublicAffairs
Hachette Book Group
1290 Avenue of the Americas, New York, NY 10104
www.publicaffairsbooks.com
@Public_Affairs

Printed in the United States of America

First Edition: August 2020

Published by PublicAffairs, an imprint of Perseus Books, LLC, a subsidiary of Hachette Book Group, Inc. The PublicAffairs name and logo is a trademark of the Hachette Book Group.

The Hachette Speakers Bureau provides a wide range of authors for speaking events. To find out more, go to www.hachettespeakersbureau.com or call (866) 376-6591.

The publisher is not responsible for websites (or their content) that are not owned by the publisher.

Editorial production by Christine Marra, Marrathon Production Services. www.marrathoneditorial.org

Book design by Jane Raese
Set in 12-point Bulmer

Library of Congress Cataloging-in-Publication Data has been applied for.

ISBN 978-1-5417-5695-3 (hardcover), ISBN 978-1-5417-5696-0 (ebook)

LSC-H

10 9 8 7 6 5 4 3 2 1

In loving memory of Mary Wells.
Without her wit, humor, and steady hand
this book would never have been written.

CONTENTS

Prologue

INTRUDER AT THE WHITE HOUSE

IT WAS A WARM AFTERNOON in late March as two intruders stepped onto the grounds of the White House.

It wasn't the secure compound in Washington, DC. Rather, it was the Winter White House—Mar-a-Lago—the gilded palace on the fabulously wealthy South Florida island of Palm Beach that President Donald J. Trump calls home. In its maze of rooms and walls decorated with Genovese Doria stone, colorful Spanish tiles, ornate Venetian tapestries, and marble from Cuba, the unexpected leader of the free world holds court with an odd assortment of billionaires and crooks, conspiracy theorists and political fixers.[1]

On March 30, 2019, one of the intruders came walking down the beach.[2] He stepped onto the club's pool deck, located in front of the luxurious beach penthouse where the president's senior advisor Ivanka Trump and her family stay when they are in town.[3] It was under this same pool's white-and-banana-yellow-striped umbrellas, within full earshot of other guests, that the First Daughter once jealously demanded that her young children tell her they loved her more than the nanny who raised them.[4]

The midday sun was baking the skin of millionaires at Mar-a-Lago's Beach Club when the man arrived. Socialites peeked out from under the brims of their floppy sun hats as they sipped coconut water through lips plumped with hyaluronic acid fillers. Few could look more out of place in the WASP-y beachfront enclave of Palm Beach than the man, who was large enough to prompt double-takes from most passers-by and had a tribal tattoo stamped across one side of his face.

He was impossible to miss as he walked onto a property guarded by Secret Service agents and local law enforcement officers typically stationed near the pool. The agents and officers formed part of the outer ring of security protecting the estate of the president—who at that moment was out golfing at his club in West Palm Beach four miles away.[5] The man was known to be physically dangerous and had a long rap sheet, including multiple arrests for violent crimes. He could have walked in with a gun or explosive device. However, no one stopped him. He never went through a metal detector. He entered the president's estate through the back door without even presenting an ID.[6]

But Mike Tyson didn't mean any harm. He liked the president.[7] And, as it happened, the club was facing what seemed a *real* security threat that day—a second intruder who revealed just how much can go wrong at the place the president formally declared his primary residence in late 2019.[8]

Tyson's intrusion was strange and fluky. In contrast, the other security breach was "nefarious," a federal magistrate judge would later proclaim from the bench. But neither incident was at all hard to predict. They were both the result of the president's choice to spend so much of his time at a private club that almost anyone can enter with the right friends or enough money. At Mar-a-Lago, almost anyone can get near Trump.

It's a reality that has Secret Service agents tearing out their hair.[9]

Whereas the White House in DC is one of the most secure compounds in the world, the Winter White House is invitingly porous. Yet throughout his presidency, Trump has insisted on spending more than one month of each year at the club chatting up members and their guests.[10]

Trump has little incentive to heed caution in his interactions with strangers at his club. Hobnobbing at Mar-a-Lago is great for business, after all.

The simple chance to bump into the president sells six-figure club memberships better than any marketing campaign ever could. The number of guests entering the club on Saturday nights exploded after the 2016 election, and the club quickly approached its top membership capacity. An entire industry of online vendors peddling access to the president sprang up around the club almost overnight. On social media, grifters targeted wealthy, social-climbing individuals overseas with "meet the president" travel packages.

Safety is the top concern at the White House. But money is number one at Trump's Mar-a-Lago. Money is also numbers two and three.

In comparison, security hardly seems to factor in, especially when the president isn't in town, unless it's to keep pesky journalists off the property. Even though staffers were once warned to be on the lookout for a reporter sniffing around their apartment building asking for interviews, they say they are not informed about intruders or suspicious incidents, even in cases when someone is arrested.[11]

With dollar signs in his eyes, the president is all but holding the door open for would-be intruders.

"It's a mad, mad world up there," one senior federal law enforcement official says of Mar-a-Lago.[12]

By January 2020 there had been 141 reports of suspicious incidents and trespassers at Mar-a-Lago since Trump won the Republican nomination—triple the number from the previous three and a half years.[13] Most never resulted in charges, but tucked into court records are examples of alarming security breaches.

In the early morning on Trump's Inauguration Day a disgruntled, forty-eight-year-old woman snuck through the bushes on the northern side of the property, smeared banana on the windows of cars in the employee parking lot, typed "FuckUTrumpB" on a computer in the club's Cloister Bar, and snatched balloons from the grand ballroom.[14] She was arrested after an hour-long romp around the property, during which security tried and failed to turn her away.

Once, on a lark, a college kid visiting his grandparents at the nearby Bath & Tennis Club over Thanksgiving weekend decided to see if he could sneak into Mar-a-Lago.[15] He walked down the beach, up the steps to the pool deck, past the yellow-and-white umbrellas, and through the tunnel that runs under South Ocean Boulevard and connects Mar-a-Lago's Beach Club to the main estate. He wandered around for twenty minutes—the Trump family was staying at the club for the holiday—before he was arrested and charged with a federal crime. "I wanted to see how far I could get," he later told a judge.[16]

Mike Tyson traced nearly identical steps to those of the college kid. But the famous boxer didn't get arrested. He was a guest of a member, and that's basically all that mattered.

Tyson had been lunching with his friend, real estate giant Jeff Greene, at Greene's Palm Beach mansion just a few doors down from Mar-a-Lago when he asked to see the president's estate. Tyson had endorsed Trump for president. And although Greene bashed Trump during a bid for Florida governor in the 2018 Democratic primary (and lost—badly), he is a member of the president's private club. It's a perk of a business deal he did with the Trump Organization to provide housing for Mar-a-Lago's foreign guest workers.[17] On a whim, Greene agreed to take Tyson to the club. The men walked down the beach together and onto the pool deck at the center of the modern political universe.

At Mar-a-Lago, who can access the club largely comes down to the discretion of its nearly five hundred members.

Secret Service agents check IDs against a list of guests compiled by club security in advance of a presidential visit. Agents physically screen members and guests who might enter areas of the club where they could come into contact with the president.[18] Beyond maintaining immediate physical security of the club, however, Secret Service agents don't have much control.[19]

Agents don't even perform background checks on club guests—even in cases in which the person might be having dinner at the table next to the president.[20]

The only requirement for entering the Winter White House is an invitation from a member or a ticket to one of the many charity galas hosted at the club.

"At the end of the day, Mar-a-Lago is a club that people belong to," Greene said.[21] Sure, security matters, but, as Greene said, "they want to be gracious to the members who pay a lot of money to belong."

Tyson didn't make it far into the club that day. If he had gone through the front door, Tyson would have been turned away. Greene didn't call in advance to put his guest on the list. Tyson probably should have been asked for ID, but the rules for the back door aren't clear. Once he arrived, he was mobbed by adoring fans clamoring for pictures with him on the pool deck. After appeasing them, he left the same way he came in. Only a photo—posted to Instagram by a young Ukrainian American luxury car salesman—links Tyson to Mar-a-Lago.

If the boxer had ventured beyond the pool deck, he might have seen something remarkable: he wasn't the only intruder on the premises.

In the main lobby Secret Service agents were busy detaining an enigmatic Chinese woman wearing a flowing gray evening gown despite the early hour. The question of who she was, what she was doing at the president's private club, whether she was working for Beijing's government, and why she and a whole class of wealthy Chinese tourists had infiltrated Mar-a-Lago would endure much longer than anything Tyson did.

Some intruders at Mar-a-Lago have been caught; others evidently come and go at will. The difference largely appears to be dumb luck and circumstance.

Regardless of intention, they're all drawn to one thing: Trump.

"If anything were to go wrong, it would happen here [at Mar-a-Lago]," said a club worker who spoke on condition of anonymity.[22] "It's too vulnerable. Money buys access. Members can bring guests. Who can possibly know the intentions of all the guests?"

No president has ever owned a private club during his time in office, much less one that operates in almost total secrecy despite its semi-official function. Mar-a-Lago's importance to international politics is no secret—it's a perk the president actively markets.

"Many of the world's great leaders request to come to Mar-a-Lago and Palm Beach," Trump said just over a year into his presidency.[23] "They like it; I like it. We're comfortable. We have great relationships."

International summits are especially lucrative for Trump. Members and their guests flock to the club to witness historic events. And in seemingly complete disregard for a constitutional provision that prohibits presidents from profiting from governments, foreign or domestic, the US government also pays Trump's business directly for lodging, meeting rooms, food, and dining.[24]

The club has become a cornucopia of delights for a cast of characters who might never get near the real White House in Washington, DC: Longtime members and far-right activists trying to influence the policy of the nation far from the scrutiny of the White House press corps. Politicians and financiers hoping to spread cash around at the crown jewel of the president's business empire to earn some goodwill. Grifters using the club's open access to the president to sell the patina of power.

At Mar-a-Lago, inflating one's influence and importance is a recreational sport. In that sense, not all Mar-a-Lago "grifters" are committing crimes. But the club tends to attract wheelers-and-dealers, the used-car salesmen of politics, and a crowd of people overstating their closeness to the president to bolster their own brands.

Perhaps most concerning of all: the club is an obvious point of entry for agents of foreign governments attempting to collect sensitive information about the world's number-one espionage target—the president of the United States.

KISSING THE RING

GUIDO LOMBARDI AND his Mongolian dinner guests sat down on Mar-a-Lago's outdoor terrace a few tables away from the president.

It was sometime around April 2017, just a few months after Donald Trump became the leader of the free world.[1]

Lombardi, a longtime Mar-a-Lago member from Italy, had hatched a plan to use the club to end what he believed was one of the world's biggest obstacles to stability: the threat of a rogue North Korean nuclear state.

He just needed to get close to the president.

Trump didn't know the Mongolians were coming, but Lombardi, who considers himself something of a gentleman-amateur political fixer, had no doubt he and these emissaries from the land of Genghis Khan would succeed in implementing the first phase of their plan.

At Mar-a-Lago there is something of a secret handshake—or, better, a dance—necessary to secure an audience with *the Don*.

Lombardi fancies himself an expert at this political tango.

It all starts at dinner.

Lombardi's wife, Gianna Lahainer, had been Mar-a-Lago's very first member,[2] and the two had known Trump for three decades. Lombardi, who is in his late sixties, claims the title of Italian nobility and is listed in a member log as such. He wears a ring with a family coat of arms on his left hand and introduces himself as the Count de Canevaro.[3] His talents,

7

however, come not from any aristocratic lineage but from his career as a political fixer on the fringes of relevance: making matches, setting up deals, and always watching, quietly, for opportunity.

For decades Lombardi has campaigned for far-right candidates, mostly in Europe, who border on the fascist, like Marine Le Pen of France.[4] A recent wave of right-wing populism across Europe and other parts of the world has increased Lombardi's influence. Where his associates were once fringe candidates, many now hold leading positions within governments around the globe. Lombardi's biggest break came when his longtime friend was elected president of the United States.[5]

Lombardi wasn't in politics for the money. He did it part time, as more of a hobby than a profession. He was mostly interested in leveraging his access to Trump to change the world. For Lombardi, disarming North Korea, ridding the world of the last remnants of communism, and protecting "the West" from what he saw as the threat of Muslim invasion were anointed missions. Trump would help him advance his political causes.

But influencing international politics wouldn't be as easy as simply whispering into Trump's ear, Lombardi knew.

When it comes to Trump, it is impossible to play to his political ideology—because he doesn't have one. Appealing to his business plans might work, if anyone really knew what they were. Lombardi always said the biggest mistake most people make when dealing with Trump is assuming they know what he really wants and why. From Lombardi's perspective, the best option is to take Trump at face value. Trying to interpret his mind or why he says the things he does is a fruitless exercise. Only Trump knows what Trump wants.

The best one can ever hope to do is to move ideas into Trump's orbit and see what sticks. To get close enough to do that requires years of loyalty to the man in charge. Certain advisors to the president didn't understand that, Lombardi knew. He was already telling people Anthony Scaramucci's days in the administration were numbered even before his disastrous six-day tenure as White House communications director in July 2017.

"He's too much of a 'me' man, and with Donald it doesn't work. You have to be a boss man," Lombardi said.

Most important, the Italian understood that Mar-a-Lago is not just a historic mansion or a millionaire's playground—it is a castle. And Donald Trump is king.

Its court had been decided long before Trump ever thought of being president, giving Palm Beachers an insurmountable lead on the Washington establishment.

Each person's rank in the king's court is discernible not in their title but in seating arrangements at dinner at the club. The closer you are to the president, the higher your rank in the shadow administration that has taken shape at Mar-a-Lago.

Red velvet rope stanchions mark the president's table, no matter where he chooses to sit. Sometimes he eats in the club's intimate main dining room, its walls adorned with painted seascapes copied from those in the Palazzo Chigi, the Renaissance-era home of Italy's prime minister in Rome.[6] More frequently he dines in the open-air terrace decorated with one of the largest collections of Moorish tiles in the world.[7] Trump never eats alone. His wife and young son sometimes join him. But more often than not, he invites guests to dinner.

When the president isn't in town, his favorite table is bestowed to the next in line to his crown: his adult children, then his closest friends.

"If Eric's there, Ivanka's there, or Don. Jr.'s there, we'd always offer them the table," said a former staffer.[8] Next in the order of succession were his oldest friends.

"It was a prestige thing. The families that would sit there were personal friends of his for years and years and not just since he became president," the staffer explained.

But when court is in session and the king at his table, Trump's adult children and his most trusted advisors dine just outside the velvet barricade. Although this inner circle sometimes includes select members of his official Washington, DC, administration, the nearest tables are always filled by Mar-a-Lago members who have known Trump for decades.

To dine at those inner-lying tables is an honor bestowed rather than requested.

Everyone who calls for a dinner reservation at Mar-a-Lago wants the table closest to the man in charge. And while the club tries to rotate seating arrangements, there's still a clear pecking order.[9] (Only members and their families may book tables at the club's private restaurant, although Trump has been known to give access to nonmembers who have gained his favor.)[10]

Within Trump's tight-knit inner circle—the men who dine closest to power—are Christopher Ruddy of conservative media company Newsmax, the so-called Trump whisperer; Isaac "Ike" Perlmutter, chairman of Marvel Entertainment, who is said to have used his connection to the club to exert extraordinary influence at the Department of Veterans Affairs; New England Patriots owner and longtime Trump friend Robert Kraft; and Howard Kessler, an introverted Boston-based businessman.[11] Both Kessler and Kraft are major donors to the Democratic Party. But at Mar-a-Lago blood is thicker than politics. The most devoted club members become adopted members of the Trump family and vice versa.

"Loyalty and friendship trumps politics for me," Kraft once said, recalling Trump's response to the 2011 death of his wife, Myra.[12] "I always remember the people who were good to me in that vulnerable time, and he's in that category."

Other well-established members are placed at tables one circle removed from Trump's closest courtiers. Among them are South Florida restaurateur Lee Lipton as well as William Koch, the once-estranged brother of Charles and David Koch, the fossil fuel magnates and ultrapowerful Republican donors.

That's where Guido Lombardi and his wife sit too.

"They [the staff] know we have a relationship. We are friends," explained Lombardi, who is also Trump's neighbor at Trump Tower in Manhattan. "We have known each other for a long, long time."

Anyone who really knows Trump knows better than to disturb him while he's eating dinner. The two inner rings of tables create an extra barrier between the president and the crowd of fawning fans who have taken to mobbing Mar-a-Lago on weekends and holidays in hopes of getting a picture with the president.

The reward for loyalty is power—or at least some semblance of it. During the presidential campaign and after the election Lombardi served as an informal liaison connecting the European far-right to Trump. His rolodex includes Le Pen as well as Matteo Salvini of Italy, Geert Wilders of the Netherlands, people close to Hungarian prime minister Viktor Orbán, and members of Austria's Freedom Party.[13] (Lombardi says Le Pen and Wilders have both stayed at his home.)

In previous administrations someone like Lombardi could never have possessed the influence necessary to turn the gears of US foreign policy. But the Trump administration—or, rather, the Trump business empire— offered points of entry that had never before been seen in modern-day American politics. Lombardi and his Mongolian dinner guests planned to use that access.

MAR-A-LAGO WAS ALWAYS intended to be a palace for America's equivalent to nobility.

Marjorie Merriweather Post, a liberal Democrat and beacon of the early days of American society, started building the mansion in 1923 on a seventeen-acre plot that spans the width of Palm Beach island from the Intracoastal Waterway to the Atlantic Ocean. So magnificent was the location that she even named her estate after it: Mar-a-Lago. Sea to Lake.

A visionary of her time, Post traveled extensively, gaining inspiration for her home from castles she visited in Europe and collecting near-priceless artifacts—twenty thousand roofing tiles from a Cuban castle, for example—and luxurious furnishings for her Palm Beach palace.[14] Mar-a-Lago's striking two-story stucco mansion sits at the center of a maze of cloisters and entertainment areas, all organized in a crescent shape around the terrace dining area and "Parrot Pool"—named for the hand-carved avian statues decorating the deck. In total, the club advertises more than thirty rooms, suites, and cabanas where guests can spend the night. The mansion's southern cloisters include the Gold and White Ballroom, where Post once held her famous square-dance parties. On the second story is the owner's suite. Southern Boulevard runs along the southern property line. It's so close to some of the buildings that drivers can catch glimpses inside.

Within the northern cloisters are the guest shop and the spa, where Jeffrey Epstein's recruiter found a sixteen-year-old attendant and lured her into his sex-trafficking network.[15] Epstein was a member for a time, but a membership log shows his account at the club was closed in October

2007.[16] Lombardi said Trump kicked Epstein out after another member complained that the pedophile had made an advance on her teenage daughter.[17] (The Trump Organization has acknowledged Epstein spent time at the club but said he was not a member.[18])

A seventy-five-foot watchtower accessible from the main mansion overlooks the entire estate. Michael Jackson and Lisa Marie Presley were said to have spent their honeymoon locked away in the tower's suite. "He was up there for one week with her and he never came down," Trump said. "I don't know what was going on but they got along."[19]

Looking west from the tower, one sees a sprawling green lawn that extends past a guest house, garages, and clay tennis courts and butts up against the Intracoastal's Lake Worth Lagoon. The expanse of green was once a nine-hole golf course, but under Trump, who owns a much better course in nearby West Palm Beach, the backyard has become a wedding and event venue. Yet another way to make money.

Looking east, one sees the front lawn where wealthy retirees clad in all-white outfits play croquet. A path cuts toward the property's south-eastern corner, leading to a tunnel under South Ocean Boulevard that gives access to the estate's ocean-front pool deck featuring a high-end snack bar.

As impressive as the buildings are, Mar-a-Lago would be nothing more than a house—albeit a large, impressive house—if it weren't for the careful details that mark it as a vestige of a long-lost Gilded Age. The Mediterranean-style villa's grand archways are adorned with intricate bird and vine motifs. Oriental rugs and tiles collected from castles cover the floors. Because Mar-a-Lago was named a national historic landmark in 1980, Trump has been unable to remodel in his signature gaudy style.[20]

Mar-a-Lago was built as a dwelling for the oldest of old money—the kind that few possess in modern times. The estate was so extravagant that no one could afford to live there after Post's death.

Trump tried. He bought the property from Post's estate in 1985 after it sat vacant for years.[21]

For Trump, the palatial private residence served as a winter home, a notice to the world of his tremendous success, and a ticket into an exclusive upper crust that no amount of money can typically buy. For its part, Palm Beach society was horrified to learn their new neighbor was a tabloid-chasing womanizer, a tasteless vulgarian. He was *not* one of them.

Trump's wave of bankruptcies in the early 1990s[22] forced the young tycoon to turn his second home into a moneymaker: Mar-a-Lago became a club.[23] Just as Trump would later identify a huge slice of the American electorate that felt cast out by coastal elitists, the developer recognized that Palm Beach was full of outsiders too: new-money billionaires who hated the island's stuffy old confines. Wealthy Jews who had been excluded from the other WASP-y country clubs. And people who just wanted to party with the Donald, the era's ultimate playboy.

The club, as members simply call it, was popular. Even some of Palm Beach's old guard began to gravitate toward the parties Trump hosted. No one could deny that with the Donald in town, Palm Beach got a lot more fun.[24]

Nearly everything at Mar-a-Lago comes with a reminder that the old-money estate is now owned by a man the town once despised. There's Trump-branded water, Trump-branded wine, and even hamburger buns with the word "Trump" stamped on top.[25]

Trump's biggest addition since taking over Mar-a-Lago has been the construction of the Donald J. Trump Grand Ballroom. Now the estate's largest event space, the freestanding seventeen-thousand-square-foot ballroom stands to the south of the historic twentieth-century mansion. (The club's promotional materials boast that the building is twenty thousand square feet, contradicting the Palm Beach County Property Appraiser.[26])

"The exterior was designed to keep up with the vision of Mrs. Post, but the inside is more me. It's got the feel and look of Louis XIV, and that's my favorite style," Trump told the *Palm Beach Daily News* soon after his ballroom opened in 2005.[27]

Lavish coats of gold used to create the world's most opulent palace at Versailles made Louis XIV one of the most memorable monarchs in history. Gold and gilding provided the king "a look so unique, so self-aggrandizing, that it granted [him] a kind of material immortality," the *Atlantic* wrote.[28] In his own mind, Trump was already America's Sun King.

Appearance means everything to Trump. The president is known for his ability to spot a crumb on the floor from across the room. The first thing he noticed when a contractor showed him around his new ballroom was that the vaulted ceilings weren't shiny enough.[29] The seventeen crystal chandeliers, priced at $250,000 apiece, glittered just as they should, but the gilding on the walls and ceiling moldings looked flat.[30] The contractor had used paint instead of real gold leaf.

"That doesn't look very good. That doesn't really look rich," Trump said to the man.[31]

He wanted the paint replaced with the real stuff, and he told the contractor to spare no expense. In the end, Trump spent $7 million putting sheets of twenty-four-karat gold on the walls and ceiling of his new ballroom, just shy of what he paid for the entire property a decade earlier.

What Trump didn't worry about fixing—either because he didn't notice or didn't care—were the acoustics. The mirrored walls of the ballroom may evoke the palace of Versailles, but they and the rest of the architectural elements refract even the slightest sound, converting the niceties of polite society into a deafening chorus of noise. And God help anyone trying to have a conversation if an event includes a live band or singer.

"He is a perfectionist in all things that he is concerned with," said Mar-a-Lago member Fred Rustmann, a former CIA officer and founder of a corporate intelligence firm in West Palm Beach. "Certainly, acoustics is not one of them."

FOR DONALD TRUMP, every day at Mar-a-Lago goes much the same.

He is up early in the morning to watch *Fox News* and to tweet.

Then it's time to hit the links at Trump International Golf Club in nearby West Palm Beach or, sometimes, Trump National Golf Club in Jupiter.[32] He eats lunch at the golf course, where he is joined by the famous golfers he recruits for his foursomes, like Tiger Woods and Jack Nicklaus, or celebrities like the talk-show host Rush Limbaugh, who owns a home in Palm Beach.[33] Back at Mar-a-Lago Trump retires to his suite for some pre-dinner tweeting. Before he became president he would often emerge for an afternoon ice cream at the Beach Club. But since the election he's cut back. In the evening Trump makes a grand entrance to dinner—but only once he's sure the restaurant is full—and basks in the applause of his members and guests.

"He comes down to Mar-a-Lago to recharge his batteries," said the billionaire and club member Jeff Greene. "He's the king of the castle."[34]

Mar-a-Lago is the Trump family home.

Don Jr., forty-two, can often be found playing the family man, grilling hot dogs for his five children on the lawn. He and his now ex-wife, Vanessa, were once seen tussling in the grass in front of their kids in full daylight. A person who saw it called it an out-and-out "dry hump."[35]

Ivanka, thirty-eight, hangs out by the pool, often escorted by an entourage of terrified attendants. Her husband, Jared Kushner, works out frequently and hits the gym almost every morning.[36] At the tennis courts Ivanka can sometimes be seen flouting the club's all-white dress code. Once, her daughter Arabella was hitting the ball well and yelled, "Mommy, look at me! Look at me!" Ivanka, sitting off to the side, didn't look up from her phone.[37]

Eric Trump, thirty-six, now runs the club, in name at least, following his father's election. He and his wife, Lara, enjoy walking their two beagles near the water.

Tiffany, twenty-six, doesn't frequent Mar-a-Lago as much as her older half-siblings. A University of Pennsylvania graduate, she prefers to keep a lower profile. But people still come looking. Once, a total stranger showed up to her cabana proposing marriage. Staff had to chase him away.

Barron, fourteen, kicks a soccer ball around the lawn, sometimes accompanied by a trainer.[38]

Members try to exploit their closeness to Trump's family. Even his brood of ten grandchildren are sometimes corralled for selfies.

But the kids are hard to catch. It's not uncommon to see Secret Service agents in pressed suits running across the grounds, trying to keep up with a fleet-footed child.[39]

For their part, the children think "lose your security detail" is good sport for sunny afternoons spent at Grandpa's house.

Before he became president, Donald Trump's preferred dinner table was along the far wall of Mar-a-Lago's main dining room. The table had a sort of public privacy to it. Perfect for a notorious introvert who built his brand around being a man of the people.

On the way to and from his chambers—a trek that takes him straight through the main dining area—Trump yucks it up with guests, remembers names, asks about sick family members, tosses out generic compliments ("lookin' good"), and poses for selfies. Though the notorious germaphobe used to back away in alarm from any hand extended in his direction, things changed as he grew more accustomed to glad-handing, and he even began to occasionally shake the hands of his dinner guests on the way to his seat.[40]

Staff leave an antibacterial towelette waiting for him at his table to wipe the grime from his hands.

Trump's main table along the wall has just one downside: it is so near to a swinging service door that Trump is in constant danger of getting hit every time an overstressed waiter runs through carrying a tray of food or dishes.[41]

Once, a young server dropped a dirty fork straight into the president's lap. Her heart stopped as she waited for the inevitable outburst. Trump is not a forgiving boss. She cringed as the germaphobe-in-chief, who demands individually wrapped packets of butter rather than smearing his pretzel rolls with butter from the communal dishes shared by the rest of the table, looked down at the fallen utensil.[42] But after considering for a moment, he simply picked it up, wiped it off, and handed it back to the mortified waitress without a fuss.

Brand is everything to the Donald, and every public interaction matters.

"He's always careful about everything. Anything that can tarnish his name, his brand," Lombardi said.[43]

At Mar-a-Lago the Trump brand is associated with high-end service. Everything has to be about the members who line his pockets with millions of dollars each year. Even a dirty fork in the lap wouldn't cause him to spoil their evening.

The president is the ultimate maître d'. He's also the ultimate chameleon. His drive to be the perfect host overrides most of his other personality quirks. When Trump stops in at a party hosted by a member of his club, the notoriously picky eater will have some of whatever is being served.[44] When his club is having a holiday buffet, the man who hates not being first will wait his turn in line just like everyone else. When he talks to a member of his club, the world seems to melt away, and they feel as though they have his full attention. No one is a better listener, they say. It is the kind of charisma possessed by only the most successful politicians and dinner-party hosts.

"I'm not a fan of his politics, but he's a very gracious host. He makes people feel good," said Jeff Greene, who had smuggled Mike Tyson onto the property in 2019.[45]

Trump's behavior as the perfect host is both an act that benefits his bottom line and a genuine reflection of who he is—a man obsessed with having people love him and the empire built in his name.

After Trump's election, members began to applaud when their new president strolled from his suite to dinner. And there was little doubt that his Pavlovian response to positive attention caused Trump to opt for an even higher-profile dining location: *al fresco*, in the center of the outdoor terrace. The longer walk to the more prominent table gave his guests longer to clap.

The president's frequent public appearances at the club are great for business—his business.

Mar-a-Lago is owned by the Trump Organization, a group of companies of which Donald Trump is the sole owner. Every person who walks into the club to eat a steak, play tennis, dance the night away, or relax in the spa benefits the real estate mogul's bottom line.

The club is more popular than ever now that he's president, as members invite friends to show off their proximity to the leader of the free world.[46] These days, on any Saturday night during Palm Beach society's high season, which runs roughly from Thanksgiving to Mother's Day, more than a thousand people may patronize Mar-a-Lago between the restaurant, ballrooms, and various events.[47] Some members and their guests have gone so far as to slip managers money to try to bribe their way to a table close to the president.[48]

"People want to see the president," said Valentina Deva, a Palm Beach real estate agent from Estonia who can often be seen at the edge of events wearing horn-rimmed glasses and livestreaming the parties out to the world.[49] "Many people love him."

In the months between his victory in the Republican primary and his January 2017 inauguration, dozens of new members joined the club—bringing in at least $5 million in additional revenue for the president's business and perhaps quite a bit more. Tables at Mar-a-Lago events were selling out well in advance. Club members started planning ahead, booking twelve-person tables months before holidays that Trump was known to spend at home in Florida. Show-offs began trying to reserve such large tables that the club soon had to limit each member to only two dinner guests while the president was in town.[50]

"For some people it's a really, really big deal, and they will jump on that and they will pay a lot of money to go there and kind of hob-nob with the president," Rustmann said.[51] "But you're not hobnobbing with the president. That's the point. When you go there you may see him and he may pass by and even put his hand on your shoulder while you're sitting there having dinner, but that's about it."

Name dropping and social-media selfies aside, in truth, most people who come to Mar-a-Lago have little to no special influence on Trump or his administration.

It's a select few of the most loyal members who hold the real power. They have spent years nurturing the relationship at Mar-a-Lago. Kissing the ring.

"He's got layers of people—they're political, they're personal—that he's known [for so] many years," said a Mar-a-Lago member.[52] "These people have been members for years. It just happens that he became president. So they like it even more."

SINCE THE 1980S one of Guido Lombardi's pet projects has been to negotiate a rapprochement between North Korea and the West.

The fixer believes that seeking a formal peace with the world's most dangerous rogue nation is one of the most pressing issues of modern times.[53]

And given Trump's inclination to conduct diplomacy at high-profile summits, Lombardi hoped to set up a meeting between the president and North Korean leader Kim Jong-un. In his eyes there was an ideal place, although few Americans could find it on a map: Mongolia.

The formerly communist Asian nation was not a random choice. Lombardi, who also goes by George, was thinking pragmatically. Kim would feel most at home in Mongolia, a country near his own that shares significant history with North Korea and is somewhere North Koreans can travel without a visa. Since breaking away from the domination of the collapsed Soviet Union in 1992, Mongolia has maintained itself as a neutral state with close ties to North Korea.[54] It had already hosted talks between Kim and the Japanese.[55] A Mongolian summit between Trump and Kim was, in Lombardi's opinion, the thing most likely to lead to a positive outcome: peace. It even had the backing of Mongolia's then president Tsakhiagiin Elbegdorj, who called his nation the "Switzerland of Asia."

"Mongolia would be a neutral third party," Elbegdorj once said.[56] "World and regional peace is Mongolia's [utmost] important mission."

That was Lombardi's mission too in early 2017 when he invited several Mongolian government officials to dine with him at Mar-a-Lago.

Lombardi didn't really know the men he had brought to see the president. But he needed them to help him broker the summit—and Mongolian politicians and businessmen had long used him for his high-level connections in Europe and the United States.

"I'm a little of a national hero there," Lombardi explained. "My dad actually was more the national hero."

As a United Nations diplomat, Lombardi's father had helped anticommunist Mongolians facing violent repression escape their native country, earning young Guido a Mongolian godfather. A tenth of the country's population was killed or imprisoned during the Stalinist purges of the 1930s.[57]

After communism fell, newly capitalist Mongolians looking to do business abroad began calling on Lombardi for his contacts. ("I tried to help them," he said. "I'm a friend to anybody coming knocking.") They were impressed to learn he had connections to Trump.

Even before the election, he said, the Mongolians "already had a sense that Trump might be a winner."

They were right.

It was a perfect Florida evening as Lombardi and his Mongolian guests sat on Mar-a-Lago's terrace just tables away from Trump. The president kept looking up from his well-done steak to make eye contact with his old friend. It was all the confirmation Lombardi needed. Trump was curious: Who were these Asian men at his club?

Upon finishing his meal, Trump stood up and walked to Lombardi's table, just as Lombardi knew he would. The count rose and introduced the Mongolians to the president of the United States.

"How do you like our country?" Trump asked the group.[58] "How do you like Florida?"

Lombardi had carefully prepared his guests for this exchange. The Mongolians tactfully responded with a round of scripted pleasantries.

"Oh yes, we love it."

"Thank you so much. You're doing a great job."

Then, as coached by Lombardi, the Mongolians explained they were in town on a diplomatic mission. The words "North Korea" never came up—Lombardi had cautioned them against being too specific. After all, courting the Don of Mar-a-Lago required subtlety. Trump's advisors could fill in the gaps for him later. The way Lombardi saw it, what else would bring these Mongolian diplomats to the home of a US president?

There was a handshake. The men posed for a picture with Trump.[59] The connection had been made.

The exchange was obvious enough that even Bill Koch wandered over to find out who Lombardi's guests were and why the president was so interested.[60]

Nothing happened immediately after the Mongolians met Trump at Mar-a-Lago.

Although the snail's pace of this kind of back-door diplomacy might bother someone with less experience than Lombardi, the Italian count remained steadfast. Seeds had to be planted and watered. Not all of them sprouted. But experience told him that enough of them would that sowing them was worth the effort.

At Mar-a-Lago, he says, "that's how things get done."[61]

Lombardi moved slowly, bringing some of the Mongolian delegation to Trump Tower in New York later that spring. In June 2017 he visited the Mongolian capital, Ulaanbaatar, posing for a classic tourist photo in front of a statue of Genghis Khan.[62]

Two weeks later a gift presented itself: Khaltmaa Battulga won Mongolia's presidential election.[63] Since the fall of the Soviet Union Mongolia had been governed, for the most part, by Western-style liberals. Battulga was no such thing.[64]

A fifty-four-year-old former wrestling champion, Battulga venerated the greatness of Genghis Khan—most notably by building a giant statue of the man who conquered much of the known world and killed millions along the way. Battulga also drew far closer to Russia, the country's former overlord in all but name, than was normal in wary post-Soviet Mongolia. He frequently appeared at the side of Russian president Vladimir Putin. *Bloomberg News* once called Battulga the "Trump of the Steppe."[65]

Like his predecessor, Battulga was enthusiastic about a Trump-Kim summit that could make Ulaanbaatar a household name around the world.

"I believe that our two countries' 70 years of friendship, [the] foundation of which was strongly laid by generations of leaders of Mongolia and [North Korea], will be consolidated even more in future," he told Kim in a letter.[66]

All Lombardi needed to do was get Trump on board with the Mongolian summit.

But that dream was dashed on April 30, 2018, when, as so often happens, the president logged onto Twitter.[67] "Numerous countries are being considered for the meeting, but would Peace House/Freedom House, on the border of North & South Korea, be a more representative, important and lasting site than a third party country?" the president wrote. "Just asking!"

Overnight the DMZ became the favorite.

But Lombardi wasn't giving up.

After all, there could always be more than one summit. Trump and Kim had met in Hanoi, Vietnam, just a few months before, and already the president was planning this new meeting.[68] The one after that could very well be in Ulaanbaatar.

But in the meantime Lombardi needed to make sure he kept the Mongolians interested—and he wanted another ally who could float the idea in Trump's ear.

He chose Pastor Rodney Howard-Browne, who has been as up close and personal with the contact-averse Trump as just about anyone.

Howard-Browne was one of seventeen evangelical pastors photographed laying hands and praying over Trump in the Oval Office.[69] The MAGA missionary had founded his Tampa church in the legacy of evangelist Billy Graham.

He was born in South Africa, where he spent his childhood collecting stamps from far-away places and wondering if he would someday be able to visit them. Mongolia captured his imagination. The young Howard-Browne grew fascinated with the history of Marco Polo and his journey across Asia. And when he began to plan a trip to preach the gospel in various countries around Asia in 2019, he added one night in Mongolia.

Lombardi learned of the trip through a mutual friend, who called Howard-Browne on his behalf to ask if the pastor would like to meet the Mongolian minister of foreign affairs, Damdin Tsogtbaatar.

"Sure!" Howard-Browne said into the phone, though he had never heard of Tsogtbaatar. "Where would you like me to come?"

"Mar-a-Lago," was the reply.

BETTER THAN SEX

GIANNA LAHAINER JOINED Donald Trump on the steps of Mar-a-Lago around the time the estate became a private club in 1995.

The sixty-year-old socialite had curly red hair and a dedication to society life that was shocking even by Palm Beach standards.

Earlier that year Frank Lahainer, an Italian count who had been Gianna's husband for nearly forty years, died in the middle of the Palm Beach social season. Instead of mourning, she put the Dom Pérignon—and her husband—on ice and threw a party. Frank's embalmed corpse waited at a West Palm Beach funeral parlor for more than a month until the Palm Beach social season ended and she had time to fly back to Italy to bury him.

"I wanted to go to the parties," Lahainer told Palm Beach ethnographer Ronald Kessler.[1] "He was ninety. I am sixty. So why should I wait?"

Lahainer had known Trump for years. They were neighbors in Trump Tower in New York, where she had bought a condo when Trump opened up the building in the early 1980s, as well as several more in the years that followed. Although the condo numbers imply that Lahainer's primary apartment is below Trump's, the open floor plan and high ceilings of the penthouse mean that, to this day, Trump and Lahainer share a landing in the tower on 5th Avenue.

As his Palm Beach club was set to open, Trump invited Lahainer to come see the property.[2] Without that invitation, Guido Lombardi, who later married Lahainer, might never have found himself at Mar-a-Lago.

Trump's invitation to Lahainer may have been a subtle effort to sell her some of the elaborate furniture that had come with the estate, Lombardi later speculated. The New York real estate developer was having serious liquidity problems at the time, with several casinos in bankruptcy,[3] and the upkeep of the estate was bogging him down financially. But Lahainer wasn't interested in the near-priceless sofas and linens. She wanted to be a member of his new club, she told Trump. The first member.

"If you want to be a member, you'll be a member," Trump told her.

"I brought the checkbook," she replied, pulling it out of her purse. Lahainer couldn't have known at the time that her $50,000 payment would, two decades later, buy the European far-right a backdoor key to the White House.

LONG BEFORE TRUMP came to town, Lahainer hit the Palm Beach social scene with her first husband, Frank, who had made a fortune of around $300 million in real estate.[4]

Gianna had been Frank's secretary in Italy when she was a teenager. In 1957 they married, and Lahainer's life became one of globetrotting, vacation homes, Rolls-Royces, thirty-something-carat jewels (but who's counting), and not much more to do than climb the ladders of high society. The two bought a condo in the Palm Beach Biltmore for just that purpose.

Frank died in 1995, just three weeks shy of his ninety-first birthday.[5] He left his beloved Gianna everything. Lahainer wasted no time in celebrating her "new life."

Within months there was a new man in the picture.

Lombardi and Lahainer had first met at the annual gala for the National Italian American Foundation held in Washington, DC, in 1994.[6] It was the kind of bipartisan gathering where one might bump into Italian American movie stars, businessmen, ball players, and even President Bill Clinton, who was the keynote speaker that year.[7] Supreme Court Justice Antonin Scalia was also a frequent attendee.[8]

Lombardi was always networking. Though his main job was real estate, Lombardi was also an up-and-coming fixer for far-right Italian politicians, and a member of Lega Nord, or Northern League. The Italian political party was dedicated to separating Italy's northern provinces from those in the south.[9] Historically, Lega Nord promoted a narrative that the Italians of the south were lazy criminals leeching off the more prosperous and industrialized north.[10] Some factions within the party openly celebrated the nationalism of former dictator Benito Mussolini's fascist state.[11]

As Lega Nord gained popularity and seats in government in recent years, the party dropped its northern-centric political stance, finally accepting all Italians as equals in their nationalist mission.[12] The party rebranded itself "Lega"—dropping "Nord"—and focused its once-broad intolerance into an anti-immigrant, anti-Muslim agenda.[13] Its program could easily be summed up as "Italy First."

But before this rebranding, in 1993, Lombardi founded an American chapter of Lega Nord to whip up support for the party among Italians living in the United States.[14] When he met Lahainer a year later, Lombardi was forty-four years old. His already receding hairline was accentuated by the thick brown bristles shaped into a mushroom cap around the sides of his head. He was a charmer with a Cheshire grin and wore a bowtie as well as any Upper East Sider. Lombardi immediately hit it off with the saucy redhead from Palm Beach society.

But at the time she was married, and he was seeing someone. So they went their separate ways.

THE DREARY WEATHER of March in New York matched Lombardi's mood in 1995 as he sat in his twenty-ninth-floor apartment in Olympic Tower in midtown Manhattan.[15]

It was the same building where Jackie Kennedy and her second husband, the Greek shipping magnate Aristotle Onassis, had lived for a time. Onassis had developed Olympic Tower, the crème de la crème of New York real estate until Trump Tower went up a few blocks away, partially obscuring Lombardi's view of Central Park. Lombardi admired the business acumen of the brash Queens playboy. "He knows his stuff," Lombardi said. Although he himself worked in real estate, Lombardi had always dabbled in matchmaking. He had already met his flashy new neighbor on a few occasions and even arranged a meeting between Trump and a Japanese businessman friend of his. Lombardi was still congratulating himself for making that introduction.

Then his phone rang.

"Hi, how are you?" said the voice on the other end of the line. It was Lahainer.

Truth be told, Lombardi had been better. His father had just died in Italy and his lovely Brazilian girlfriend had grown tired of the cold in New York and gone back home.

"Well, you know, not so good," Lombardi replied. "What about you?"

"My husband just passed," Lahainer said. She explained that she was coming through New York in April after the season in Palm Beach wrapped up and asked if he'd like to have dinner with her. He said he would like that very much.

She cooked spaghetti with vodka sauce and salmon. They held hands.

Lahainer and Lombardi married in Palm Beach in 2000, five years after she became Mar-a-Lago's first member, but their relationship was serious from the beginning.[16]

Lombardi moved in with her at Trump Tower, where she already owned several units. It was at their parties that Trump became acquainted with the Italian far-right. A photo of one such occasion shows a younger Trump, smiling broadly, with both hands on Lahainer's shoulders. To their left is Roberto Maroni, a member of Lega Nord and interior minister to Italian prime minister Silvio Berlusconi from 1994 to 1995.[17] To their right stand Lombardi and Maxwell Milton Rabb, the ambassador to Italy during the Reagan administration. Lombardi calls Rabb his mentor. "Through him, from Reagan's time, I've been able to do some things," the tantalizingly guarded Lombardi acknowledges.

Lombardi sold his vacation home in the Florida Keys to take up residence in Palm Beach with Lahainer during the season. She extended her Mar-a-Lago club membership to include Lombardi and began to introduce him to Palm Beach social circles. Charming, soft-spoken, and still fastidious about making sure he picked the right English word, Lombardi was never interested in dominating his new social scene. He was playing a longer game, "planting seeds," as he liked to say, in the minds of the influential people he met, then watering them over time to see which ones took root. He did enough to earn the trust and respect—and dare he say friendship—of the future president.

"Two of my great members, Mr. and Mrs. Lombardi. They've been my friends for a long time," Donald Trump announced to a crowd gathered at Mar-a-Lago in March 2011.[18]

Trump had just come from golfing and wore a pink polo and white hat. He slung his arms casually over their shoulders for a photo op and gave Lahainer a kiss on the cheek before departing. It was the inaugural event for The United West, an anti-Muslim group dedicated to maintaining the purity of Western civilization and the "Judeo-Christian World." It was listed as a hate group by the Southern Poverty Law Center.[19] Lombardi cohosted the event and served as a featured speaker, saying the North Atlantic League—an organization he had founded with a vague mission to bring together the United States, Italy, and Israel—stood with the mission of The United West, and he led the group in a prayer.[20]

For years Trump had been stopping by Lombardi's table after dinner at Mar-a-Lago to talk politics. Trump's favorite question to ask was "How's Berlusconi?"

Silvio Berlusconi fascinated Donald Trump, who considered the Italian media magnate to be cut from a similar cloth as himself.[21] Both were billionaires, at least on paper, and famous outside of politics, although Berlusconi was richer. They were also both infamous cads, chasing after supermodels and cultivating images as sex-soaked playboys. (Berlusconi's liaisons with young women would even lead him to a criminal trial in which he was ultimately acquitted.[22])

It hadn't hurt either man in the public eye. Berlusconi had been elected prime minister of Italy in 1994, having no prior experience in political office. He had parlayed his celebrity and wealth into the highest office in the land, capitalizing on investigations into his feuding political rivals and outmaneuvering them by forming an alliance with Lega Nord.[23] Trump was intrigued. He had also been considering politics as his next avenue for stardom and even ran a half-hearted bid for the Reform Party's nomination in the 2000 presidential election.

For years Lombardi, who claimed to be an informal advisor to the Italian prime minister, tried to broker a meeting between the two men.

On several occasions he invited Berlusconi to Mar-a-Lago for Christmas. The mogul never came. Lombardi said he always assumed the offer was ignored because Europeans at the time hardly considered Trump a man of import—that, and Berlusconi had a place in Bermuda where he usually went instead. (Or was it because Lombardi had less influence than he let on?)

Over time Trump's political curiosities shifted. On his after-dinner jaunts by Lombardi's table, Trump started asking about the meteoric rise of the Tea Party and the groundswell of support for politicians lining up outside of traditional party lines. To Trump, anything popular or notorious was worth examining.

"Do you think they have any chance?" Trump would ask Lombardi.

Lombardi assumed Trump's interest was mostly in the viability of an outsider candidate rather than the ideology of the GOP's far-right fringe.

"He was always interested in having his own movement or his own thing," Lombardi said. Trump had even been putting out feelers about a bid to challenge President Barack Obama in the 2012 election, repeatedly advancing the racist conspiracy theory that Obama had faked his birth certificate and been born abroad.[24]

Although Trump didn't really see himself as a Republican, he was alarmed by what he saw as a left turn in the Democratic Party toward a more European-style social democracy that promised hefty taxes for the rich. The Donald was not interested in anything that threatened his fame or fortune.

"He's very Reagan-esque in that sense. He's very anti-communism, socialism. That ideology is still part of this," Lombardi said.[25]

It was the Italian who would introduce the once-registered Democrat[26] to far-right circles in Florida. Lombardi, always seeking to bring conservatives from around the world together, had founded a group called Tea Party Italy and had grown close with several conservative activists in South Florida. When the local Tea Party planned a Tax Day event in April 2011, Lombardi pitched Trump as an ideal speaker.

Event organizer Pam Wohlschlegel was admittedly skeptical.[27] Trump's politics were unknown, and she wasn't sure they would really resonate with Palm Beach conservatives. But Trump could draw a crowd. So organizers went ahead with the plan. A flier promised that the host of *The Apprentice* would tell Congress: "You're fired."

They had expected a thousand people.

They got double.[28] The day started off rainy, but the skies cleared in time for the event. It was still windy as Trump took the stage in Boca Raton, a prosperous coastal town twenty-five miles south of Palm Beach filled with retirees. It's the kind of place that makes old-money Palm Beach turn up its nose but puts transplanted New Yorkers right at home. Trump showed up just before he was set to go on stage.[29]

"Wow, this is really amazing. Woah!" Trump said as he went to the podium, James Brown's "Living in America" fading out as he approached the mic. "You know, my second home is right down the road in your little competitive community called Palm Beach. You know that, right? I love Florida. I love it." The crowd cheered in appreciation: he was one of them.

As a strong breeze whipped the red, white, and blue balloons over-head, Trump joked to the crowd, "With all this wind, now at least you know it's my real hair, right?" His hairspray must have been aerosol cement. Barely a strand shifted. The self-deprecating line earned him some chuckles. The ice was fully broken. There was no stopping Trump. He spoke for the next forty-five minutes—twice as long as his allotted time—forcing organizers to cut the rest of the planned entertainment.[30] His speech took on what has now become a familiar, freewheeling pattern.[31] He pandered to the egos of those he wished to impress: Florida governor Rick Scott, he said, was "doing a hell of a job." A reporter covering the event for *Bloomberg Businessweek* was "beautiful." He thanked the Tea Party "because they made Washington start thinking, both Democrat and Republican."

Trump spent most of his time on what wasn't great: the United States, Barack Hussein Obama (he always emphasized Obama's middle name when he wanted to make a point), China, Jews critical of Israel, China, "criminals" who crossed the border with ease while smart people struggled to get visas, the wars in the Middle East, China, career politicians with no business experience, India, South Korea, and more China, to name just a few of the topics that he lurched between. "All I want to do is see this guy's birth certificate," Trump barked about Obama.

Wohlschlegel breathed a sigh of relief. She was impressed with his patriotism and professed adherence to the principles of small government. "He was relating to the people. He was getting a lot of applause. They were egging him on to speak more," she said.

At the crowd's urging, Trump spent at least ten minutes spit-balling about all the people he didn't like. "Bill Ayers," someone shouted. "George Soros!" another person said. The further off script he went, the more the crowd loved him.

Trump talked about how great he was, how great his company was, how rich he was, how many other rich people he knew, and how he was not a politician but a winner. If he ever ran for president, he said, "I look forward to disclosing my financials because I built a great, great company." The disclosure would be like a scorecard of his success, Trump told the crowd. (As of early 2020 Trump has yet to make that particular "scorecard" public, blaming the delay on a tax audit, although he is perfectly free to release the records.[32])

Trump never said he was going to run, but he talked frequently about a hypothetical presidential bid. Only a businessman could fix the country, he told the crowd. Not a politician. "The United States will be great again," he concluded, foreshadowing his future campaign slogan—Make America Great Again, which he trademarked the next year.[33]

Trump left the stage to a standing ovation. He was the opposite of the polished, politically correct politicians the crowds were used to seeing. He was something new and refreshing. Someone people wanted to get behind.

"I think it was sincere and brilliant. He planted the seeds," Wohlschlegel told the *Tampa Bay Times* at the time.[34]

A giddy Trump picked up the tab for event security as a good-faith gesture after the crowd's unexpected size landed the South Florida Tea Party with a far bigger bill than expected.[35]

Trump was brimming with adrenaline as he walked to his car, Lombardi on his heels.[36]

"Donald, you like this?" Lombardi asked.

"I love it," came the developer's reply.

From the expression on his face, Lombardi knew Trump was hooked on the politician's life. The sensation of being on stage in front of a cheering crowd hanging on every word is a powerful drug, especially for someone as addicted to celebrity as Trump. Lombardi knew the feeling.

"It's better than sex," Lombardi said.

⚯

THAT DAY IN BOCA RATON, surrounded by his friends from South Florida and spurred on by a trusted Mar-a-Lago member, the businessman became a viable presidential candidate in the mind of the only person whose opinion ever really mattered to Trump—his own.

"Wow! That was unbelievable," he reportedly told right-wing political consultant Roger Stone at the time. "There's something here."[37]

But the political establishment did something that almost all establishments had done during Trump's career: it laughed at the Donald, just as Wall Street had mocked the brash developer, just as Palm Beach society had when Trump showed up to buy Mar-a-Lago in the 1980s.

Trump had made himself an easy target. The Obama administration put out a copy of the president's long-form birth certificate.[38] And Obama happily mocked Trump at the White House Correspondents' Association Dinner, which was held later that same month.[39] "No one is happier, no one is prouder, to put this birth certificate matter to rest than the Donald," Obama said, needling the man that he, least of anyone, ever expected to succeed him. Sitting in the audience, Trump grimaced, although he claimed he appreciated Obama's jokes.

Being mocked by Obama only further endeared Trump to the Tea Party crowd. The establishment didn't get it. So fixated on what Trump wasn't, they couldn't see what he was.

"There is nothing in Trump's background that would suggest he should be this popular with a family values, economically thrifty, Tea Party supporter," wrote the *Crowley Political Report*, a Florida blog.[40] "Trump is on wife number three. His gaudy lifestyle certainly does not suggest thrift, and when he speaks about issues it is clear that it has been many years since he read a book."

But Trump would find fantastic success diverting the white middle-class anger whipped up by the Tea Party into his own political movement.

"It was Trump's genius that he sensed the rot in the party and rather than making a quixotic third-party run, like Ross Perot or George Wallace, and losing, he had the vision to hijack the party of Ronald Reagan," Florida GOP operative Mac Stipanovich told the *Orlando Sentinel*.[41]

Trump is not an ideologue. Nor is he even particularly right wing, Lombardi said. "He's not terribly intellectual," he said. He doesn't much personally care about abortion one way or the other. He never sat down at a table and thought out an anti-immigrant platform. "He just went with the feel of the people," Lombardi said. He wasn't a Democrat or Republican. He was Donald Trump, the outsider who always managed to outflank the "in-crowd" and eventually usurp its power. That doesn't mean Trump had a master plan. "I don't think he wanted to build the movement consciously. I don't think he had the design to reshape the party in his own image. That's not him." Lombardi said.

The Donald was going to do politics the same way he did dinner parties—by being a great host and pandering to those who paid his bills.

At the club "it was about his clients being happy," said Maycol, a Mar-a-Lago lounge singer and keyboard player who publicly goes by a single name.[42] In 2012 Maycol and his musical partner, Lilian, were scouted by Mar-a-Lago manager Bernd Lembcke at a nearby country club. Lembcke asked them to perform at Trump's club. On the night of their first performance they were surprised to find the billionaire making rounds in the dining room, asking his guests what they thought of the new performers. Unlike most other wealthy Palm Beachers they met, Trump's own opinion came second.

"His focus was to see how his clients were accepting us," said Maycol.

Trump had always been that way. More than a decade earlier, when Trump needed a favor from the city government in Phoenix to help launch a condo project, he flew in to meet the Democratic mayor, Phil Gordon. Trump's only aim was to please.

"I hear you're a great Democrat. I'm a Democrat," Trump told Gordon. "You should come to New York, and I'll introduce you to a lot of people."[43]

The future build-the-wall president also praised Gordon for his battle against anti-immigration activists in conservative Arizona.

After the Boca Raton rally, politics became Trump's newest business venture. Conservative voters were his club members to whom he offered various amenities. If they didn't like one thing, he got rid of it and gave them something new. It was only when Trump received an impassioned response to an offhand remark about immigration that he began rallying his supporters around the plan for a wall on the border with Mexico.[44] He talked about being tough in trade negotiations with China not just because he was a fervent nationalist but because he got such a positive reaction every time he mentioned it.

"He kind of plans it as he goes," Lombardi said.

Trump's off-the-cuff politics often don't line up with his other business interests. Since he announced his platform for bringing "good-paying jobs" home to American workers, Mar-a-Lago has applied for visas to hire more than two hundred seasonal foreign workers.[45] The club hires international staff from labor agencies across the world, sometimes paying the workers half of what Americans said they expected for a similar job. The Trump Organization claims there aren't enough experienced Americans who want the service jobs, although dozens have applied.[46]

Trump was so lacking in defined ideology that billionaires David and Charles Koch—the intellectual authors and biggest financiers of the Tea Party movement—put just a few thousand dollars into his 2016 campaign.[47]

Before his death in the summer of 2019, David Koch was a part-time Palm Beacher and a dedicated libertarian. He admired Trump's ballsiness, he once told his friend, the author Harry Hurt III, over lunch at Trump International Golf Course in West Palm Beach.[48] But Koch knew a huckster when he saw one. Koch told a story about Trump trying to sell him half ownership of a Trump-branded hotel at the same price Trump had paid for the whole building. When Koch called him out, Trump got angry and walked away, muttering, "art of the deal, art of the deal" under his breath.

"David had a very clear-eyed view of what Donald Trump was all about," said Hurt, who met Koch while writing *The Lost Tycoon*, a Trump biography. "I would not say he's a Trump hater. He wouldn't lower himself to hate a guy who was sort of a clown like that."[49]

Although Trump would become the face of the new Republican Party, he sought advice from a former Democratic president before he decided to run. In 2015 Trump called Bill Clinton to talk about his political ambitions and intentions to run for president, four people told the *Washington Post*.[50] Clinton listened carefully, and while he never told Trump to run outright, he did reportedly tell the billionaire that "he was striking a chord with frustrated conservatives and was a rising force on the right." (Clinton's aides acknowledged the conversation took place but said the two men did not discuss the presidential race.)

Trump got into politics because of the high he got from the adoring crowds. And his political agenda tended to mirror whoever could get close enough to talk to him.

Suddenly, chit-chat over Mar-a-Lago's famed chocolate cake became an avenue for affecting global politics.

AROUND NOON ON April 20, 2019, the day before Easter Sunday, Pastor Rodney Howard-Browne made his way through Mar-a-Lago security with his adult son Kenneth Howard-Browne.[51]

After passing a bust of Cicero, the Roman statesman famous for his opposition to tyranny, the two walked past the ornate sofas in the entryway where Trump once took official photos with the Chinese president. They were going to meet Guido Lombardi in the walnut-paneled Library Bar where a famous portrait of Trump in tennis whites, titled "The Visionary," hangs.[52] Shortly after their arrival, the Mongolian ambassador to the United States, Yondon Otgonbayar, and the Mongolian minister of foreign affairs, Damdin Tsogtbaatar, entered the bar. Lombardi made the introduction, explaining that the pastor was planning a trip to Mongolia.

There, the high-ranking Mongolian officials gave "a strategic briefing of Mongolia" to the pastor, his son, and, somewhat inexplicably, the South Florida saxophonist Edwin Sepulveda.[53]

Sepulveda serves on what he calls an unofficial Mar-a-Lago "welcoming committee" for the American Pro-Israel PAC, a fly-by-night political committee set up to "elect candidates who embrace the Judeo-Christian worldview and support the Nation of Israel as America's closest ally."[54] Founded in 2018, the PAC hosted a dinner at Mar-a-Lago during the Trump family's Thanksgiving holiday, paying the club nearly $40,000.[55] One car dealer from Ohio donated $100,000 to the group in order to attend.[56] The PAC put on two more events at Mar-a-Lago, but it's not clear how much Trump made because the PAC didn't file its required financial disclosure forms with the Federal Election Commission.[57] (At one of those events Lombardi gave the opening address.[58])

When reached, Sepulveda said the Easter discussion with the Mongolians in the Library Bar was "classified."[59]

But Howard-Browne laughed off that characterization. The Mongolians simply ordered drinks, he said. They chatted about Mongolia and its need for foreign investments and tourism dollars.

Then they had lunch out on the terrace.

Interested in trying American cuisine, several members of the Mongolian delegation ate burgers.

Lombardi was a fixer doing what he did best: connecting people who could help each other—and him too. The Mongolians were looking for influence in the Trump administration—and he had shown them the perfect backdoor at Mar-a-Lago. He hoped the connection might someday lead to his long-hoped-for summit between Trump and Kim and, eventually, peace.

More than a month later Lombardi got a call from his friends in Mongolia.[60] John Bolton, then Trump's national security advisor, was in Ulaanbaatar meeting with Tsogtbaatar and Otgonbayar, the high-ranking Mongolian officials Lombardi had brought to lunch at Mar-a-Lago.[61]

The trip made Bolton something of a laughing stock in the press and foreign-policy circles.[62] At the time Trump was holding his summit with Kim at the demilitarized zone between North and South Korea. There he became the first sitting US president to walk across the DMZ line—a true act of showmanship made for TV.[63] The timing of Bolton's Mongolian expedition made it look as if Trump had banished his national security advisor from the historic moment. After all, Trump had always been a little embarrassed by Bolton. Specifically, Bolton's *looks* embarrassed Trump. His big bushy mustache was just a bit *too much* for the Trump brand, a White House insider once told the *Washington Post*.[64] (Bolton, a North Korea hawk, probably didn't mind missing out.[65] And as it turned out his trip to Mongolia was planned long before Trump's jaunt to the Korean peninsula.[66])

Lombardi's Mongolian friends were delighted by Bolton's visit.

"When are you coming?" they asked. "Our president would like to meet you."

Lombardi said he politely deflected, although he's planning to make another trip to Mongolia at some point soon. The way things were looking, he had already done his job.

In Mongolia Bolton's visit was seen as a huge success.[67] The relationship between the two nations took off. Weeks later President Battulga was visiting with Trump in the White House. He offered a gift: a prized miniature horse from Mongolia for Trump's youngest son, Barron.[68]

Of course, Barron didn't really get to keep the horse, a fragile and near-priceless creature that would not have been easy to ship across the Pacific. Instead, the horse stayed in Mongolia, but Barron got to name it. He chose "Victory."

A *Washington Post* headline declared, "The Trump administration and Mongolia are getting cozy."[69]

Over the summer Donald Trump Jr. went to Mongolia to trophy hunt an endangered species of sheep.[70] Then, Lombardi's associate, the foreign minister Tsogtbaatar, met Trump and Melania after the UN General Assembly on September 24, 2019.[71]

Lombardi was as close to real influence as he had ever been. He clearly relished it, though he never said as much.

His agenda was being heard—not in the cloistered confines of Washington, DC, but in the place that actually mattered: Mar-a-Lago.

KING OF THE SWAMP

A FEW YEARS before he became president, Donald Trump walked down the lawn to Mar-a-Lago's tennis club on an early morning jaunt.

He took a seat on a chair and looked out admiringly over the five clay courts where, years earlier, he'd played pro/am tournaments for charity.

Trump always won the tournament. Not because he was a fantastic tennis player—he was average—but because he always picked the best professional player to be his partner. In 2001 he partnered with South African star David Adams, then the world's number seven doubles player, to beat pro Vince Spadea and his partner, the disgraced junk bond king Michael Milken, whom as president Trump would later pardon.[1] (The tournament raised $2.5 million for a prostate cancer cure.[2]) It wasn't cheating, per se. Trump just hates losing, so he always stacked the deck in his own favor. Staff say that the other players also used to let Trump win.

"He had to win. And if he didn't win, he was not happy," said Fred Rustmann, who attended some of the tournaments. "You could see it in his face. His face gets all red. He's not happy. If he made a bad shot, not happy."[3]

"The Donald would always rig the match," he added.

Hardly anyone was around that day as Trump sat alone. In the early morning, the sun bakes the eastern-facing courts. A staffer offered him water. "No," he snapped. The staffer scurried off. On the nearest court, one instructor was teaching a beginner how to hit a backhand.

"These are the greatest courts in the world," Trump suddenly said.[4]

The staff were pretty sure their boss was talking to himself. It would be very rude to shout something like that at a beginner who was trying not to trip over their own feet.

"Aren't these the greatest courts in the world?" Trump continued loudly. "That Serena Williams, isn't she great," he said of the star, an honorary Mar-a-Lago member who had just broken the record for match victories at the Australian Open.[5]

They all pretended not to hear as the Don of Mar-a-Lago marveled to himself about the greatness of his own kingdom, perched on the edge of the nation's largest swamp.

MALARIA WAS ELIMINATED from Florida in the 1940s.[6]

It was a modern miracle.

Only a decade earlier the mosquito-borne disease—which induces its victims to sweat heavily while sitting on the toilet clutching a bucket to accommodate the sick coming from "both ends"—had been killing Floridians at an alarming rate.

The major about-face in malaria mortality was brought about not just by modern medicine but through an aggressive government initiative to eliminate the kinds of mosquitoes that carry malaria by draining the swamps where they breed.[7] The program was so successful that the process for rapid and systematic eradication of disease-carrying insects became a popular political metaphor for rooting out corruption.

"Drain the swamp!" goes the cry.

The problem is that politicos can't seem to agree on exactly where the swamp is, what the mosquitos are, and who ends up fouling their pants.

The idea of draining the political swamp is thought to have been first used by Milwaukee-based socialist Winfield R. Gaylord in a letter to the *Daily Northwestern* in 1903.[8] "Socialists are not satisfied with killing a few of the mosquitoes which come from the capitalist swamp; they want to drain the swamp," wrote Gaylord.[9]

To Gaylord, money and the economic interests of the Gilded Age robber barons, carried to Washington by corrupt politicians, would infect American democratic institutions with "industrial despotism."

Candidate Donald Trump used the same metaphor to appeal to coal miners, laid-off auto workers, and others dispossessed by the financial crisis. He first tried it out in Gaylord's Wisconsin.[10]

But unlike Gaylord, who saw "capitalism" as the swamp, Trump supporters see Washington, DC, as the swamp and career politicians and staffers as the carriers of the corrupt plague known in their circles as "the deep state." They say Trump, a billionaire in his own right, wouldn't fall victim to the kind of corruption seemingly endemic in Washington precisely because he is so wealthy.

It's not clear that Trump himself initially understood his own metaphor or the historical uses of the same phrase. The slogan, modeled on Ronald Reagan's description of Washington's entrenched bureaucracy, had been suggested to him during the campaign. Trump was more than a little skeptical.[11]

"I hated it," Trump explained later. "Somebody said, 'Drain the swamp,' and I said, 'Oh, that is so hokey. That is so terrible.'" But for whatever reason, Trump decided to try it on October 17, 2016, in a speech about ethics reform in Green Bay. The crowd went crazy. They loved it.

Whoa, what's this? Trump thought.

"Then I said it again. And then I start saying it like I meant it, right? And then I said it—I started loving it, and the place loved it," Trump marveled. "Drain the swamp. It's true. It's true. Drain the swamp."

Ever the crowd pleaser, Trump continued to promise to drain the swamp and rid the country of swamp creatures like his opponent Hillary Clinton, whom he has called the "most corrupt person to ever run for the presidency of the United States."[12]

He would know, he said. Few have spent more time mucking around this particular swamp than Donald J. Trump. For decades Trump has played to politicians on both sides of the aisle in an effort to grease the wheels for future favors.

"I give to everybody," Trump said at a debate during the Republican primaries in 2015.[13] "When they call, I give. And you know what? When I need something from them two years later, three years later, I call them, they are there for me."

At the debate Trump also said he had once donated to the Clinton Foundation—and thus secured Hillary's presence at his Mar-a-Lago wedding to Melania Knauss.

Trump had given thousands of dollars to Clinton's various campaigns over the years—to her US Senate race in New York and then later during her primary defeat against Obama.[14]

"I said be at my wedding and she came to my wedding. You know why?" Trump asked the debate crowd. "She didn't have a choice because I gave."

The jibe hurt Clinton's feelings, her spokeswoman said after the debate.[15] Clinton thought she had been invited to the wedding because the Trumps and Clintons were friends.

On the campaign trail Trump called the pay-to-play system broken.

But after his election he went straight back home to the swamp he'd promised to drain.

When Congress passed his sweeping tax cuts in December 2017 that largely benefited the wealthy and corporations, Trump celebrated at Mar-a-Lago.

Over dinner he crowed to his friends: "You all just got a lot richer."[16]

HAMILTON DISSTON WAS the first part-time Floridian to promise to drain the swamp.[17] Though the two never met, in some ways Disston laid the groundwork for Trump's political career. Like Trump, Disston was born in the northeast, made a fortune by expanding his father's company, was considered a "nouveau riche . . . society club man," had business interests in Atlantic City, and came to Florida, where he was charmed by both the weather and the great business potential.[18] Unlike Trump, in Disston's case the swamp drainage he promised was quite literal. And it began around 1880.

Disston had landed a contract with the state of Florida to drain large swathes of government land in the northern Everglades, which, once dried out, he thought would become rich in potential for citrus farming and other agro-industry. In exchange for the work, Disston's company received 50 percent of the drained land, which he then sold to railroad companies. He recruited wealthy financiers from the north and Europe to invest in this new land, "making him one of the largest promoters of Florida."[19] As he dredged canals and pumped water, Disston was planting seeds in Florida's southeast for another kind of swamp to replace the marshland.

"From the time Mr. Disston's purposes became known . . . more miles of railroad were built [in Florida] in proportion to population than in any other state of the Union," one scholar wrote in 1939.[20] Snowbirds seeking warmth and beaches during the winter months began to flock to Palm Beach as soon as the swamps were dry enough to lay down railroad tracks that far south. Within two decades of Disston's drainage, the far more celebrated Henry Flagler of Standard Oil had opened his first hotel in Palm Beach in 1894 and established the area as the winter getaway for the nation's wealthiest and best-connected class. Thirty years later Marjorie Merriweather Post took the train to Palm Beach and built Mar-a-Lago.

If the swamp refers to the place where special interests commingle with powerful political operatives, then it's safe to say that Mar-a-Lago became the palace of the swamp creatures quite early. At her lavish estate, which took a staff of seventy to run, Post entertained politicians, lawyers, and businessmen who were crafting the industrial capitalism of the twentieth-century American state.[21]

Post "furnished [her home] with the same gaily plumed abandon as a Ziegfeld Follies set, filling it with furniture, tapestries and paintings from decaying ducal palaces and stone carvings reminiscent of ancient Greece and Egypt," Nancy Rubin wrote in *American Empress*, a 1995 biography of Post.[22] "The parties held at Mar-a-Lago were equally fabulous. Guest lists often exceeded 200 and included some of America's most celebrated tycoons, moguls and movie stars, as well as European aristocrats." She even brought Ringling Bros. and Barnum & Bailey Circus to perform.[23]

Post hoped to make Mar-a-Lago's role in statecraft official. The year before she died in 1973 she bequeathed Mar-a-Lago to the federal government, saying her home should be used as a "Winter White House"—a term she may have borrowed from her Palm Beach neighbor Joseph P. Kennedy Sr. His son John Fitzgerald Kennedy had taken his wife, Jackie, and their children to the family home in Palm Beach so often while he was commander-in-chief that people began to call Joe's home the Winter White House.[24] It was enough to spark envy in any Palm Beacher with a taste for one-upping the neighbors.

Mar-a-Lago "really was the perfect place for visiting dignitaries before they came to Washington, if they needed to rest up, or as a winter White House," Post's daughter Dina Merrill said.[25]

President Richard Nixon, who vacationed in Key Biscayne, liked the idea, although Watergate put the kibosh to that. In the end, Mar-a-Lago proved too expensive for the government to maintain and was given back to the Post Foundation in 1981.[26] The estate went up for sale. For years it languished. Post's mansion was a gem in Palm Beach—but a hideously expensive and impractical investment, costing $1 million per year to maintain.[27]

Trump first learned about Mar-a-Lago while being chauffeured to a dinner party in Palm Beach in the early 1980s. The Manhattan mogul was fascinated by Palm Beach, admiring the status and longevity it represented. Trump may have inherited his wealth, but he didn't inherit status. His grandfather was a German immigrant, not old money.[28] Trump was possessed by the notion of buying his way into a society where access is typically only granted through birthright. He asked the driver what was for sale as they drove through the streets lined with hedges.

"Well, the best thing by far is Mar-a-Lago," the driver replied.[29] Trump, who had never heard of Mar-a-Lago, ordered an immediate detour. They arrived at an estate as overstated as the real estate mogul himself. Peering through the hedges from South Ocean Boulevard, the thirty-nine-year-old got his first glimpse. The property needed work, "like an old, beat-up, overgrown Rembrandt waiting to be restored," he said in his book *Trump: The Art of the Comeback*.[30]

As soon as he saw it, Trump knew Mar-a-Lago would be his crown jewel.

"I feel it is one of the diamonds of real estate, and I love diamonds, as you know," he said.[31]

The king had found his castle.

SUN-KISSED PALM BEACH was a far cry from the first place Trump had sought to rule.

As a boy, dissatisfied by being the rich kid in the safe, insulated Queens suburb he called home, Trump would sneak off to the F train and cross the East River into the bustle of Manhattan, which his parents considered too dangerous.[32] It was there, gazing up at the skyscrapers, that he decided how he would make his mark. It certainly wouldn't be by building the dull, gray, Soviet-style projects on Coney Island that his father had. Fred Trump's business was good, but Donald knew he could do better. And bigger. His real estate empire would be a manifestation of his own larger-than-life ambitions.

Trump's father thought his son was crazy and initially tried to keep him within the outer boroughs, overseeing projects in Brooklyn, Queens, and Staten Island from a modest office on Avenue Z—well away from Manhattan.[33] It was there that the father and son ran into a major issue with the law. In 1973 the Justice Department sued Fred and Donald Trump, alleging they denied housing to prospective black tenants.[34] At the time it was one of the biggest Fair Housing Act cases ever pursued by the government.[35] Trump called the suit ridiculous and consulted Roy Cohn, the former counsel to Senator Joseph McCarthy as well as suspected mob bosses.[36] Cohn urged him not to settle.[37] They hit you, the pugnacious Cohn advised, you hit them back a hundred times harder. Trump filed a $100 million countersuit, accusing the Justice Department of defamation. Though that countersuit was dismissed, Trump later settled the case without admitting guilt.[38] Cohn's advice would set the stage for how Trump would handle conflicts to come:[39] There's nothing a multi-million-dollar lawsuit can't fix. (Gratitude may not have been one of the lessons Trump learned. Years later Cohn came to visit Mar-a-Lago. He was dying of AIDS. After Cohn left, "I had to spend a fortune to fumigate all the dishes and silverware," Trump reportedly told his guests.[40])

It was on New York construction sites that Trump learned the art of emotional manipulation. He was a tough boss, prone to tirades and micromanaging, with little regard for the opinions of his chief engineers or lawyers.[41] It was his way or no way.[42] But for the working guys—apart from, of course, the ones whose paychecks he shorted—he was generally a likable boss.

Guido Lombardi gave an impression of the mogul's construction-site manner.

"Hey Joe!" Trump might say to a guy on the site. "How are you doing? How's your wife? I know she was having an operation." The worker's heart would melt that the big boss remembered his family. "Oh yeah, she's doing good. Thank you, Mr. Trump." (It was a skill that would later come in handy in politics.)

Trump cares what other people think about him almost as much as he cares about getting his way. He always wore makeup to the job site in case someone with a camera stopped by, something the workers laughed about behind his back.[43] Ultimately Trump is an opportunist, ready to jump at any enticing prospect. In New York he learned that the best deals came from waiting for a seller to be just the right amount of desperate. And in the 1970s New Yorkers were desperate.

New York City was at a breaking point—on the brink of bankruptcy and with a serial killer on the loose.[44] Tax incentives were offered to anyone willing to invest.[45] So, amid the turmoil and despite the naysayers, Trump was able to carve out his first Manhattan real estate venture: the decrepit Commodore Hotel near Grand Central Station. Trump picked it up for a mere $9.5 million from the bankrupt Penn Central railroad and pitched the deal as an act of civic-minded selflessness to the press.[46]

At a time when public employees were being laid off for the first time since the Great Depression, Trump was wearing three-piece, flared-leg suits and riding around Manhattan in a limousine with DJT license plates, driven by a laid-off cop who played the role of armed chauffeur.[47] He opened Trump Tower on Fifth Avenue and billed the condos as intended exclusively for "the world's best people" and "totally inaccessible to the public."

"I tried to bring Donald down to earth many times," Fred Trump told *New York* in 1980. "But he always had a nose for quality, and we could never get it out of him. Once when he was a little boy, a friend was having a birthday, and he wanted to buy him a fancy baseball glove—$35 it cost, can you imagine anything so crazy!—so I took Donald to see a $5 glove Herman's was advertising, and seeing those cheap gloves, he almost threw up."[48]

His father, who had sent Trump to military school to whip out his obsession with glitz and glamor, wasn't his only critic. One detractor speaking to the *New York Times* called the Donald "overrated" and "totally obnoxious."[49] His competitor, Sam LeFrak, said, "Kid only knows how to talk, not to build."[50] (LeFrak's son, Richard, would later become a member of Mar-a-Lago.[51])

The lack of recognition for his hard work and contributions to the city seeped under Trump's skin.

"In Houston, I would be the most important man in the city—but here, you bang your head against the wall to try to get some nice buildings up, and what happens? Everybody comes after you," Trump once said of his reception in New York.[52]

The problem wasn't him, he almost certainly thought. It was everyone else who didn't understand what he was doing.

And no one, not his father, not the doyennes of Palm Beach, was going to change Trump's bull-in-a-china-shop approach.

PALM BEACH IS NOT friendly to strangers. As the journalist Ronald Kessler pointed out, the town doesn't even have a sign indicating visitors have entered the municipality. "If they have to ask where Palm Beach is, they shouldn't be there," Kessler wrote.[53]

"They think they are above the world," said one Palm Beacher, Ildikó Varga, of her fellow islanders.[54] "They think that they are more than everybody else."

Varga immigrated to the United States from Hungary, where she had amassed a small fortune in the crystal business. She opened a crystal boutique in Palm Beach in 1994.[55] She spared no expense, launching her store on Worth Avenue, a posh shopping district that is the town's answer to Fifth Avenue in Manhattan and Rodeo Drive in Beverly Hills.

The day before the grand opening a group of people knocked on the shop door. Varga's son, inside sweeping, ushered them in.

"What brings you from Budapest to Worth Avenue?" one inquired. "It's like the top of the world."

Varga was an intruder, and Palm Beach intended to show her that. Still, the young man didn't flinch.

"My mother likes the best," he responded. "My mother always wants the elegance."

That's why they chose Worth Avenue, he explained.

The group sized him up, unsure at first what to do with this bold outsider. Then a woman in the group stepped forward.

"Give me a piece of paper, and I am going to write my name and number so your mother can call me," she said.

In clear penmanship the woman wrote: Eunice Kennedy Shriver.

Shriver was John F. Kennedy's younger sister. The Kennedy clan, Palm Beach regulars, were as much a royal family as the United States had.

Still new to the country, Varga's son didn't recognize Shriver's name. Varga called her back that day. Shriver loved Budapest, she told Varga. The two became fast friends. Shriver brought Varga to all the best parties, and their photos began to show up together in the society pages. The Kennedys commissioned a crystal portrait of the late Rose Kennedy, the family's matriarch.[56]

"That really helped me in the social life," Varga explained. "People didn't know who I am, but they saw me with influential people, so everybody was inviting me everywhere. That's how I basically got into the social life of Palm Beach, Washington, DC, and New York."

Unspoken rules dictate that to be part of Palm Beach society is to be born into it. But if you wanted an alternate route, being welcomed by Kennedys was a pretty good start.

RATHER THAN DEPENDING on friends for an entree into Palm Beach, Trump tried to buy his way in.

In 1983 Trump made his first offer for Mar-a-Lago.

His $9 million bid was contingent on rezoning, as he planned to build fourteen single-family homes on the property alongside the mansion.[57] It was less than half the listed asking price of $20 million. (The highest sale price for a home in the United States at the time was believed to be $14.5 million.[58]) The Foundation said no.[59] Even his business proposals were offensive to old money. Trump didn't make a new offer right away. He could afford to wait. The Foundation was struggling and buyers that wealthy were scarce. The estimated costs of keeping up the estate had soared to $2 million per year, plus $400,000 in property taxes.[60]

Triump kept a shrewd eye on Mar-a-Lago, watching deal after deal with other potential buyers fall through. In the summer of 1985 O. W. Smith, the Scottish president of a gold refinery, offered to buy the property for $14 million, contingent on securing the strip of beachfront property across South Ocean Boulevard.[61] The quaint cabanas and pool overlooking the beach had once made up the "Mar" side of Mar-a-Lago but had long since been sold off to the former owner of Kentucky Fried Chicken. Desperate to close the deal, the Foundation signed a contract to buy the beach property back for a whopping $2 million, only to have Smith back out at the last minute. The Foundation ended up with more land—and fewer options. Trump swooped in.

From an outsider's perspective, he looked flush. He had just completed some of his first real estate projects: the Grand Hyatt Hotel, Trump Tower, and an Atlantic City casino, among others. As the owner of a team in an upstart football league, he sued the NFL on antitrust grounds. But while he managed to keep it quiet at the time, his casinos, hotels, and other core businesses lost $46.1 million in 1985, a *New York Times* investigation found.[62] By the mid-1990s his losses would total $1.17 billion. But that didn't stop him from making an opportunistic offer on Mar-a-Lago when Smith and other interested parties like the Houston developer Cerf Stanford Ross got cold feet.

BACK AT TRUMP TOWER in New York, the mogul ran into one of his neighbors, Gianna Lahainer, future wife of Guido Lombardi.[63]

"Donald, how are you?" Lahainer greeted him. She had heard the chatter in Palm Beach about Trump's intention to buy Mar-a-Lago. "I hear that you're buying this place."

"Yeah, we are still debating the final contract and everything," Trump replied.

Lahainer knew everything about everyone. And she knew there were lots of problems with Mar-a-Lago. She was curious about Trump's decision to buy.

"Well, don't the planes bother you?" she inquired, in that Palm Beach fashion of softening one's critique by placing a question mark at the end.

Trump was confused. "What planes?"

Lahainer explained that Mar-a-Lago sits directly below the flight path to Palm Beach International Airport. On some days the planes fly so low that diners on the terrace must pause their conversation and wait for the deafening engines to pass.

"You know I was up for a house there and I didn't buy it because of the planes," Lahainer told Trump. The brokers showing Trump the property certainly knew about the noise—everyone in Palm Beach did—and no doubt planned for it by showing the property only during particular times of day.

In the end, Trump bought Mar-a-Lago for even less than his first low-ball offer—$5 million for the property and $3 million for its furnishings—in part because he negotiated around the inconvenience of the airplane noise.[64] (At least that's how Lombardi tells the story.[65]) Trump paid another $2 million for the beachfront land, bailing the Foundation out of its bad deal.

Trump barely put up any of his own money. Instead, he secured an unrecorded $8.5 million loan from Chase Manhattan Bank as well as a loan from the owner of the beachfront property to finance the purchase.[66]

Still, he told the world he had paid all cash.[67]

(Decades later he would also try to inflate the value of his original offers, saying he had bid $28 million—and been rejected by the Foundation—only to eventually beat the aristocrats down.[68])

Embellishments aside, it was still Trump's best business deal to date. In 2018 Forbes valued the property at $160 million, meaning Trump's investment had outpaced the S&P Index's return.[69] This time there was no talk of subdividing the property, which had proven unpopular with the townsfolk. As thanks for her tip about the planes, Lahainer was made vice president of the Trump Tower condo association in New York.[70]

"She saved him a lot of money," Lombardi would later explain.

In palm beach Mar-a-Lago's new owner was a pariah.

Trump was crude. He was distasteful. And he had no desire to kiss ass.

He was everything that was hated in the reserved, insular, high-society town—which banned men from jogging shirtless until the mid-1990s.[71]

On his private Boeing 727, Trump flew in friends from New York to see his grand new winter palace. The Prince of Wales and Constantine, the deposed king of Greece, came for tea. As a souvenir, visitors received a brochure about Mar-a-Lago embossed with the names Donald and

Ivana Trump in eighteen-karat gold.[72] (Ivana, a Czech model, was the Donald's first wife.)

Where most Palm Beachers hid behind the hedges that blocked their homes and clubs from the public, Trump basked in the limelight. He invited reporters to Mar-a-Lago and called up the tabloids or radio shows to offer salacious commentary. He appeared regularly on the *Howard Stern Show*, sharing opinions on everything from J. Lo's butt to his various sexual exploits.[73] This was a shock to Palm Beachers, who typically kept to themselves and their circles, save for write-ups about their charitable events in the *Palm Beach Daily News*, nicknamed the Shiny Sheet.

After divorcing Ivana, Trump threw a "Bachelor Ball" to celebrate. The party infuriated the rest of Palm Beach. For on that very night, just up the road, the Breakers Resort was hosting the International Red Cross Ball—the crown jewel of the social season. As the ladies and gentlemen of Palm Beach donned their splendor for a tasteful evening, across the way at Mar-a-Lago pro football and basketball players, cheerleaders, and 350 Miami models were filling Trump's halls, with paparazzi eagerly waiting to snap their photos.[74]

As much as old-world Palm Beachers hated this immoderate outsider, he held an irresistible appeal.

Palm Beach before Trump was boring. Every season it was the same people, from the same families, going to the same galas at the same clubs. For the most part a night out consisted of eating dinner and perhaps a bit of live music. Trump provided a different option—parties with pretty girls and celebrities, Hawaiian night–themed bashes and world-class performers like the Beach Boys.

But behind his nouveau-riche bravado, Trump was not immune to the heavy financial burden of Mar-a-Lago.

A year after he bought the estate Trump sued the county property appraiser's office after receiving a property tax bill of $208,340.[75] Trump said the county had overvalued Mar-a-Lago by $4.5 million. His real tax bill, he claimed, should be cut in half. Trump won the initial ruling[76] but lost in the appeal, leaving him to foot the full bill.[77]

That first tax bill might have seemed like small change to a billionaire, but two of Trump's casinos were hurtling toward bankruptcy.[78] The Trump Taj Mahal Casino, his Castle Casino, and the airline Trump Shuttle all reported multi-million-dollar losses in 1990.

When his sumptuous winter home proved to be a white elephant—too expensive for any individual to maintain—Trump was forced to look for alternatives.

In 1991 he again proposed subdividing the seventeen-acre lot in order to build and sell eight multi-million-dollar homes.[79]

"I'll call the project the Mansions at Mar-a-Lago. I'll turn it into a moneymaker," he told his fretful bankers. ("When you owe billions of dollars, and then you journey down to Mar-a-Lago on your 727 for weekends, it irks them," he later wrote of the tense exchange.[80])

The town shot him down. It wasn't interested in rezoning a historic property. After two years of strife, including a $50 million lawsuit and a threat to sell the estate to the Reverend Sun Myung Moon and his Unification Church if he didn't get his way, Trump folded.[81] Facing the prospect of personal bankruptcy, he needed a new plan.

It wouldn't be the Donald who came up with the idea that saved his Florida home. Trump's Palm Beach attorney, Paul Rampell, was the real visionary behind turning Post's property into a social club, according to Laurence Leamer's *Mar-a-Lago: Inside the Gates of Power at Donald Trump's Presidential Palace.*

Trump himself didn't think it would work. "I just don't like it," he told Rampell. "It's just not right."[82] Still, Trump didn't have any other options. And despite some grumbling, the town council consented.[83] (Trump later tried to take credit for his lawyer's stroke of genius.[84] He would also give up his right to develop Mar-a-Lago as anything but a club, knocking roughly $250,000 off his tax bill overnight.[85])

The matrons of Palm Beach society clutched their pearls at the news. They had built their lives around clubs like Bath & Tennis and the Everglades. Now a paparazzi-chasing Queens developer wanted to upend their social order.

"Many old-money Palm Beachers did not want to become members of Mar-a-Lago at the beginning because anybody could buy a membership, and they believed membership should be something you inherit," said Ildikó Varga, the Hungarian crystal merchant.[86] She quickly signed up.

Trump was about to capitalize on a growing pool of like-minded and incredibly wealthy high-society outcasts who wintered—bored and isolated—on the island of Palm Beach: people the other WASP-y clubs wouldn't touch. Jews and African Americans would pay good money for a membership. So would the simply gauche, like one Palm Beach billionaire who had been rejected from Bath & Tennis after raising a glass of dessert wine and saying the only thing sweeter than a bottle of Château d'Yquem were his wife's private parts.[87]

Trump planned to open his doors to any of these "un-clubbables"—so long as they could pay.

"If you were a member of the Bath & Tennis Club or the Everglades, you were horrified that this man whose parents didn't come over on the *Mayflower* took over Mar-a-Lago and was going to let in anybody who could afford it," said Shannon Donnelly, a transplanted northeasterner who has spent years covering Palm Beach society for the Shiny Sheet. "They said: 'That's not a club. That's Triple A.'"

Trump's inclusivity did not arise from any particular sense of tolerance but because money, which he equated with prestige, meant more to him than almost any ideology.

Certainly Trump had a well-earned reputation for racism.

Several years before he turned Mar-a-Lago into a club, he walked into a recording studio in New York to find several black musicians recording music for a commercial for one of his Atlantic City casinos.

"I really don't want any n****** on my project," he said loudly to the composer Fred Weinberg, one of the only white people in the room.[88] Trump also immediately asked about Weinberg's accent, asking where it was from. Weinberg explained that his parents were Holocaust survivors and had fled to Colombia, where he was born before moving to the United States.

"Oh, so you're a Jew, spic, aren't you," Trump replied. (Weinberg's account was confirmed by another person who worked at the company and heard about the incident at the time.[89])

Trump's intolerance seemed to disappear in Palm Beach. He was okay with anyone who could pay his club's $50,000 entry fee. And as a result, Trump opened what remains the most diverse club in town.

"Palm Beach is very much changing for the better," Trump told the *Wall Street Journal* in 1997.[90] "A lot of that is because of Mar-a-Lago."

ON JANUARY 22, 2005, Melania Knauss walked down the aisle of the Church of Bethesda-by-the-Sea in Palm Beach wearing a $100,000 Dior dress.[91] Fifteen hundred crystals—which had taken more than five hundred hours to sew into place—made the dress almost too heavy for the thin model to carry as she approached Trump at the altar.

The wedding was a coronation in Palm Beach—the christening of a new king.

"Donald is our Prince Charles," Mar-a-Lago member Robin Bernstein told the *Palm Beach Post* at the time.[92] "It's a great honor to be invited. He knows so many people that an invitation is a form of acknowledgement." Bernstein's husband sells insurance to the Trump Organization.[93] The couple had been members since the 1990s,[94] and their twin daughters grew up best friends with Tiffany Trump.[95]

In Mar-a-Lago's largest ballroom Trump's court celebrated with caviar, tenderloin, and Cristal. Among the revelers were celebrity entertainers like Billy Joel, Paul Anka, Tony Bennett, Russell Simmons of Def Jam Records, *American Idol*'s Simon Cowell, *Apprentice* producer Mark Burnett, infamous boxing promoter Don King, supermodel Heidi Klum, and a who's-who of TV personalities, including Barbara Walters, Katie Couric, Kelly Ripa, and Kathie Lee Gifford.[96]

There were also business tycoons like Kathy and Rick Hilton (parents of Paris) and a smattering of political elites, including Rudolph Giuliani and his then wife Judith Nathan. Laughing alongside the Trumps at the reception—the first event held in his new, Sun King–style ballroom at Mar-a-Lago—was Hillary Clinton in a yellow gown. Bill Clinton placed his hand on Donald's shoulder, giving it a squeeze.

These were Trump's friends—or at least the people he considered more than acquaintances.[97] The creatures of the swamp had come to pay him their respects.

A decade later, as the president established his administration, the early Mar-a-Lago members and honored wedding guests began to make appearances with Trump as he leaned on them to extend his empire to Washington, DC.

Bernstein, who reportedly spoke "basic" Spanish, was named the US ambassador to the Dominican Republic, where the Trump Organization was actively reviving a real estate project.[98]

Giuliani would continue to serve as Trump's lawyer and fixer, performing a wide variety of tasks, including pressuring the Ukrainian government to dig up dirt on Trump's political rivals.

WHEN AIR FORCE ONE touched down at Palm Beach International Airport in February 2017, dozens of supporters gathered on the tarmac to greet a newly sworn-in President Trump, who was making his first trip to Palm Beach as commander-in-chief. The crowd cheered, passing him baseball caps to autograph.[99] Trump flashed thumbs up and clapped alongside his supporters.

After a few minutes he turned to get into his motorcade, pausing only to toss his uncapped black Sharpie to the crowd. People lunged for the prize. A few miles east, more locals lined the roads to Mar-a-Lago, waiting to catch a glimpse of America's new leader.

If you'd asked any longtime Palm Beacher a decade earlier if they thought such a scene was possible, they'd have scoffed. The old guard, whose wealth and status spanned generations, could never have dreamed of a moment when they might be forced to cede control of Palm Beach society to the gaudy newcomers and their poster boy, Donald Trump.[100]

But now that he was president, Palm Beach revolved around Trump: roads were closed, planes were barred from flying overhead, and crowds were beckoned at his command. The old guard retreated to their mansions and learned to accept—or at least quietly ignore—their grand new seigneur.

In the end it wasn't so much that Donald Trump drained the swamp as that he consumed it.

THE WINTER WHITE HOUSE

INCOMING WHITE HOUSE spokespeople Kellyanne Conway and Jason Miller spent their holidays after Trump's election branding Mar-a-Lago as the new White House. Their makeshift, outdoor studio for network TV interviews was positioned so that viewers could see the estate's palm trees and turrets in the background. It was an image of sunshine, perfect tranquility, and control.

Like most things in Palm Beach, appearance did not match reality.

A quick camera pan right would have revealed that Conway was actually seated in a dusty, public boat launch paces away from the busy Southern Boulevard bridge that thousands of people use every day to get to and from the barrier island. Supporters begging for autographs converged on the site. Enraged feminists biked over the bridge to flip the bird or spit in the direction of Trump's palace. Gunboats turned away jet skiers who got too close to the property while enjoying the sunshine on the public waterway.

After the biggest electoral upset in American history, chaos was the new normal.

Trump's transition team rampaged around Mar-a-Lago, breaking every norm of both Washington, DC, and Palm Beach.

It was the most exciting thing to happen to Mar-a-Lago in years, maybe ever. Helicopters hovered overhead. Secret Service agents popped out of bushes and walked bomb-sniffing dogs around cars. Media swarmed from all over the world. The president-elect was seen wandering the terrace and dining room, consulting members on whom he should tap as secretary of state and what he should say in his inaugural address.[1] (When he tweeted a photo of himself "writing" the speech, he appeared to be sitting not in his quarters but at the receptionist's desk in Mar-a-Lago's main entryway.[2])

People flew in from across the country to interview for jobs in the new administration. Fabio, the famous model from the front of romance novels, chatted with the president-elect. (What he hoped for was never exactly clear, although he reportedly offered his assistance on veterans' issues to White House press secretary Sean Spicer.[3]) Actor and director Sylvester Stallone presented Trump with a framed article that praised the *Rocky*-inspired political ad Stallone had produced for the campaign.[4]

"To President Trump, a Real Champ! Greatest knockout in History!" Stallone wrote on the glass in black sharpie. The actor said he had turned down consideration for a position at the National Endowment of the Arts.[5]

Mar-a-Lago's more than thirty guest rooms booked up. Events sold out.

"Everybody wants a piece of whatever is happening there," said Lexye Aversa, a Palm Beach travel agent and event planner.[6] "They want to go to the parties. They want to feel part of it."

Palm Beach philanthropist Lois Pope was dead set on using her proximity to Trump to get a nine-week-old rescue puppy into the White House.[7] Pope had named the goldendoodle Patton, after Trump's favorite World War II general who believed himself to be the reincarnation of a marshal in Napoleon's imperial army.[8] Trump didn't take the bait.

Trump's golfing buddy Greg Norman—an Australian golf star and South Florida resident known as the "Great White Shark"—clinched a spot as an unofficial liaison between the Trump administration and Australia by grabbing White House Chief of Staff Reince Priebus as he walked through the dining room.[9] He had very important information for Trump about the "alliance between Australia and the US," Norman told Priebus at the time.

"That's how I started back-channeling the whole thing because to me I am a very proud Australian," Norman told the *Australian*. "I wanted to put it in front of him so it is on his radar screen in the Oval Office."

Niall O'Dowd, founder of the online diaspora publication *Irish Central*, joined his friend, Palm Beach attorney Brian Burns, for lunch at Mar-a-Lago on the last Friday afternoon of 2016.[10] Despite O'Dowd's distaste for Trump, Burns assured him it was a good opportunity for the Irish American journalist to make connections with the new administration.

O'Dowd was surprised to find he quite liked the club. It was classy, unlike other Trump properties he knew. When he mentioned it, someone proudly told him the gilding at Mar-a-Lago was *real* gold. Trump's other properties used the fake stuff.

The tables on the terrace filled up with members backslapping and reveling in a sense of occasion and self-importance. O'Dowd suspected that many of those lunching on overpriced burgers and salmon were expecting official ambassadorships or positions in the administration. A hint of mania permeated the air.

"The rest of the world was spinning around this axis now," O'Dowd said. "They had pulled off something that even they themselves were a little bit bewildered by."

O'Dowd's visit to Mar-a-Lago was enjoyable, if not quite peaceful. Members of Mar-a-Lago kept interrupting their lunch to chat with Burns about the victory.

The Burns family was well established in Palm Beach. His father, a Harvard Law School professor, had been a friend and advisor to the Kennedys. As a young man, Burns had caddied for JFK.[11] As a friend of Trump's, a respected member of the Irish American community, and a member of Mar-a-Lago, Burns seemed a shoo-in for ambassador to Ireland. The president had already run into him one night in the club's lobby and eagerly asked if he'd take the job.

"Brian, are you ready to go to Ireland?" Trump had said.[12]

Burns had always admired Trump. "He saw Trump as an outsider in Palm Beach," O'Dowd said.[13] "A guy who was prepared to break some of the glassware to get his way. And he kind of admired that." Trump was a king who rewarded loyalty.

Although Burns wasn't the only member in the running for an ambassadorship, he was certainly the most qualified. Mar-a-Lago member Patrick Park was tapped to be ambassador to Austria, receiving the unofficial offer from Trump via a handwritten note early in 2017.[14] A concert pianist and businessman, his only apparent qualification was his love for

The Sound of Music, a movie set in Austria that Park says he's seen "like seventy-five times."

"I know every single word and song by heart. I've always wanted to live in the Von Trapp house," he told Palm Beach society writer Shannon Donnelly.

In the end, both Burns and Park declined the offers for ambassadorships for personal reasons. But two other club members, Lana Marks, a well-known Palm Beach handbag designer, and Robin Bernstein, whose company insured the Trump Organization and who called Trump "Prince Charles" at his third wedding, did become the ambassadors to South Africa and the Dominican Republic, respectively.[15] In both cases it's unclear what their qualifications were aside from being wealthy and well connected. (Marks was born in South Africa but hadn't lived there in forty years.[16])

"This is how influence works. It doesn't work the way people think it does," O'Dowd said. "It's a quiet kind of lunch at Mar-a-Lago. It's meeting the right kind of people at the right time at the right place."

"These are the people he's clasped to his bosom the last thirty years. Who stood with him when he was an outsider," he said.

AFTER LUNCH BURNS took O'Dowd to meet the new administration.[17] They entered a small room off the main foyer that had been hastily converted into an operations center at the Winter White House. The modern communications equipment must have seemed out of place against the elegant decor.

The room was empty except for three men sitting at a table: White House Chief Strategist Stephen Bannon, Chief of Staff Reince Priebus, and a man O'Dowd didn't recognize.

Years earlier O'Dowd had visited the Clinton transition team. He was taken aback by the difference between that experience and what he witnessed briefly at Mar-a-Lago. Clinton's drab Arkansas office was full of young men running between cubicles. They were ready to rule. In contrast, Trump's transition team relaxed in the gilded mansion. O'Dowd got the impression the men spent most of their time looking at each other and saying, "Can you believe this?"

"There really wasn't much sense of people doing much serious work, to be honest," O'Dowd said. "Frankly, I think they were still a little bit stunned that they were doing what they were doing. . . . Stunned that they were running the world."

Though it didn't seem like it at the time, O'Dowd had walked into the transition team's war room in the middle of a moment that would haunt Trump through the first two years of his presidency.

The previous day the Obama administration had announced the expulsion of thirty-five Russian government officials from the United States and closed two Russian government compounds as part of sanctions against Russia for Moscow's interference in the US elections.[18] Without a clear plan, the Mar-a-Lago transition team flew into action.[19] The team had agreed "tit for tat" retaliation wouldn't end well.[20] National Security Advisor Michael Flynn relayed the message to Russia's US ambassador Sergey Kislyak, who he hoped could encourage Putin to show restraint in his response to the sanctions.

Sometime around 5:00 P.M. on December 29, Flynn's second-in-command, Deputy National Security Advisor K. T. McFarland, briefed the president-elect. Also present were a group of advisors working from Mar-a-Lago, including Bannon, Priebus, and Press Secretary Sean Spicer.[21]

Did the Russians do "it"? Trump asked McFarland. By "it" he meant attempts to electronically intrude on and influence the elections.

"Yes," she responded.

Trump wasn't convinced. But, he said, the sanctions provided him leverage against the Russians. At the time Trump seemed to have more pressing things he wanted to discuss with his transition team.

Immediately after the briefing was over, Trump led the group of advisors out of the main building on a tour of his beloved estate. They navigated the cloisters via curving stone paths decorated with tropical plants and statues, past the terrace where dinner guests were beginning to gather, hung a left at the pool, and walked under the long yellow-and-white awning into the Donald J. Trump Grand Ballroom. Trump pointed to one of the Corinthian columns along the wall, puffing out his chest and telling war stories about the permitting process with the town.[22]

"He's very proud of all that stuff, and he can't get over it. He just talks about it all the time," Mar-a-Lago member Fred Rustmann said. "He's a braggart."

Bannon was in a good mood again by the time O'Dowd and his crew showed up the next day. The Mar-a-Lago team's quick response through their back channels had "stopped the train on Russia's response."[23] Kislyak later told Flynn as much, though Flynn admitted that he didn't document the part of his conversations with Kislyak about the sanctions out of a concern it could be perceived as interfering with the Obama administration's foreign policy.[24] (Flynn would plead guilty to lying to the FBI about those conversations.[25])

Bannon immediately got up to shake hands with O'Dowd and the rest of the group. He seemed to know Burns and was quick to explain that his ex-wife was Irish. He absolutely loved Ireland, he told the group affably, and chatted about various trips he had taken there and enjoyed. Bannon's warmth surprised O'Dowd. "This was a guy who had been portrayed as this monstrous entity who had brought this troglodyte into the White House, and he was in fact very effusively friendly," O'Dowd said.

Behind Bannon, Priebus wore a bemused expression. Still, he was game enough to chat and take pictures at Burns's request. "You just missed Kellyanne," Priebus told them as he shook hands.

The third man stayed seated, sourly observing the group. He looked very young, O'Dowd thought. The man never introduced himself, but O'Dowd later realized the glowering man was Stephen Miller, the immigration hardliner and chief architect of Trump's travel ban as well as his policy of separating children from their parents at the southern border.[26] Miller had been tasked with helping Trump write his inaugural address—a job that had seemingly been taken over by members and guests.

"I think a lot of it is opportunism. Everybody wants to be on the winning side," O'Dowd said. "You'll never get more sycophantic than the people around Trump."

If Trump is a shark, then those angling to be closest to his new administration were the remoras. It's a symbiotic relationship, if a bit lopsided. Remoras keep the parasites off the shark and, in exchange, receive protection and food from the much larger predators. But nature is cruel, and remoras tend to subsist off the shark's feces.

O'Dowd's visit with the transition team left him with little desire to pursue another Mar-a-Lago meet-and-greet. He had seen enough.

"You're looking at the unfolding of a right-wing dream, which is a strong man in the White House," O'Dowd said. "At Mar-a-Lago—that's his kingdom—Trump looks out over his minions and they all bow down. And after that it's bread, then it's circus."

WHEN TRUMP DID his first impromptu press conference as president-elect in front of Mar-a-Lago's three-hundred-pound, wrought-iron door, it wasn't his new press secretary who introduced him but an old friend—a convicted killer.[27]

"You all know Don King?" Trump asked the reporters, spreading his hands wide to the side.

The famous boxing promoter had been friends with Trump since the two had turned Atlantic City into a boxing mecca.[28] On the campaign trail Trump called King a "phenomenal person."[29] The two stood under the main door's archway.

"It's just great to be in America," a beaming King said, taking on his usual role of hype man. "Now, with our leader, we're going to make a new day, Make America Great Again."

King wore sparkly chains and an American flag around his neck, his iconic hair still standing straight up like he'd just been hit by lightning. He clutched a handful of tiny flags from various nations in his left hand.

Perhaps because of his odd appearance, it so happened that the first question at the first press conference held by the president-elect was addressed not to Trump but to an allegedly mobbed-up eighty-five-year-old who had once stomped a man to death.[30] (He was pardoned for manslaughter in 1983.[31])

"Is your Israeli flag a message for Obama?" a reporter in the group asked King.

"The Israeli flag is about peace, you know, peace in the Middle East," King said, not answering the question and rambling until Trump jumped in. The president-elect said he thought the press would be very impressed come January 20 and turned to leave. They stopped him with a barrage of questions about job creation, Russia, Obama, and health care.

Trump told reporters he had invited the leaders of the Mayo Clinic, Johns Hopkins Medicine, and the Cleveland Clinic to Mar-a-Lago that day for discussions.

"They were all in a room together with myself—and some others— and we're working on something to make it great for the veterans," Trump told reporters.

What he didn't say was that the "others" in that meeting were Mar-a-Lago regulars who planned to run the show in Washington.[32]

DAVID SHULKIN, A HOLDOVER from the Obama administration who was promoted to become Trump's first secretary of Veterans Affairs, saw firsthand how the levers of power under the new president ran through Mar-a-Lago.

His job interview happened there, although he didn't know it.

After Trump's surprise election, Shulkin, then the number-three official at the VA, was summoned to Florida. He wasn't sure why. Walking into the club was like "stepping into a James Bond film," Shulkin wrote in his 2019 memoir *It Shouldn't Be This Hard to Serve Your Country*.[33] On the terrace waiting for him was a short, elderly man with the bronzed skin, slicked-back hair, and confident manner of a man in charge: Ike Perlmutter, the chairman of Marvel, who was also one of the Trump campaign's biggest financial backers and a member of Mar-a-Lago.[34] Alongside him was Perlmutter's friend, the West Palm Beach doctor Bruce Moskowitz.

They talked of Perlmutter's service in the Israeli army during the Six-Day War of 1967 and of Moskowitz's connections to prestigious institutions like Johns Hopkins and the Mayo Clinic. They asked Shulkin about his time at the VA, and he told them he hoped the new president would let him stay on, however unlikely it seemed for an official appointed by Trump's hated Democratic predecessor. It felt bizarre. "The purpose of the meeting still eluded me," Shulkin wrote. Ninety minutes later it was over.

The Mar-a-Lago breakfast began a whirlwind courtship that ended with Shulkin meeting the president-elect at Trump Tower in Manhattan just a few days later on January 9, 2017. Perlmutter was patched through on speaker phone.

"Donald, he's your guy," the comic-book magnate said of the stunned Shulkin. "I wouldn't steer you wrong."

That's all Trump needed to hear. He turned to his then-trusted fixer Michael Cohen. "Next time you see him [Shulkin], you can call him Mr. Secretary," the president-elect declared.

That was how the head of the federal government's second-largest agency was hired.

As it turned out, Perlmutter wasn't just Shulkin's ticket into the administration; he also considered himself the secretary's puppeteer, at least according to Shulkin.

"Jared Kushner joked that Ike had become my adopted father," Shulkin wrote.

Perlmutter, Dr. Moskowitz, and the physician's squash partner, an attorney named Marc Sherman, formed a fearsome troika that ruled the VA from Palm Beach.[35] They said the president had empowered them to reform the agency, which had been crippled by scandals over the poor treatment it provided veterans. Shulkin—the only Trump cabinet member granted unanimous Senate confirmation—was their implement. The threesome quickly became known as the "Mar-a-Lago crowd," although only Perlmutter was a member.[36] All they wanted, the Palm Beachers said, was to help.

"The three men pushed the agency's health care system toward the use of more privately provided health care, tried to derail a critical contract [and] blocked moves to fire employees they considered allies," the *New York Times* would later report.[37]

None of the men had served in the US military or government or even visited a VA hospital, according to Shulkin's book. "These gentlemen were, in my opinion, well-intentioned, even if sometimes off base with their advice," Shulkin wrote. Still, the secretary spent nearly as much time dealing with them as doing his job. He knew the president was getting most of his information about the VA not from him, the secretary, but from the Mar-a-Lago crowd.

The idea of Trump as a monarch and Mar-a-Lago members as his court went beyond metaphor. When another club regular, the Pennsylvania dentist Albert Hazzouri, wrote a note to Trump about the American Dental Association and the Veterans Administration, he addressed it "Dear king." (Trump forwarded the note to Shulkin.[38])

Shulkin became so sidelined that he was literally forgotten. Once, at a televised White House meeting, Trump turned to the secretary and asked if he would be attending a discussion on VA issues with Perlmutter that night at his "Southern White House." Shulkin shook his head no.[39] "You heard about it right?" Trump asked. Trying to save face on live TV, Shulkin nodded with an awkward smile. The secretary hadn't even been invited. In fact, that *was* the first he heard of it.

In a statement Perlmutter, Moskowitz, and Sherman said their only goal was to improve health care for veterans: "We didn't seek or receive any personal or financial gain. We never imagined that volunteering our personal time to improving veterans' healthcare would open us up to criticism. In hindsight, it is clear we underestimated the coarseness of an environment in which even well-intentioned efforts can be twisted to fit pre-conceived narratives."[40]

After Shulkin tried to buck their directives over a $10 billion contract for electronic health records, he found himself out of a job. In March 2018 Trump fired him with two tweets. The reported reason for his ouster? An inspector general's report critical of Shulkin's taxpayer-funded travel to Europe with his wife, as well as disarray within the agency.[41]

But the real reason seemed clear: Shulkin had dared to cross the Mar-a-Lago crowd.

Under Trump, the real center of power wasn't Washington, DC.

It was Palm Beach.

WHEN MAR-A-LAGO MEMBER Guido Lombardi approached Steve Bannon with an offer to introduce two former Colombian presidents to Trump, the president's strategist shrugged the Italian off.

Lombardi had a friend in common with Andrés Pastrana and Álvaro Uribe, the ex-Colombian leaders, and thought Trump would benefit from their advice on Latin American policy. Bannon wasn't interested.

"Your friend is a nobody," the strategist replied.[42]

He refused to facilitate the meeting.

No matter. In April 2017 Uribe and Pastrana briefed Trump at Mar-a-Lago anyway.

The White House tried to downplay the encounter.

"They were there with a member from the club and briefly said hello when the president walked past them," spokeswoman Sarah Huckabee Sanders said at the time. "There wasn't anything beyond a quick hello."[43]

Pastrana contradicted the official messaging, tweeting his thanks to Trump for a "cordial and very frank conversation" about regional issues.[44]

Lombardi 1, Bannon 0.

It takes years to earn Trump's trust—and the old-time Mar-a-Lago members had a near-insurmountable head start on people like Bannon, who'd practically just stepped off the plane from DC.

After the election a Mar-a-Lago membership was worth its weight in gold to people trying to get a thumb on the pulse of American politics. Even the chance to have a cup of coffee with Ivanka Trump sold for nearly $60,000 at a charity auction.[45]

In the six months between Trump winning the Republican primary and being sworn in as US president, Mar-a-Lago welcomed fifty-two new members—accounting for 10 percent of the total capacity of the club.

Price of entry at Trump clubs has always been fluid and strikes a balance between whatever a person is willing to pay and how much Trump wants them to be a member.

In response to the new demand, the standard entry fee skyrocketed from $100,000 to $200,000, but according to staff, new members, and news reports, the price of entry has jumped again to $250,000—or whatever the newcomer is willing to pay. Trump is known for cutting deals for his friends and gouging the desperate and unpalatable.[46]

Even a conservative estimate suggests that the spike in membership in the year before Trump's inauguration brought in over $5 million in new revenue for the club.[47]

On New Year's Eve 2016 then president-elect Trump got up on the Grand Ballroom's golden stage to address his sold-out event.

New Year's Eve at Mar-a-Lago is legendary, with almost annual performances by the famous cover band Party on the Moon. There is a new theme each year, from Studio 54 to Moulin Rouge.[48] In 2016 the unofficial theme seemed to be "Welcome to the White House," and it was more popular than ever. More than eight hundred people attended the party, where tickets ran $525 for members and $575 for guests, bringing in at least $400,000 from ticket sales alone.[49] But Trump wanted to make sure everybody knew it was about more than that.

"I want to thank my members. I don't really care too much about their guests because the ones I really care about are the members, I don't really give a shit about their guests," Trump said.[50]

To be a member at Mar-a-Lago is to become a member of the extended Trump family, a royal entourage.

"I love my members," Trump repeated.

But it isn't always clear who *is* a member. Media outlets often erroneously report that frequent guests or other celebrities belong to the five-hundred-member club. Vaguely defined "honorary members" like tennis stars Venus and Serena Williams further confuse matters. Even club staff get mixed up.

For instance, staff have repeatedly called the best-selling mystery author James Patterson, who is not a Mar-a-Lago member, when trying to reach Long John Silver's founder James Patterson, who is, to remind him of his dinner reservations.

"I've even had reporters insist I'm a member," Patterson (the author) said with a laugh.[51]

Trump himself added to the uncertainty—intentionally. Soon after Mar-a-Lago opened, he began claiming that luminaries like Prince Charles, Princess Diana, and Henry Kissinger had joined the club. But it turned out Trump had simply added them to the membership rolls—without them asking or paying a dime. "If Mr. Trump has made them honorary members," a Buckingham Palace spokesman said curtly in 1995, "that's up to him."[52]

After 2016 doors at Mar-a-Lago began to open directly into the White House.

Conservative radio host Howie Carr and his family were among the New Year's Eve crowd at the club. They had recently joined Mar-a-Lago during Trump's campaign for president. But prior to that they had the green light to dine at the club whenever they wanted, Carr told his old friend Ron Kessler when they ran into each other that night.[53] As they mingled with the president-elect near the pool during the pre-dinner cocktail hour on New Year's Eve, Carr's twenty-two-year-old daughter Charlotte piped up.

"Can I intern in the White House?" she asked, crossing her arms and giving her father's friend a sassy look.[54]

"Yes!" Trump replied.

Charlotte Carr had already interned with the Trump Organization the previous summer and spent her winter break meeting members of the incoming administration around Mar-a-Lago.[55] In May 2017 she started a summer internship at the White House press office.[56]

A year later she took a job as a "confidential assistant" at the Overseas Private Investment Corporation, the US government's development finance institution that channeled private money into international development projects in an effort to assist US foreign policy and national security.

Mar-a-Lago has always been the place businessmen go when seeking a deal with the Trump Organization.

During his New Year's Eve speech Trump made a point to mention one member in particular—Hussain Sajwani, an Emirati real estate mogul and chairman of luxury developer Damac Properties.[57] The Trump Organization has two licensing deals with Damac for Trump-branded golf courses in Dubai.

"Hussain and the whole family, the most beautiful people from Dubai, are here tonight," Trump announced.[58] "And they're seeing it and they love it."

When Sajwani and his family stay at Mar-a-Lago they usually rent Beach Club Penthouse I, a luxurious suite along the Atlantic Ocean that is a favorite of Tiffany Trump when she is in town.[59]

Known for his ability to cultivate friends in high places, Sajwani had spent the week from Christmas to New Year's hanging out at the club and getting acquainted with the new administration. He and his wife had dinner with Kellyanne Conway, who later called them "absolutely lovely people."[60]

"They had no formal meetings or professional discussions. Their interactions were social," Trump's spokeswoman, Hope Hicks, said.[61]

At the time, Sajwani was in negotiations with the Trump Organization over a $2 billion real estate proposal. Trump turned it down a few days after New Year's in an effort to avoid the appearance that he was taking advantage of the office of the president for his own personal gain.[62] He also announced that the Trump Organization would not be engaging in any new international development projects while he was president for the same reason.

Just a few months later Don Jr. visited Sajwani in Dubai. The two talked "new ideas and innovation" over a lunch of chicken nuggets, served on Sajwani's elegant china.

Sajwani returned to Florida the following year for Thanksgiving and Easter.

Sajwani is one of the guys some staff call "fake members"—people from out of town who pay club dues but only use their memberships opportunistically. Prior to the Trump presidency Mar-a-Lago was always full of wealthy snowbirds who spent their winters playing tennis and croquet and dining in the club's restaurants several times a week. But many of the new members come just a few weekends a year—when the president is sure to be in town.[63]

"It's a very, very new crowd right now," said Ildikó Varga, who was an early Mar-a-Lago member. Her membership lapsed when she spent three years living in Monte Carlo a decade ago. To get it back she'd need to pay the new, higher rate. Varga isn't the only member of the old guard that has been sidelined by the special interests with deep pockets banging down the club gates.

"Right now the attraction is to be close to the president of the United States," Varga said. "They would like to get a membership at Mar-a-Lago, and of course, if they have the money, they would buy it."

Chapter 5

THE MAN IN CHARGE

TO SAY NO ONE KNEW what they were doing at the beginning of the Trump presidency isn't exactly true. The staff and members of his private club certainly knew how to work with the Donald. And Secret Service, White House staff, and others from Washington knew how to work with a president.

At the Winter White House everyone knew what they were doing. They were just doing different things.

Mar-a-Lago's food and beverage director, Aaron Fuller, knew, for example, that the dinner table selected by an uptight Secret Service detail for the new president's first Mar-a-Lago visit was never going to fly with his boss.[1] It was too far removed from the limelight. But he also knew it was pointless to argue with the agents who had pragmatically selected the table for safety reasons.

The problem was that the agents had no experience at all with the kind of fit Trump would throw when he saw the table they had picked. It's not that Trump cries or makes a scene when he doesn't get his way—at least not in public. He just digs in his heels like a stubborn child and refuses any way but his own.

Fuller didn't have a problem with Trump's behavior. He figured a billionaire has a right to have things done exactly to his fancy, and Fuller's job was to make that happen. The Trumps paid his paycheck, not the White House, so it was clear who he had to please at the end of the day.

So Fuller did the only thing he could. He reserved the table Secret Service wanted for Trump while simultaneously reserving a second table—one nearer the center of the dinner action that he was sure his boss would like.

Sure enough, when Trump arrived in Palm Beach after his election, he took one look at the table the agents had selected for him, didn't like it, and, upon further survey of the dining area, noticed an empty table near the center of activity (the one Fuller left purposely empty) and declared he would sit there instead. Powerless to change his mind, the agents took their stations on either side of the president's chosen table without another word.

It wasn't long before the White House started calling Mar-a-Lago staff to find out where the president was going to sit during his visits to the club.[2]

The almost psychic ability to predict the Trumps' whims and cater to their every need was how Fuller made himself indispensable—that, and his spaghetti Bolognese.[3] For many years the meat sauce was one of Barron Trump's favorite foods, so much so that Melania would jar it up to bring to New York. It didn't seem to matter that Fuller's track record wasn't pristine. There was the DUI he got while on his way home from work and the "show me your boobs" text he allegedly sent to a twenty-year-old employee. The man who reported Fuller to HR on behalf of the woman claimed he had his position eliminated in retaliation.[4] (Fuller pled no contest to the DUI. The retaliation case is in arbitration. In a statement Fuller denied any retaliation, saying the food and beverage department had a revenue shortfall: "The club has a fantastic human resources director and all issues involving the club and its team members are always handled in a professional way."[5])

Fuller remained in his job through the first year of the Trump presidency before leaving to open Aaron's Table and Wine Bar in the nearby town of Jupiter.

THE DINNER TABLE was the first of many losing battles government staffers would face at Mar-a-Lago. They knew how to protect a president at the White House, but they didn't know how to protect the king of the castle from himself.

"Nobody tells Donald Trump where he can and cannot go," Trump's former campaign advisor Roger Stone told the *Washington Post*.[6] At Mar-a-Lago, Stone said, "you don't have the minders." (Stone was later convicted of obstructing a congressional inquiry, lying to federal agents, and witness tampering.)

Especially in the early days, Trump would run outside the ranks of his Secret Service detail to greet someone he recognized in the crowd.[7] He would invite people at the club to government meetings and interviews and get their opinions on his future plans. There was no way to track these informal encounters. Unlike the White House, Mar-a-Lago keeps no visitor logs.[8]

"He's very gregarious," said club member Fred Rustmann. "He loves to come along and meet people and just walk through. I guess he considers this his family, so he feels very safe and secure with members. He kind of enjoys mingling."

The Winter White House is in a constant state of rebellion against the norms of the White House in DC.

Former chief of staff John Kelly spent his tenure trying to keep Trump from receiving certain bits of news that were sure to cause the volatile president to blow his lid on Twitter. Kelly understood that the lack of transparency was necessary.[9] Without it, five minutes and six tweets later, Kelly would be faced with an international relations fiasco that staff would spend weeks cleaning up.

In Washington Kelly was more or less in control. But he was all but powerless at Mar-a-Lago, where longtime members frequently slide information and news articles to Trump that his staffers would have otherwise squirreled away.

The fact that Mar-a-Lago is a club—one where dues-paying members and their innumerable guests expect the royal treatment—has further complicated things for presidential security.

"I think it is quite hard to regulate because members of the club expect to have and do have full access to the relevant areas for them . . . and the president is going to routinely, predictably, be spending a lot of time there," said David Kris, an assistant attorney general for national security in the Obama administration and founder of the consulting firm Culper Partners.[10]

Trump has always stayed in a large suite overlooking the pool in the main mansion. Melania and Barron both have separate rooms.[11] The shortest path from the main entrance to the grand ballroom passes right by Trump's door.

At first, the Secret Service required members and their guests to take the long route so as to avoid the presidential suite on their way to their parties. But the tenfold increase to club security was already damaging its luxury brand, and another inconvenience was too much to ask of members. Agents agreed to a compromise: guests could pass the rooms—except for the moments when the president might be coming or going.

In theory that should have been enough to keep the president safe, but Trump had a habit of ducking his security detail while he was in his home.

"No set of protocols will suffice if people don't follow the protocols," Kris said. "If he's told the Secret Service 'Don't disturb the guests! Don't block them from walking on the beach,' ultimately I think they will take an order from the commander-in-chief on these things."

One evening after Trump became president, a Mar-a-Lago member and her husband were walking past his rooms on the way to an event when Trump suddenly stuck his head out the door.[12]

"There was nobody around him," the Mar-a-Lago member said. "He just jumped in front of us like Mr. Clean and said, 'Hi folks.'"

Even the children have joined the rebellion.

Secret Service agents can sometimes be heard desperately asking into their radios if anyone had eyes on Barron, whom they had lost sight of more than once already that day.[13]

In reality Mar-a-Lago is nothing like the White House, a highly controlled location to which the public has limited access. It isn't even really a country club. It doesn't have a golf course, and it isn't run by a board of members who act as the gatekeepers for polite society.

Mar-a-Lago is a palace, and the only rule is that of the king.

TRUMP RULES MAR-A-LAGO with an iron fist. Not an oven is bought without Trump's approval. Nothing at the club happens without him hearing about it. As a boss, he expects nothing short of excellence.

If a server is standing around for too long, Trump will call over a manager. "Who's that?" he'll ask. "Why aren't they moving? Why are they standing around?"[14] Every time Trump sees a member of his club he asks them about their experience. If a dinner guest tells him their asparagus is cold, Trump is in the kitchen minutes later breathing down the necks of the line cooks.

Trump is not an intellectual or a policy wonk—he hates reading—but when it comes to details about his condo towers, casinos, and Mar-a-Lago, he misses nothing.

Trump remembers everything. Once, at the end of a season, he had been displeased by the size of the shrimp served during his final meal at the club.[15] Nearly six months later it was still bothering him. The first thing he did when he arrived in Florida for the start of the next season was to go down to the kitchen to follow up with the chef.

"Hey chef, you changed that shrimp, right?" he asked.

Who remembers stuff like that?, the chef wondered to himself.

"What he doesn't remember you couldn't find on the bottom of the sole of my shoe," said Mar-a-Lago member Toni Holt Kramer. "That man, it's bizarre how much he remembers. It's almost like you never want to do anything wrong because you know he'll never forget it."[16]

Now that he is president, some of the responsibility for running the club falls on Eric Trump, the second of his three sons. But Eric is not hands-on. He never visits the athletic facilities. He's rarely seen by the members. On one occasion a member browsing merchandise at a club store took a $60 shirt, stuffed it into a bag, looked up at a security camera, and smiled—before walking off without paying. When staff gently confronted the man, he played it off as if he had intended to pay later.[17] Eric waited until the end of the season, when all the dinners and parties were over, to suspend his membership for four months. The man was welcomed back at the beginning of the next season with open arms. "No one gave a shit that he was a thief," one staffer said.[18]

Almost by default the club's general manager, Bernd Lembcke, and the other staff run the Winter White House.[19] But no one has any illusions about who is really in charge.

The forty-fifth president of the United States is still *il capo dei capi*.

A year into his presidency Trump walked into the usually spotless kitchen to find it filthy. He blew his top and nearly fired both the general manager and head chef, according to a member familiar with the story.[20] Just because he wasn't around every day did not mean his employees could get lazy, Trump yelled.

"He's the six-star general," said Rustmann, who worked with Trump on several real estate projects in the 1990s. "There's no question about it, he's in charge. Particularly now that he's president of the United States. He is in charge. And he lets you know that right off the bat."

Mar-a-Lago has a reputation in the service industry for being a difficult place to work. Pay is lower at Mar-a-Lago compared to other Palm Beach country clubs, and workers are sometimes promoted without pay raises.[21] Staff go through a preseason boot camp, where they're expected to learn the names and faces of all members, especially those closest to Trump. They're quizzed on the history and layout of the club. They're also taught about Mar-a-Lago's VIP list: anyone with the last name "Trump."

When the Trumps are in town staff are on their toes, waiting to cater to the Trumps' every whim.[22] The chefs prepare chicken breasts for Eric Trump's dogs, which they deliver to his cabana near the Intracoastal. They never forget that Ivanka doesn't like mushrooms or that she drinks her morning lattes with skim milk. Everyone knows Jared Kushner drinks iced tea, Tiffany Trump prefers virgin piña coladas, Melania usually drinks water but will occasionally sip red wine with her mother, and Melania's father prefers single-malt scotch, either Chivas or Macallan 18, when he's feeling fancy.

Specially vetted staff stock the "Trump cooler"—a refrigerator in the main kitchen filled with family favorites: Coca-Cola, ice cream, crab cocktails, Trump wedge salads (a wedge of lettuce slathered in Roquefort dressing that is practically the only vegetable Trump will eat), bottles of Trump-brand water, and sugar-free Red Bulls for Trump's two adult sons.

For years Trump hand delivered annual bonuses to his staff. He would walk into the kitchen with a wad of cash in hand and, starting with the dishwashers, ask how long each one had worked for him. "One year," the first dishwasher said. Trump handed him a hundred-dollar bill. "Two years," the next dishwasher would say. Trump handed him two Benjamins. By the time he got to the servers and chefs, the staff were inflating their tenure at the club so much that Trump gave up. The next year he just told the managers to divvy up the cash.

Just like on his construction sites in New York, Trump knew how to endear himself to regular people. Even if he didn't always treat them well, he was the working man's billionaire. Those who work at Mar-a-Lago occupy a special place in his heart.

"This is home. He loves it. It's what he loves and where he's comfortable," said a Mar-a-Lago member.

On October 4, 2019, Trump changed his legal residence from Trump Tower in Manhattan to Mar-a-Lago.

He was simply making official what everyone already knew.

As TRUMP FILLED UP his White House, he turned not to lifelong DC staffers but to people he could trust—those who had already proven themselves loyal. What better pool of applicants to draw from than Mar-a-Lago and the Trump Organization?

Brooke Watson went from being Mar-a-Lago's catering and events director to the assistant manager of Blair House, the president's guest house in DC.[23]

Dan Scavino climbed the Trump ladder from personal caddie to executive vice president of the Trump National Golf Club in Westchester and then, finally, social media director for the White House, becoming one of the president's longest-standing aides and closest confidants.[24] Hope Hicks, formerly the Trump Organization's communications director, became the youngest-ever White House director of communications and one of Trump's highest-paid staff members.[25]

Not everyone has made such a clear transition from Trump Organization employee to White House staffer. Some appear to hover in between, such as Heather Rinkus. In 2017 Rinkus, Mar-a-Lago's guest reception director, reportedly received an official White House email and a government-issued phone to help Trump prepare for the G7 Summit in Italy.[26]

Her husband, Ari Rinkus, who pleaded guilty to wire fraud in a Ponzi scheme, is said to have attempted to leverage his wife's connection to the president to secure business deals. (Several years earlier a federal prosecutor described him as "a grifter . . . who has participated in a series of fraudulent schemes and shady business deals in an attempt to get rich quick.")

"He immediately brings up his wife's job," one source told *BuzzFeed News*.[27] "That's how he ropes investors in."

When Trump decided to christen his Winter White House by holding a bilateral summit with Japanese prime minister Shinzo Abe in February 2017, it fell to Aaron Fuller to pull off a state dinner.

What, Fuller wondered, do you feed the leader of another country? Better question: What do you feed an Asian head of state that a president with the palate of a nine-year-old boy will also eat?

More or less directionless and facing a huge learning curve, a very nervous Fuller began to put together a meal plan. Steak, he thought, would be a safe bet—not the New York Strip that Trump usually wanted but filet mignon, which his boss would eat and was better for a larger event. After adding a few Japanese flourishes to the proposed meal plan, he sent it to the White House for approval, which in turn sent it to Japan.[28]

The Japanese, it turned out, were not interested in Asian-fusion additions. "Please don't do anything special for us," they responded. The White House passed the message back to Fuller, who modified the menu again to something strictly American.

The real problems began just a few days before the state dinner.

Florida Department of Health officials showed up to inspect Mar-a-Lago's kitchen and found thirteen separate violations.[29] Meat coolers were not functioning properly, so chicken, duck, beef, and ham were all being stored at dangerously high temperatures. (Staff were ordered to empty and repair the coolers immediately.) Fish intended to be served raw or rare had not undergone proper parasite destruction. (Inspectors ordered the chefs to either cook it immediately or throw it out.) The tap water was too cold to properly sanitize staff's hands.

The infractions were immediately corrected, and preparations for Trump's first state dinner moved forward.[30]

Everything was set for Abe's visit, down to the selection of Marjorie Merriweather Post's china that Trump had purchased along with the property in the 1980s. The Trump wedge salad would be the same that is served every weekend. The steaks would be cooked as standard American fare. No flourishes needed.

Against all odds, Mar-a-Lago's staff had pulled it off.

6

"IT'S JUST NUKES"

TRUMP HAD BEEN PRESIDENT of the United States for exactly three weeks when he met Japanese prime minister Shinzo Abe on the outdoor terrace at Mar-a-Lago.

The dimly lit patio was packed with members and their guests as Trump and the prime minister made their grand entrance. Their wives followed, along with an interpreter and a horde of media and security.

Trump is a fashionably late kind of guy. Every time he arrives for dinner the packed terrace is ready to give him a standing ovation. The Abe meeting was no exception.[1] Staff planned around his whims, always prepared to give him the entrance he desired.[2]

"Hail to the Chief" played from the speakers, as is customary for a presidential entrance. At Mar-a-Lago the staff had begun doing this long before Trump actually became president in an effort to divert their boss's stormy moods.[3]

"He loves it. He loves all the fuss made. And to be treated like a king," said one club employee who spoke on condition of anonymity.[4]

Things had not gone well with Abe up until that point. Normally a smooth talker, Trump had been decidedly awkward when the Japanese leader arrived in DC.

Entirely out of his element, the new president had greeted Abe most uncharacteristically—by pulling him in for a hug. Not only is that not very presidential, but also Donald Trump *hates* hugs.[5] Touching other people in general makes him uncomfortable. Even in photos he generally poses with his hands hanging at his side rather than touch the people around him. The hug was so unusual that Trump addressed it in a press conference later that day.

"I shook hands, but I grabbed him and hugged him because that's the way we feel," Trump told reporters.[6] "We have a very, very good bond—very, very good chemistry."

There was also the nineteen-second handshake at the end of their meeting in the Oval Office.[7] The two leaders had been seated in mustard-yellow chairs, gripping each other's fingers, sort of smiling but mostly grimacing for the cameras, as they yanked their clasped hands tug-of-war-style back and forth across an invisible centerline, neither really gaining the upper hand. Eventually a staffer ended the excruciating exchange with an "All right, thank you, press!"

Abe gave a world-class eyeroll, his jaw literally dropping as he moved to rise from his chair. Trump gave the cameras two thumbs up. "Strong hands," Trump commented, imitating a golf swing.

Abe let out a small laugh before getting up.

It was with a sigh of relief that the president and Abe boarded the plane to Florida.

Out on Mar-a-Lago's terrace for dinner with his friends and family, Trump finally began to relax. The press cameras clicked away as Melania planted a kiss on each cheek of New England Patriots owner Robert Kraft, who, somewhat inexplicably, had been invited to participate in Trump's first diplomatic dinner as president.

Kraft also brought a friend from Palm Beach, Peter Bernon, of the Massachusetts-based milk-and-plastics fortune. (That friendship wouldn't make national headlines until *Vanity Fair* magazine outed Bernon for driving Kraft to a South Florida massage parlor where the Pats owner received sexual favors before the AFC Championship.[8] At dinner with Abe, Bernon was practically invisible.)

"Does anybody know Bob Kraft?" Trump kidded, playfully diverting attention from himself and the prime minister as the group sat down.[9] Kraft's team had made a historic comeback in the Super Bowl the weekend before.

"He knew he was going to win the game," Trump said for the cameras. "Even when he was down 28 to three."

No one pointed out that Trump hadn't shown the same faith. He had left his own Super Bowl party during the third quarter with the Patriots down by several touchdowns.[10] Kraft laughed at Trump's jokes, nodding to the camera. Leaning over to Abe, Trump said quietly: "He's been my good friend for a long time."

Abe grinned.

Trump was back in the driver's seat.

THE SATURDAY MORNING of Trump's first summit as president took place on the links at Trump National Golf Course in Jupiter, an eighteen-hole course designed by Jack Nicklaus about twenty miles north of Mar-a-Lago.

Golf appeals to Trump. He celebrates the game as one of tradition, respect, and rules.[11] It is both Trump's primary "love language" and the internationally understood tongue in which he has always conducted business, according to Guido Lombardi. Lombardi recounted a time in the nineties when he introduced Trump to a Japanese businessman. "I was shocked because out of the one-hour conversation, forty minutes was about golf," Lombardi said.[12]

When Trump was elected, his business became the presidency, and as such, golf became his preferred avenue for international diplomacy. (That was only a problem when it came to leaders like Chinese president Xi Jinping, whose government once banned Communist Party members from playing the sport.[13])

Abe, also a golfer, seemed to understand this side of Trump.[14]

At their White House press conference Abe had mentioned golf in a not-too-subtle play to Trump's ego. "My scores in golf is not up to the level of Donald at all," Abe said.[15]

Abe had also taken a leaf out of his grandfather's book when he visited the president-elect at Trump Tower in November 2016. He presented Trump with a golf club. (His grandfather, former prime minister Nobusuke Kishi, had famously given golf clubs to President Dwight D. Eisenhower.) The savvy Abe knew just any old club wouldn't be enough for America's new president. So he presented Trump with a gold "Honma Beres S-05 with 9.5 degrees of loft and a 5S Armrq Infinity stiff shaft"—a state-of-the-art club that cost $3,755 and featured the kind of gold accenting usually reserved for the *ancien régime*.[16]

Trump, it seems, may have forgotten to get Abe anything. He perhaps offered Abe a golf shirt from one of his clubs, although media accounts conflict.[17]

The new president had struggled with classic diplomacy in his first months. But the morning of "golf diplomacy" was curated perfection.[18] It was a beautiful, sunny morning on the links in Jupiter, and no one was around to mess it up. Trump wore a white MAGA cap.[19] A white cap was a good sign, according to his former butler.[20] Red caps are a warning sign of a bad mood.

In order to maintain that good mood, Trump's staff had sequestered the press corps in a basement suite at the clubhouse with black plastic taped over the windows to give the two leaders privacy while they golfed.[21]

For Trump, privacy is a relative term. His home is a club, and his daily life an open book to all of its members. Privacy never means actual solitude but rather the experience of having no one around to give him a hard time. Thus, the sequestration of the gaggle.

Out on the golf course Trump seemed to enjoy the mob of people watching him. There were Secret Service agents in summer wear, police officers dressed in bullet-proof vests, other golfers who got the chance to meet the Japanese prime minister, and a crowd of admirers, including a golf cart of Trumpettes, the fan club of aging Palm Beach socialites dedicated to lavishing praise on the president.[22] Trump joked with golf buddies, high fiving and laughing in a way rarely seen by a world familiar with his stiff-armed photo ops that always seem to capture his "resting pout face." Joining the leaders was South African golf legend Ernie Els, known as "the Big Easy." (Els took heat from his friends after the round. "They kind of needled me a little bit, saying I was a suck up," he told the *Wall Street Journal*. "I just said, 'Go eff yourself. I played with the president and you haven't.'"[23])

While the press corps sat blind and bored, club members like retired investor Richard DeAgazio had spent the weekend following Trump everywhere. DeAgazio was clearly thrilled that his newly acquired Mar-a-Lago membership had gotten him a front-row seat to history.[24] On the golf course Trump pointed in his direction as DeAgazio snapped a photo. "There's my guy!" DeAgazio wrote in a Facebook post that included the picture.[25]

Society photographer Paulette Martin shot dozens of exclusive photos, which she put up for sale on her website.[26]

From the green, Trump called out to her: "Make sure I look skinny, Paulette!"

MARTIN ALWAYS TRIED to make her clients look good in photos. That's why they loved her. She is known around Palm Beach for her flattering shots.

She had been one of the photographers hired by Mar-a-Lago to document grand occasions for more than a decade. She'd gotten the job the same way many people had—by approaching the president with a pretty girl.

Twenty years before the Abe visit, Martin ran into Trump at Dan Marino's charity golf tournament.

"Hello, Mr. Trump," she said. "I heard you're having a party tonight. Do you need a photographer?"

"Well, I think we have that covered, but why don't you come and bring some pretty girls," Trump replied.

So Martin arrived at Mar-a-Lago with her twenty-three-year-old daughter in tow. Martin's daughter competed in the Miss Florida beauty pageant, and Trump was transfixed.

"Well, hello there," Trump said, kissing the young woman's hand. He was single at the time, having separated from his second wife Marla Maples the previous year.[27]

"Donald, I'd like you to meet my daughter," Martin said.

"Daughter?" Trump replied.

The playboy mogul whisked the young woman away. "She was his shoulder candy," Martin said.[28] After the pary, the three of them rode his limo to a night club, and then at the end of the evening Trump took mother and daughter out for pizza.

"Do we have to go back to the real world?" Martin's daughter asked her mom on their way home.

The answer came a week later. Bernd Lembcke, Mar-a-Lago's general manager, called Martin. "Mr. Trump would like to hire you," Lembcke said. "He wants to know how much you're going to charge."

For years the Trump Organization paid Martin and her daughter to photograph major events and holidays at Mar-a-Lago. But Martin shot the Abe visit just for fun.

On February 11, 2017, Martin got a phone call from her friend Annie Marie Delgado, who worked as an organizer for the Trump campaign in Florida and had known the president for years.

"Paulette, I'm going up to Trump Jupiter. Donald's in town," Delgado said. "Do you want to come?"

That sounded good to Martin, who packed up her long lens and got ready to go. Delgado called ahead to the club to let them know Martin was coming with her to photograph the occasion.[29]

After Martin took some photos near the club house, the two women drove a golf cart to the home of a friend who lives on the course. They walked into the backyard to find Trump and Abe right there on the green. After sinking his putt, Trump turned to the women.

"How you doing, folks?" Trump asked as he walked closer. He kept a bit of a distance but got close enough that the exchange felt intimate.[30]

"I'm good. I'm good, sir," Delgado responded. She didn't close the several-yard gap. Nor did anyone else. Everyone who knows him knows that Trump doesn't like to be approached.[31] If he wants to get close, he will. Otherwise keep your distance.

Trump continued as if on autopilot from his campaign days.

"Everything good? How's our campaign? Looking pretty good? You ready in three, three and a half years?" he said, one sentence running into another.

Trump motioned Abe to come over, prompting a flurry of excitement and Martin to cry, "Let me get my camera!"

"She's great," Trump told Abe, motioning in the general direction of Martin and Delgado. It wasn't clear which one of them he was talking about. Both women took his words as a personal compliment.

It was the easy exchange of a lifelong crowd pleaser: Make everyone feel like an old friend. Insert a little humor. And then move on before the inevitable awkward silence. Lifting his club to gesture at Martin, who was frantically getting her camera ready, Trump said, "Paulette, get us on the next hole."

Trump headed back to his golf cart, patting Abe on the back and saying something that no one in the crowd could really hear. Abe laughed. It wasn't the polite laugh of a politician but a real, open-mouthed laugh of someone genuinely enjoying himself.

Trump bent down and picked up a green jug from the ground next to the golf cart. "Is this us?" he asked in a tone that a good-natured uncle might use with a young nephew. Trump handed it to a caddy, who stowed it in the cart before hopping on the back. Trump got in the driver's seat, with Abe on the passenger's side, and pulled away.

Later Trump tweeted a picture of the two men engaged in "golf diplomacy."

"Having a great time hosting Prime Minister Shinzo Abe in the United States," Trump tweeted.[32]

Not all of the wheeling and dealing at the summit was government business. Out of nowhere, the president brought up casino licenses in Japan, which had recently been legalized after years of debate.[33] The market was predicted to be worth as much as $25 billion annually.

The president suggested that Abe should consider giving one of the lucrative licenses to his friend and top political donor Sheldon Adelson, owner of Las Vegas Sands, according to *ProPublica*.[34] (A spokesman for the prime minister said Abe never received such a request from Trump.[35]) Adelson had dined privately with Trump in DC the night before the Abe summit and also had breakfast with Abe and a small group of American CEOs before the prime minister departed for Palm Beach.[36]

According to Japanese media, Trump also brought up casino magnate and former RNC chairman Steve Wynn.[37]

A bit taken aback, Abe didn't say much, but he jotted down the two names Trump suggested.

TRUMP ALSO USED Abe's Mar-a-Lago visit to bolster the value of his club's brand.

After golf, Trump and Abe returned to Mar-a-Lago mid-afternoon and walked the grounds, where a couple had just been married.

"Come on, Shinzo," Trump said.[38] "Let's go over and say hello."

And so, in addition to the classic photos of stuffing cake into each other's faces, Carl Lindner IV, whose family once owned the Chiquita banana empire, and Nashville socialite Vanessa Falk added candid shots of themselves with two world leaders to their wedding album.[39]

Trump loves dropping in on weddings held at his clubs. So Mar-a-Lago staff always have to keep a careful eye to make sure that their over-zealous boss doesn't accidentally interrupt the bride walking down the aisle or her father giving a toast.[40]

When he stopped by the Lindner-Falk reception later in the night, Trump played up his unusual contribution to their special day. "So they have pictures, pretty good pictures, with the prime minister of Japan," Trump said, pausing slightly. "And the president. Don't worry about the president." The crowd laughed at his self-deprecating joke.

This was the Trump Palm Beachers know and love. Their "crazy uncle Donald," as one woman once described him.[41] He was charming, funny, and honest almost to a fault.

Trump had begun his impromptu speech by saying that he knew the families of the bride and groom very well. "One of them has been members of this club for a long time. They paid me a fortune," he said.[42]

More laughter.

In Palm Beach it's entirely acceptable to make money off your friends. Trump didn't mention the $100,000 Linder's father had donated to political action committees that supported his campaign.[43] Or that Falk's parents had just recently joined Mar-a-Lago, part of the influx of new members that drove membership prices to double.

"You really are a special, beautiful couple," Trump said. "And I hope everybody right now is going to get back to dancing. Go and have a good time and congratulations." He kissed the bride on the cheek, posed for a few more photos with bridesmaids dressed in hot pink, and then returned to schmoozing around the club.

It was a side of Trump that club members—and just under half of American voters—say the "fake news media" never reports.[44]

The way the Mar-a-Lago in-crowd sees it, the reason reporters missed the smiles and lighthearted exchanges that day was *not* because they were locked in a windowless room. They could have been standing right there, witnessing the same good-natured banter as everyone else and would have seen Trump's behavior entirely differently—perhaps as an inappropriate and unpresidential exchange or as an effort to sell more memberships to his club. In other words, even if they had been there, "the media" would have missed what makes Trump so appealing.

"The president loves people," said Toni Holt Kramer, a Mar-a-Lago member and founder of the Trumpettes. "He has a real genuine feeling. He has a great sense of humor, a magical sense of humor."

The people around him know that Trump is not exactly presidential, and many people love him for it. Kramer said she doesn't mind his belligerent tweeting because at least she knows what he is thinking. And she thinks that Trump making some extra money is not only acceptable but also expected.

"I think he's motivated by money. We all are," said Kramer.[45] "He has a brain. He's motivated by money. I have a brain. I'm motivated by money. But not at the risk of selling the country out."

MAR-A-LAGO WAS BUSTLING on the second night of Trump's Southern White House summit with Abe in 2017. The Lindner wedding reception was in full swing in the grand ballroom, and both the terrace and dining room were packed with members and their guests eager to catch a glimpse of such a historic moment or, better yet, have a chance to brush shoulders with some of the most powerful people in America.

At dinner Trump's team took the terrace with a newfound swagger. They posed for pictures with members. DeAgazio posted several to Facebook, including one with a man he identified as "Rick," saying he was the aide-de-camp who carries the nuclear football—the briefcase that serves as a mobile command center from which the president can launch a nuclear attack.[46]

Steve Bannon sauntered to his seat, glancing to the side and giving a sort of celebrity-style finger point and nod to some nearby diners.[47] Ildikó Varga congratulated him for masterminding such a successful campaign.

"Thank you, but it was a team effort," Bannon responded. The notoriously camera-shy man then posed for a picture with her and a few other dinner guests.

The Saturday dinner was a stately affair. The small round table of the previous night had been replaced by a long table where various aides also joined the mix.

Dawn Basham, one of Trump's favorite lounge singers, was the evening's entertainment. A few years before Trump took office Basham had performed at Trump International Golf Club in West Palm Beach, where the former beauty queen's voice—and her ability to stun in an evening gown—caught the Don's attention.

Intent on showing off to Abe, Trump sent his aides to bring Basham right up to their table. This happens a lot to performers at Mar-a-Lago: they are asked to stand next to the table and sing his requests. Usually something from *Phantom of the Opera* or *Cats*.

As Abe listened, Trump requested four songs and told Basham what a great job she was doing.[48]

Then the president asked Basham to twirl around for the men.

If Trump's behavior bothered the singer, you wouldn't have known it. Basham is a Marilyn Monroe type—but with a much better voice.

Asking her to twirl for a foreign head of state probably wasn't the most embarrassing thing Trump had ever done to her either. A few years earlier Trump sang "Happy Birthday" to Basham in front of a full house at the club. Before he began, Trump declared to the crowd that singing was something he wouldn't even do for his wife.

Basham's perfect facade never slips. She is well versed in the coded vernacular of society. Her Facebook page is full of shout-outs to the designers who dress her and posts about "what an honor it was" to perform for the president, to meet so-and-so, or to be accompanied by this or that pianist.

"It was awfully nice having Mr. Trump sing Happy Birthday to me," she wrote on Facebook at the time.[49]

Standing in front of Abe, she began to twirl, careful not to slip on the slick terrace made of surf-polished stones that Marjorie Merriweather Post collected from the shores of her Long Island hunting preserve. Her silvery evening gown glittered in the dim light. Almost precisely at midtwirl, things began to change. A flurry of activity began at the president's table. Something had happened. Something with North Korea. Basham tried to make her exit.

"Mr. President, I shouldn't know this," someone heard the performer say.[50]

Trump shrugged.

"It's just nukes," the president said. "Sing us a song."

TRUMP'S OPERATIC PRIORITIES were quickly overruled. North Korea had launched a missile in the direction of Japan.

Basham retreated. Aides with laptops and sheets of paper converged on the table, using cell phones to illuminate the documents for Trump and Abe. The president got on a phone—possibly his unsecure Android that he had tweeted from before the dinner.[51]

"Wow . . . the center of the action!!!" DeAgazio wrote on Facebook.

Press had not been allowed into the dinner, so DeAgazio and others on the terrace posted photos and reported what they saw. "Trump and Abe will delivery [*sic*] joint statement soon about North Korea Missile," Lombardi tweeted from his nearby table, along with a photo of Trump and Abe.[52]

Behind the scenes Mar-a-Lago was chaos. "All of a sudden, when you see people running around, you think, 'Oh shit, something's happening,'" said a staffer. White House staff scurried to outfit the Gold and White Ballroom with flags and an appropriately presidential blue curtain so that the leaders could hold a press conference.

Within about ten minutes of the calls interrupting their dinner, the two grim-faced leaders walked past Lombardi's table to get a briefing on the North Korean missile test and face the cameras.

"North Korea's most recent missile launch is absolutely intolerable," Abe said in Japanese. "During the summit meeting that I had with President Trump, he assured me that the United States will always be with Japan 100 percent. And to demonstrate his determination as well as commitment, he is now here with me at this joint press conference."

Trump stood stiff armed, off to the side, wearing his resting pout face until it was his turn to speak. He said very little.

"I just want everybody to understand and fully know that the United States of America stands behind Japan, its great ally, 100 percent," Trump said, giving the classic "okay" sign with his fingers. "Thank you."

After the press conference Trump stopped by the wedding, where he delivered his impromptu toast and then went back to the terrace to continue mingling with his guests. Some members expressed their awe at how he handled the situation, even celebrating Trump's apparent transparency with concerns of national security.

"He chooses to be out on the terrace, with the members. It just shows that he's a man of the people," DeAgazio said to the *Washington Post*.

Much of the rest of the world was horrified.

Sean Spicer spent the next several days trying to explain away what had happened in front of the diners at Mar-a-Lago. No classified information had been discussed, Spicer assured the press gaggle.

"Apparently there was a photo taken, which everyone jumped to nefarious conclusions about what may or may not be discussed," he said, in reference to DeAgazio's Facebook posts, which had been subsequently deleted.[53] According to Spicer, Trump and Abe had already been briefed in a secure room set up at Mar-a-Lago before dinner and then again after. The discussion at the table was just about logistics for the press conference, he said.

Despite the national media blasting DeAgazio, he said he faced no repercussions from the club for his social media posts. "Quite the contrary," he said. "I was welcomed enthusiastically."[54] He added that he was wrong about a briefing taking place on the terrace and parroted Spicer's explanation that the nation's security had never been in jeopardy.

Many members brushed off the whole thing as no big deal.

"We really didn't see anything. We saw people came over with a piece of paper, and the translator was reading something. But we didn't see anything," Varga said. "Anybody who tells you that they knew what was going on is lying. They didn't know anything."

While the terrace was probably too noisy for guests to hear anything, the abundance of unsecured cell phones connected to the club's public WiFi network alarmed national security experts. John Kelly would later ban personal cell phones from the West Wing, although no such prohibition was put in place at Mar-a-Lago.[55] (Trump, who stills talks about TiVo like it's a new technology, considers security precautions on his own cell phone "too inconvenient."[56])

The president did not seem to grasp the weight of the situation.

"It was a party for him. It worried me," said one Mar-a-Lago employee. "I thought I was in the twilight zone."

Behind the scenes the club took the smallest of steps to improve security.

Future dinners with foreign leaders would be held in the Gold and White Ballroom—away from the prying eyes of other patrons.

And the club imposed a "no photos" rule when the president was around, though it was almost impossible to enforce at larger galas—and there was a general exception for selfies.

When John Havlicek, an eight-time NBA champion with the Boston Celtics, celebrated his birthday at Mar-a-Lago, his son tried to take a cell phone photo of the birthday cake. Immediately one of the club's private security guards intervened.

According to society columnist Shannon Donnelly, the guard snatched the phone out of Havlicek's son's hand and walked away, shouting, "No photos. The president is entitled to his privacy."[57]

"The people at surrounding tables began booing and shouting their objections at the security guard," Donnelly recounted, "but Havlicek just sort of gave a quiet 'no big deal; everybody stay cool' gesture to the crowd and went back to blowing out the candles."

Regardless of the tougher rules, a fundamental tension remained. The Winter White House is a club, one that the president depends on for part of his wealth. And the club members like to take pictures. The business exists to serve its members.

As a club owner, Trump knew what he was doing. His personality and easygoing presence were a big hit. But when it came to national security, it was pretty clear he didn't have a clue.

In response to what the *Washington Post* called Trump and Abe's "al fresco situation room," Chelsea Clinton posted the thought that undoubtedly kept many FBI agents up at night: "How many of Mar-a-Lago's new members will be (already are?) members of foreign intelligence agencies & media organizations?"[58]

7

OVER HAMILTON'S DEAD BODY

MAR-A-LAGO WAS GIVING Michael Dobbs a headache.[1]

Dobbs, a civil servant who had worked in the Obama administration, was the director of an obscure government office tasked with managing logistics for presidential travel.[2] His office was struggling to find a way to pay Mar-a-Lago for rooms and facilities used by the federal government during the president's summits at the club. Caps on government spending and Mar-a-Lago's insistence on billing in increments no greater than $10,000 were making it nearly impossible for Dobbs to find a way to pay the bills. It didn't help that the staff at the luxurious club had no clue about the government procurement process and didn't much seem to care.

By mid-April 2017, Dobbs was still dealing with invoices from Abe's Mar-a-Lago visit two months earlier. Thus, the headache.

"I don't know if I have asked this before but how is [the Office of Administration] funding the rooms at Mar-a-Lago for WH staff accompanying POTUS on the weekend? Any assistance would be greatly appreciated," Dobbs emailed a colleague at the Executive Office of the President.[3]

"WH is paying for the rooms via credit card authorization form. They can only charge our cards in increments. Hope that helps," the colleague replied.

During the summit with Abe six high-level advisors to the president stayed at Mar-a-Lago, running up an initial bill for taxpayers of $6,396, according to internal emails sent by Dobbs's office. The team included embattled National Security Advisor Michael Flynn, who would resign days after the summit; White House Chief Strategist Steve Bannon; Deputy Chief of Staff Katie Walsh; and the president's twenty-six-year-old body man, John McEntee, a former football standout for the University of Connecticut.[4]

The cost of each room: "$546 I believe which is 300% of the lodging per diem," Dobbs wrote in response to questions from another confused civil servant.[5] The bills themselves had to be corrected before they could be paid. Walsh had billed food to her room, which should have been paid with her per diem. Mar-a-Lago staff were slow to make the correction and resubmit the invoices, further bogging down the process.

Adding to the stress, on the second weekend in April Trump had hosted an even bigger international summit at the club—this time with Chinese president Xi Jinping.

The DC bureaucrats handling logistics for Xi's visit quickly realized that making deals in South Florida was nothing like the rest of the world.

The civil servants were structured, procedural, and used to people following the rules, especially those set by the federal government. A typical South Floridian couldn't care less about any of those things. To a South Floridian, being an hour late means being on time. Every business deal is a chance to con—or be conned. And rules don't exist: just look at the way people drive.

Millie Pugliese, a federal contracting officer tasked with sourcing supplies for the summit, must have thought she had stepped into another dimension when she began making calls to South Florida businesses.

One party-rental company refused to send rope and stanchions over to Mar-a-Lago unless it got billing information from the federal government first. "They didn't care who we are," an irate Pugliese wrote to Dobbs.[6]

Another party-rental company insisted on being paid in advance and refused to waive taxes despite Pugliese presenting them with the office's tax-exemption paperwork. The company told her their phones shut off at 5:00 P.M. sharp and she wouldn't get anything if she didn't give them her credit card by then. They didn't seem to believe she had one.

But the "worst vendor," she complained, was U-Haul, which demanded up-front payment for a fifteen-foot truck it didn't have at a price it couldn't name. The U-Haul employees kept writing receipts addressed not to her but to "Andrew Crook," whom she had never heard of. The disagreement took more than an hour to straighten out, with another federal employee holding on the other line the entire time.

How did something that should have been so simple get so complicated, she fumed. Explaining some of these transactions to the auditor was going to be "impossible."

"We have to try to do something better as this visit tied up my entire night," Pugliese wrote.[7] "It's apparent that these firms have been burnt before as they don't trust anybody."

The State Department agreed it should probably send someone down to South Florida in person next time.

The Trump Organization was no better. Prior to Xi's visit the Office of Presidential Travel Support had tried to get the president's business to agree to a standard billing rate for rooms at Mar-a-Lago in order to comply with federal spending caps. In the end the club turned down the blanket agreement, and Dobbs was back to square one, with tens of thousands in bills for lodging and facilities rentals and no easy way to pay them.

The Xi visit was massive, with at least twenty-four senior administration officials staying at Mar-a-Lago. At the club's standard government billing rate of $546 per night, their lodging alone would have cost taxpayers more than $30,000.[8] Other lower-level officials stayed at far cheaper hotels, including the Hampton Inn in West Palm Beach, which was billing at $195 per night.

Mar-a-Lago was also charging the government $4,000 for the use of ballrooms, the main dining room, and the Teahouse over five days. The press corps chipped in $250, half the cost for the Grand Ballroom on the Friday of the summit. But that still stuck the government with a $3,750 bill—a point of contention because of the government's $3,500 spending cap on small purchases. Mar-a-Lago refused to adjust the bill.

"They need to understand that is our max limit," wrote one frustrated government employee.

So it wouldn't violate the spending cap, the government asked the Trump Organization for a 10 percent discount on conference space. After a month of haggling, Mar-a-Lago relented. (In 2018 Trump signed a law lifting the cap on small purchases from $3,500 to $10,000.[9])

Then Mar-a-Lago sent Dobbs's office an even more baffling bill: $3,169.20 for "Chinese delegation room charges."[10] It didn't seem to make sense. Xi and his entourage had stayed at the ultra-luxury Eau Palm Beach Resort & Spa, not the club.[11] And Dobbs's office wouldn't cover a bill for Chinese officials anyway.

"Presidential Travel Support does not pay for foreign delegation rooms," a State Department official wrote back to the club's persistent membership billing coordinator, Beverly VanEvery.[12]

Everyone was confused. It may have been just another Mar-a-Lago mix-up. Yet again the bureaucrats and the club employees seemed to be speaking different languages. From the emails it's not at all clear if the guests were American or Chinese or whether it was Trump or Xi's government that ended up paying the president's club. Neither the White House, the State Department, nor the Chinese Embassy commented. (To avoid any political blowback over taking foreign money, Trump had personally paid for Abe's lodging when the prime minister stayed at the club two months earlier.[13])

For his part, Dobbs was still grappling with the question of what credit card his office could use to pay the bills it *was* on the hook for. In the end, he had to open a new account at Citibank and assign a federal employee to manage it.

"Mar-a-Lago has given me a headache," Dobbs wrote in an email to a State Department colleague.[14]

He ended the message with a smiley face.

WHILE DOBBS WORRIED about paying the bills, Alexander Hamilton was rolling over in his grave.

Trump's presidency embodied everything Hamilton had feared for the nation.

"In republics, persons elevated from the mass of the community, by the suffrages of their fellow-citizens, to stations of great pre-eminence and power, may find compensations for betraying their trust, which, to any but minds animated and guided by superior virtue, may appear . . . to overbalance the obligations of duty," Hamilton wrote in 1787.[15] "Hence it is that history furnishes us with so many mortifying examples of the prevalence of foreign corruption in republican governments."

When he wrote those words, Hamilton could never have imagined a global business empire that compared to Donald Trump's: hotels, restaurants, condos, golf courses, and his famous club in Palm Beach. All potential avenues through which a president could be "purchased by the emissaries of [foreign] kingdoms," as Hamilton wrote. Although Trump turned his company's operations over to his sons when he became president, he remains the sole owner of his business—from which he can withdraw money at will.[16] He is the only recent president with significant assets who did not set up a blind trust.[17]

Of course, Trump believes he *is* of the "superior virtue" as described by Hamilton—or at least superior wealth. He and his supporters maintain he is too rich to be bought or corrupted.[18] That hasn't stopped foreign leaders in search of influence in the Trump administration from spending money at the president's properties.[19]

Hamilton had tried to prevent that—with laws Trump would later label "phony."[20]

In two small sections of the US Constitution known together as the "Emoluments Clauses," the Founding Fathers forbade the president from receiving compensation of any kind from US federal and state governments beyond the normal presidential salary. The founders also barred the president from accepting any compensation, gifts, or titles from foreign nations or leaders without the explicit permission of Congress.

Since Trump's election, at least twenty-eight individuals or entities associated with foreign governments have spent money at Trump businesses, according to a 2019 analysis by the consumer advocacy group Public Citizen.[21]

Rather than being concerned, Trump has seemed to throw open the doors.

"He talks up his properties every chance he gets with anyone—with staff, with members of Congress, with the press, with the public, with foreign leaders, with anyone," a former White House official told *Politico*.[22] "He's been a salesman. He's been a PR person for his properties for the last fifty years, so almost out of force of habit, that's what he does."

Three days after Trump's inauguration he was sued for allegedly violating the foreign emoluments prohibition. (The lawsuit would be followed by others.)

"Never before have the people of the United States elected a President with business interests as vast, complicated, and secret as those of Donald J. Trump," stated the complaint filed by the watchdog group Citizens for Responsibility and Ethics in Washington (CREW).[23] "Now that he has been sworn into office as the 45th President of the United States, those business interests are creating countless conflicts of interest, as well as unprecedented influence by foreign governments."

The Justice Department and Trump Organization maintain that fair-market payments for hotel rooms are not "gifts" and do not violate the Constitution.[24]

Even so, the Trump Organization has put together what it calls a "voluntary" repayment plan to donate its estimated profits made from foreign governments back to the US Treasury.[25] In order to be counted, the money has to come directly from a foreign government. Per its own rules, the Trump Organization is not required to donate money spent at unprofitable Trump properties. Because the president's company is private, it's impossible to check the math.

"It's awfully strange to see the Trump Organization claim that this constitutes fulfillment of a pledge to operate ethically. It does not, not even close," Robert Weissman, president of Public Citizen, told *ABC News*.[26] "If the Trump Organization won't say how much they paid, let alone how they calculated it at each property, why in the world should we believe they actually have delivered on their promise to donate foreign profits to the US Treasury?"

ON THE EVENING of April 6, 2017, the first day of the Xi summit, a group of US government officials retreated to Mar-a-Lago's Library Bar, the wood-paneled study where Guido Lombardi would entertain the Mongolian ambassador.[27] The group asked the bartender to leave the room so they could "speak confidentially," *ProPublica* reported.[28]

Then they started pouring drinks—in total, fifty-four—made with premium liquor: Chopin vodka, Woodford Reserve bourbon, and Patron and Don Julio Blanco tequila. A week later Mar-a-Lago sent the State Department a bar tab of $1,005.60: $838 for the booze plus a 20 percent service charge. They weren't charged sales tax. The participants were never confirmed, although Steve Bannon was listed among them in emails between government employees. (He denied it and said he doesn't drink.)

The State Department refused to pay, so the White House cut a check.[29]

Anytime a US government official goes to Mar-a-Lago as part of their job, taxpayer dollars are funneled into the president's coffers, though the bills are usually not for late-night benders.

The Secret Service spent more than $471,000 at Trump properties while performing its duty to protect the president and his family between January 2017 and April 2018.[30]

"That's exactly what the Domestic Emoluments Clause prohibits," constitutional experts Ron Fein and Brianne Gorod argue.[31]

Mar-a-Lago was one of the top recipients of this taxpayer spending. The receipts were released through a Freedom of Information Act request by Property of the People, a government transparency group, and then supplemented by reporting from the *Washington Post*.[32] The *Post* revealed the Secret Service was renting rooms at the club for up to $650 per night in 2017.[33] The next year the club reduced the per night charge to $396.15 after making the agency an "honorary member" and therefore eligible for a discount.[34] In a single month in 2019 the Secret Service spent more than $40,000 on rooms at the club, according to documents obtained by Public Citizen. (The receipts represent just a small window into the agency's total spending at the president's businesses.)

Usually, executive branch officials allow the Secret Service to stay at their properties for free. The only recent exception was Vice President Joseph Biden, who charged the agency a total of $171,600 over six years to rent a cottage on his Delaware property.[35] Those payments were disclosed in public spending databases.

The Trump Organization has repeatedly claimed it does not profit on rooms rented to the Secret Service. "We provide the rooms at cost and could make far more money renting them to members or guests," Eric Trump told the *Post*.

Other federal and state agencies and local governments have paid at least $386,000 to Trump's businesses, according to records that cover parts of 2017 and 2018.[36] The largest expenditures were for lodging and facilities rentals.

In total, nearly $900,000 of government spending at Trump's businesses has been publicly documented.

But the real amount of taxpayer money going into Trump's pockets is a mystery. Federal agencies have routinely fought public disclosure. Even Congress doesn't know how much the Secret Service has spent. During the first three years of Trump's presidency, the agency filed only two of a required six reports on spending at Trump properties because, it said, of a lack of staffing.[37] In the reports that were filed, the line for Mar-a-Lago was left blank. (The Secret Service says it follows the law.)

Property of the People filed lawsuits against four federal agencies to obtain the limited receipts that it did.[38] In those records, the Secret Service mislabeled $63,700 worth of payments to Mar-a-Lago as payments to "Trump National Golf Club," the *Post* reported.[39] (Trump National Golf Club is twenty miles away in Jupiter.) The agency's disclosure of spending was stripped of important details, including what the payments were for and the location of almost all the Trump properties where taxpayer money was spent.

Under the column labeled "merchant name," only one thing was consistent: Trump.

THE TRUMP BRAND is now inextricably tied to the presidential office. Buying Trump wine has become synonymous with buying presidential wine. Staying at a Trump property is like staying at the White House, especially if that property is Mar-a-Lago.

Since his election Trump has repeatedly mentioned the club in the context of official business, often referring to it as the "Winter White House" or the "Southern White House." He used Marjorie Merriweather Post's vision for the property to legitimize this marketing strategy.

"It was originally built as the Southern White House," Trump said in an official press briefing. "It was called the Southern White House. It was given to the United States, and then Jimmy Carter decided it was too expensive for the United States. So they, fortunately for me, gave it back and I bought it. Who would have thought? It was a circuitous route. But now it is, indeed, the Southern White House. And again, many, many people want to be here."

Trump gave this promotional spiel as he sat next to Abe at Mar-a-Lago for a second summit in 2018.[40]

"Many of the world's great leaders request to come to Mar-a-Lago and Palm Beach. They like it; I like it. We're comfortable. We have great relationships," Trump boasted. (So great that he and Abe even wore nearly identical ties: blue with white diagonal stripes.)

In December 2019, from the same Twitter account he uses to make presidential declarations, Trump retweeted promotional materials for the club, saying, "I will be there in two weeks, The Southern White House!"[41]

It wasn't just Trump. Federal officials began parroting the boss. In an effusive blog post the State Department wrote, "Post's dream of a winter White House came true with Trump's election in 2016. Trump regularly works out of the house he maintains at Mar-a-Lago and uses the club to host foreign dignitaries."[42] After heavy criticism, State pulled the post.[43]

"The intention of the article was to inform the public about where the president has been hosting world leaders," the department said. "We regret any misperception."[44]

All four of Trump's clubs in South Florida have seen a surge of revenue since he entered politics. By 2018 Mar-a-Lago's revenue had more than doubled compared to the year before Trump declared his candidacy.[45] (The number is calculated by taking the monthly average of income declared on his financial disclosures, where experts say Trump is actually reporting gross revenue.)

But by all appearances that money isn't being reinvested into the club. Grass grows from the aging roof faster than it can be pulled by the club's skeleton maintenance crew.[46] Health inspectors cited the pool because its tiles and finish were stained a "yellow mustard color."[47] On one visit Eric Trump's bungalow was growing so much mold he couldn't stay there.[48] The ceiling sometimes drips so badly into guest rooms that staffers have to put down buckets.[49] And while the food was never good, "since he became president, it's gotten worse," a regular said.[50]

"They're always looking to save money in all the stupidest places," said one staffer.[51] "Every one of these rooms is a disaster. It's like a bad motel."

But that doesn't stop people from banging down the doors. The presidential rebranding has paid off. The newcomers aren't there for the food. They're paying for Trump.

"Mar-a-Lago is a vehicle for enriching the president and obtaining access to him. It's the definition of corruption—use of public office for private gain," said Virginia Canter, chief ethics counsel for CREW and former ethics advisor to the International Monetary Fund and US Treasury.[52] Trump's businesses represent "unprecedented" conflicts of interest, Canter said.

"We know they were targeting foreign governments for business. We know they used the political campaigns and parties to direct business. We know they raised the prices before he took office so they could take advantage of people's interest in having access to the president and his property."

Marketing Mar-a-Lago as a second White House also guaranteed a new revenue stream for Trump's club: political money. Republicans across the country have seen huge value in hosting events at Trump properties.[53]

It was money the club had never seen before. In the years before he announced his candidacy, federal political candidates and committees spent just $55,000 at Mar-a-Lago for events, catering, and lodging.

Since Trump entered the race in 2015, however, Mar-a-Lago brought in more than $1,175,000 in political revenue.[54] Almost all came from the Republican National Committee and Trump's own campaign committees. But there was also a 500 percent increase in spending from other political committees as compared to the previous four years. Mar-a-Lago has become a favorite haunt for groups backed by casinos, energy companies, and other special interests.

Whether the spike in political spending at the club came from a desire to capitalize on the red-hot Trump political brand or to pay a favor to the Don becomes something of a "chicken or the egg" argument. In the end a visit to Mar-a-Lago accomplishes both.

A 2018 analysis by the magazine *Fast Company* found that at least eight candidates for federal or state office received a presidential endorsement on Twitter after spending money at Trump properties.[55]

Ever the opportunist, the president milked the demand. Trump sells at whatever price people are willing to pay. These days political organizations are willing to pay a lot to get through the gilded doors of Mar-a-Lago. In March 2018 the Republican National Committee paid the club more than $224,000 for venue rental and catering.[56] (Compare that to the $17,000 the Democratic Senatorial Campaign Committee paid in February 2008 to host an event at Mar-a-Lago.) The Republican Party of Palm Beach held its annual Lincoln Day fundraiser at Mar-a-Lago in late March 2017, capitalizing on the Trump political brand in an online invitation that showed Abraham Lincoln wearing a "Make America Great Again" hat with the message: "Speaker to be announced." The $300 tickets sold out over a month before the event. The group had been hosting the event at Mar-a-Lago since 2013, but this was their best year yet.

Trump didn't show, and Melania only came for fifteen minutes to the VIP event, but it didn't matter. Each consecutive year the Palm Beach GOP was able to charge more as the Trumps continued to make appearances. The president's eldest son, Donald Trump Jr., attended in 2018, and in 2019 the president spoke at the event within hours of the Mueller Report being released.[57] Tickets for the 2020 event would go for more than double what they had cost just four years earlier.

In addition to political committees, right-wing groups have flocked to Mar-a-Lago. Even the "Bad Boys of Brexit," Nigel Farage's top advisors, scouted the club as a potential venue.[58] The draw is clear: events hosted at Mar-a-Lago often feature appearances by the president, members of his family, and high-profile political allies, juicing ticket sales.

"It is shocking," said Fred Wertheimer of Democracy21, a nonprofit dedicated to combating private money in politics.[59] "The presidency has become a family business."

But even the man behind *The Art of the Deal* couldn't close on every opportunity presented by his presidency. ACT for America, designated an anti-Muslim hate group by the Southern Poverty Law Center, promoted a gala at Trump's club, which was canceled by the Trump Organization after a round of negative press.[60] A US Marine Corps reserve unit stationed in West Palm Beach also hit a political roadblock when it tried to host its annual ball at Mar-a-Lago.[61] In the past, the unit had held its event at an airport hotel. Critics pointed out that the dramatic change in venue made it seem like the Marines were officially endorsing Trump— and lining the pockets of their commander-in-chief. The ball was held elsewhere. ("Can you imagine walking into Mar-a-Lago with your girlfriend on your arm?" one disappointed officer told the *Miami Herald*.[62] "Can you imagine what that does for the heart of a young warrior?")

Visits from heads of state are particularly lucrative for Mar-a-Lago, given the increase in room and facility rentals and the flock of members and guests who converge on the club to witness something historic.

The summit with Xi was an unparalleled money maker. The club didn't just profit from hosting dozens of federal officials for a long weekend. It was also the most successful promotional event in the club's history.

Xi's trip led to a massive surge of Chinese tourism to Trump's Florida estate. Online travel agents were quick to put together vacation packages for Chinese tourists that included stops at the club where Xi and Trump held their summit. One advertisement featured a photo from inside Mar-a-Lago and labeled it "VIP Hall of President Xi Jinping."

For Mar-a-Lago, China was a huge and previously untapped market. And Trump would soon need it. When the club's high-society gala business plummeted after Trump's controversial comments about a white nationalist march, wealthy Chinese tourists swooped in.[63]

Their cash would be critical in keeping Mar-a-Lago afloat.

"I think the Founding Fathers would be horrified at President Trump's use of his private vehicles to enrich himself," said Canter, CREW's ethics counsel. "He is encouraging something which the Founders thought was the greatest threat to the American political system: the threat of corruption by foreign governments."

At Mar-a-Lago, Trump might as well be dancing on Hamilton's grave.

8

THE GATEKEEPERS

DAVID S. GOODBOY wanted to have a party at Mar-a-Lago for one reason: he knew people would come.[1]

Goodboy was a newcomer to the Palm Beach scene. The finance
writer-turned-hedge-funder had tired of New York's cold gloom and decided he wanted to live where he vacationed. So in 2013 Goodboy moved
to Palm Beach where, knowing no one on an island home to more than
thirty billionaires, he started an association to drum up interest for what
he envisioned as a new hedge fund mecca.[2]

He struggled to get the staid residents of the exclusive enclave to buy
into his vision. Five people came to the Palm Beach Hedge Fund Association's first event, held at a divey saloon in West Palm Beach.

This time would be different.

Goodboy advertised a Mar-a-Lago poolside cocktail hour with a tan-
talizing possibility. "Should the president be in residence, another letter will follow explaining the upgraded entry/security procedures," the
March 2017 invitation read.[3]

Two hundred people RSVP'd, far more than the seventy-five-person
capacity of the Gold and White Ballroom. Goodboy had to hold a lottery
to choose the lucky few who could attend.[4] It was the most popular party
he'd ever thrown in Palm Beach.

Since the election events of all kinds were selling out at Mar-a-Lago,
as people from all over the world searched for a way to gain an audience
with Trump. "If you're not part of Mar-a-Lago, you look for any person

that can lead you there," said Palm Beach travel agent Lexye Aversa.[5] "There are people begging all of the time."

It didn't matter what the event was or even whether the cause aligned with Trump's politics.

Trump had spent his campaign attacking hedge funds that mine huge datasets to gain a competitive edge in global markets, where they trade billions of dollars in nanoseconds.

"The hedge fund guys are getting away with murder," Trump said on CBS's *Face the Nation*.[6] "They're making a tremendous amount of money. They have to pay taxes."

He vowed to get rid of a tax loophole that he said benefited wealthy hedge fund managers and private equity executives at the expense of the middle class.[7]

Nobody munching on hors d'oeuvres at Mar-a-Lago on March 16 seemed worried about his animosity.

"I believe he was simply speaking to his fan base, you know, his constituents," Goodboy told the *New York Times*.[8] "The truth is he is pulling back on those statements, the way I see it."

As president, Trump surrounded himself with behemoths of the financial world. He even tapped part-time Palm Beachers Carl Icahn, Wilbur Ross, and Stephen Schwarzman to help him overhaul regulations.

The president has every incentive to accommodate requests to attend Mar-a-Lago events. Goodboy's $400-a-head reception paid Mar-a-Lago more than $10,000 for the event space, catering, and open bar.[9] The president didn't show up, but members of his cabinet did, according to Goodboy. (He wouldn't say which ones.)

Benefits from Mar-a-Lago events go both ways. In 2017 the Palm Beach Habilation Center brought in an extra $13,000 for its annual Hab-A-Hearts luncheon after people started whispering that Trump might show up—which he did.[10] Mar-a-Lago also got its cut from the jump in attendance, taking in roughly 10 percent more than it had the year before.

The wild success of most Mar-a-Lago events was thanks to two things: the high demand for tickets to anything held at the president's estate and the club member who sponsored the event.

THOSE WHO HOLD one of the five hundred Mar-a-Lago memberships have become the de facto gatekeepers for the Winter White House.

All nonmembers interested in coming to the club must either come as a guest of a member or with a ticket to attend an event. And all events hosted at Mar-a-Lago must have a member sponsor as a sort of insurance policy for the club.

When Trump was elected president, being a gatekeeper for his private estate became a powerful position.

People have built entire careers by gaining access to the MAGA brand through Mar-a-Lago.

Wayne Allyn Root was one.[11]

Before Trump's political career, Root didn't have a TV show or a national radio show or a newspaper column. He was a fringe conspiracy theorist, his name known pretty much exclusively in the darker corners of the internet as one of the first proponents of the debunked theory that Barack Obama was born abroad. It was even a bit too much for Sean Hannity when Root appeared on his show in 2012 demanding Obama release his college transcripts to prove he wasn't a foreign-exchange student.[12]

Now the *Wayne Allyn Root Show* has the 8:00 P.M. slot on Newsmax TV. Root also has nearly eighty thousand Twitter followers and a nationally syndicated radio show at 6:00 P.M. He frequently writes op-ed columns for his hometown paper, the *Las Vegas Review-Journal*.

Root is his own favorite example of the so-called American Dream. He's just an "SOB"—a son of a butcher from New York—who worked relentlessly toward his dreams. But Root is happy to admit he built his career on the coattails of a giant. He is proud of that.

"I was smart enough to notice this was a great guy to latch onto," Root said of Trump. "I was smart enough to notice you can't go wrong with his coattails. I was smart enough to realize that the people who love him really love him. You just gotta build a show around celebrating the good stuff that Donald Trump's done."

As much as Root owes his career to Trump, he also owes it to one of his best friends, Mar-a-Lago member Lee Lipton, the South Florida restaurateur.

For years Lipton had been slipping printed copies of Root's blog posts and articles to Trump when he would see him at the club. Root was never sure Trump actually read the articles until one day in 2015, when

Root received an email from Trump's personal assistant, Rhona Graff: "See the attached from Donald J. Trump."

Attached was a scan of a handwritten note from Trump congratulating Root on a recent article suggesting that the Donald had the potential to be a real-life Jay Bulworth—a fictional movie character portrayed by Warren Beatty in the movie *Bulworth*. The title character, a Democratic senator, loses his filter and takes on Washington lobbyists for their greed and corruption. In his column Root argued that Trump's belligerent truth-telling would likewise win over the American people.

"What a great story. Enjoyed it. You're the greatest," Trump wrote.[13]

From then on, Trump was a Wayne Allyn Root fan. He even tipped Root off a few days before he announced he was running for president.

"My entire relationship for all these years with Donald Trump has been through Lee and Lee sending my columns to Donald," Root said. "I can only tell you that after I say it, usually, a couple of weeks later something comes out of the president's mouth that sounds a lot like what I would say or said on TV or I said on my radio show or I said in my column."

Root introduced Trump at his campaign rallies in Las Vegas. He also sent Trump suggestions for a tax plan to be used in the campaign, although he acknowledged Trump's final version isn't exactly what he proposed. But when Root visited Mar-a-Lago in 2018 hoping for an audience with the president, Lipton worried Trump might not recognize the pundit out of his usual Vegas context.

"I can't promise you it's going to be a great meeting. I can't even promise you that he's going to agree to see you," Lipton warned Root.[14] "And if we do see him, I can't promise you we'll even get in to see him because if he's eating dinner, he's going to be surrounded by Secret Service and a velvet rope and you only get in if he waves you in."

To better their chances, Lipton arranged for himself and Root to have pre-dinner drinks with two other members who were extremely close with the president. (Recounting the story, Root wouldn't say who.)

After drinks the foursome walked past the president's table on the terrace, where they paused slightly in hopes that the president would look up and greet his old friends. Trump waved at his members. Then his eyes locked on Root.

"Wayne Root! Come on in!" Trump said.[15]

"Oh my God," Lipton said under his breath.

A delighted Root walked through the stanchions and sat down with the president and his dinner guest, *Fox News* commentator Geraldo Rivera.

"Wayne is one of my biggest fans, one of my biggest supporters, and he takes care of me in Vegas," Trump told Rivera.

All the billionaires and bigshots stared jealously.[16] After about ten minutes Root got up and walked away. Nosy Palm Beachers who have to beg for an audience couldn't quite believe what happened.

"I'm Trump golf's partner," one man said to Root by way of introduction. "I play golf with him all the time. Who the hell are you?"

Root wrote about the experience for the *Las Vegas Review-Journal*:

> Trump is nothing like the man the hateful liberal media portray. He has a huge heart. He appreciates every supporter. Trump cares what the little guy thinks. I am living proof. In that room full of billionaires and million-dollar donors, Trump made me feel like the most important person there. And I couldn't help thinking how proud my parents must be, looking down from heaven. Only in America.

Root knew whom he had to thank for his newfound importance: a Mar-a-Lago member.

"If it wasn't for Lee," he said, "maybe that wouldn't have happened."

MANY MAR-A-LAGO MEMBERS have capitalized on their proximity to the president and the international popularity of his political brand. But few have done so as successfully as former Hollywood personality Toni Holt Kramer, who reignited her own stardom by throwing parties at the club in Trump's name.

In 2015 the seventy-seven-year-old socialite and two of her Palm Beach friends cofounded Trumpettes USA—a Trump fan club and propaganda machine that masquerades as a nonprofit.

"Your job as a Trumpette is to help get the real Donald J. Trump elected, not the one the press wants you to believe in," the Trumpettes' website instructs.[17] "No one networks better than women so introduce the real man to your family, your friends, the people you work with and anyone you come in contact with. No matter whom you meet, where or how, just take a few minutes and talk about Trump."

The Trumpettes—who almost as a rule have undergone enough plastic surgery to look several decades younger—don't make calls. They raise awareness in the style of high society: by hosting parties.

"It's all propaganda," Kramer acknowledges.[18] She and her socialite girlfriends spend their time waltzing through Mar-a-Lago, taking pictures, and sometimes even snagging shots with the president himself, which are quickly posted to Facebook with fawning messages and a strong dash of self-importance.

Club staff call Kramer and her posse the "Hooters Girls" of Mar-a-Lago.[19]

Their parties are some of the hottest in town.

"I'm convinced that the passion people have for and about the man—pro or con—is why it was easy to fill both ballrooms at Mar-a-Lago, the winter White House in Palm Beach," Kramer wrote in her memoir *Unstoppable Me*.[20]

Kramer's obsession with Trump doesn't come from any long-held Republican ideals. She has always been about glamour. To Kramer, there's little difference between Washington, DC, and Hollywood.[21]

"You've got to know how to handle a camera. You've got to know how to talk. You've got to know how to be photographed," she said. "People are very judgmental."

Kramer would know. She has a Hollywood star with her name on it. Well, not quite Hollywood. The star is in Palm Springs, the California resort town where she owns a home a hundred miles east of Hollywood's "Walk of Fame."[22]

She had achieved C-list celebrity status as the host of various TV programs in Los Angeles, including *Talk of the Town*, a show in the 1990s that took viewers behind the scenes of some of the world's most exclusive parties with actors, business elites, and politicians. Back then she didn't care about politics and could hardly tell a Democrat from a Republican.[23] Only the power and palace intrigue of DC captured her interest.[24] (Her other passions are horse racing and the stock market.)

From Kramer's vantage point, Ronald Reagan was a centrist to be admired. He was "outstanding" in every way—except for his choice to wear a burgundy sports jacket.[25] He wore the offending item to lunch at the Polo Lounge in Beverly Hills when he was president of the Screen Actors Guild. It was the first time Kramer had ever seen him in person. She distinctly remembers wondering why any *man* would choose to wear that color.

The rest of her politics follow a similar pattern. In Kramer's mind, Nancy Pelosi's biggest fault is that she wears pantsuits that obscure her stunning legs. Still, Kramer maintains that the Speaker of the House is "one of the best-dressed women in politics."[26] She also admires how Pelosi lures the unsuspecting into her lair with an appearance of doe-eyed innocence.

But Hillary Clinton was Kramer's favorite.

Kramer first met Clinton at the White House the night before George W. Bush took over the country.[27] Despite Clinton's preference for plain clothes and square heels, Kramer loved her instantly. Clinton had a giggle that made her eyes twinkle and a face that gave away everything she was thinking.[28] Also, they were both "mommy's girls," Kramer remembered fondly.

"Hillary and I got on famously," Kramer said. "She was very close to her mother, Dorothy, and I was very close to my mother, Helen. And there was really a camaraderie from that alone."

The women stayed in touch over the years, and in 2007 Kramer supported the New York senator in her presidential primary against Barack Obama.

"I really believed that Hillary, at that time, would do a magnificent job as president. Because she appeared very centrist," Kramer said.[29]

She was sure her friend was going to win and was devastated when Clinton lost to a rookie US senator. How could some nobody from Illinois overtake a former First Lady who had worked her whole life to become the nation's first female commander-in-chief?[30]

But Kramer didn't back her old friend in 2016. She was afraid of the way the country was going under Obama, who in her mind was conspiring to make the United States "a country dependent on welfare to exist."[31] She liked Clinton but was afraid the Democratic Party would force her to continue down Obama's path. Kramer was convinced that would lead to the catastrophic collapse of respectable society.[32]

Donald Trump came into her life for the first time during a New Year's Eve party at Mar-a-Lago in 2009. Kramer was in the dining room with her husband and a few friends. Trump was making his usual rounds. After her hosts introduced him to the Kramers, Trump suggested the couple join his private club. They did. They had just moved from California to Palm Beach, and Kramer felt a special connection with Trump—they were both Geminis.

Trump became the solution to her political anxiety. Kramer's inner voice, the same one she claims predicted 9/11, told her that the mogul was the only person who could return the country to the way she remembered it growing up.[33] She knew he could win.

She was ecstatic when, in 2015, Trump walked past her dinner table and—without stopping and in a voice only she could hear—said, "I'm running."[34]

Kramer had the inside scoop: Donald J. Trump was going to run for president.

"He is a genius," she said. "You may think I'm mad, but I believe this was an anointed presidency."[35]

Kramer may be a genius too. Since founding the Trumpettes USA, which now has members from around the world, Kramer's personal brand skyrocketed. She has been interviewed by major media outlets as a Trump insider. She published a book about her life. Even Trump endorsed her brand. Speaking from the stage at the Trumpettes' 2020 Mar-a-Lago gala, the president celebrated the group's unlikely success.

"They put in a little ad saying any women that want to join us and they didn't know, remember you told me, they didn't know. Was it going to be ten people? Was it going to be twenty? Maybe thirty?" Trump said as he turned to Kramer, who stood beaming at his side.[36] "And they had eleven thousand people call! Women. All women. Only women."

Trump had blown off the Hooters Girls' events in previous years. But by 2020 they had grown too prominent to ignore.

"Now, I guess [the Trumpettes are] all over the country. And we just had our best poll numbers that we've ever had. They just came in. And I said, we have to come down and say hello."

Kramer's once-fading star had suddenly never been brighter.

Chapter 9

A PROBLEM IN FLORIDA

IT WAS HER ONE CHANCE to deliver a very important message to the president, and Annie Marie Delgado had no intention of wasting it.

Delgado was standing in line with a dozen VIPs in Mar-a-Lago's grand ballroom on March 10, 2019, waiting for a photo-op with the president. She had raised $50,000 for Trump's re-election campaign.[1] A pair of tickets to the breakfast and a signed photo with the president were her reward.

But Delgado wasn't really at Mar-a-Lago for a meal or a photo. The scrappy GOP activist had come to the fundraiser because it would get her close enough to Trump to do one thing: warn him.

"At Mar-a-Lago, anyone who can get within eyesight changes the game," a former White House official told the *Washington Post*. "Everyone who is angling for something knows to be there."[2]

Delgado wanted to tell the president about everything she saw going wrong in his backyard—the "fake" Florida Republicans she believed were screwing his chances of re-election, the foreign money she'd heard was being brought into his campaign, and the grifters using his name and club to enrich themselves. "If they appear at Mar-a-Lago, they appear to be accepted by the president," Delgado said. "But the president has nothing to do with it." He had to be made aware.

Delgado was a lifelong Republican—unlike, she suspected, most of the people who started frequenting Mar-a-Lago after 2016. Their motivations weren't political but economic. "They're all sociopaths," she said, "and sociopaths cluster."

So when it was her turn to pose in front of the American flag, giving the thumbs-up with the president, Delgado leaned over and whispered into the ear of the man who had once nicknamed her "Spitfire."

"Mr. President, we've got a problem here in Florida."

DELGADO HAD KNOWN Donald Trump since she was brought in to sell condos at the Trump Plaza towers in West Palm Beach thirty years earlier.

She had accidentally stolen his chair the first day they met. Normally, he'd be mad about something like that. But when he walked into the boardroom and found an attractive woman in his seat, he laughed. They'd kept in touch over the years. When Trump announced his presidential bid, Delgado interviewed with then campaign manager Corey Lewandowski for a job running the grassroots effort in Florida. As they sat on Mar-a-Lago's terrace discussing her role, Trump came down from his apartment.

"Hire her," Trump told Lewandowski.[3]

"I already did, sir," he replied.

Working on the Trump campaign was different from anything Delgado had ever experienced.

"Mr. Trump brought out the average person who has always felt like, 'Why should I bother? My vote doesn't count. I don't have a voice,'" Delgado said.[4]

That inspired her. But along with the well-meaning new activists came a group of people hoping to use the red-hot Trump brand to inflate their own importance and build their own empires.

"A lot of these coo-coo puffs now think that because they volunteered for a couple of months that they're the new kingmakers," she said.[5]

Dozens of groups have sprung up around the country using names that include "Trump," "45," or "MAGA" to raise money in the president's name.[6] The problem for the Republican Party is that a lot of that money doesn't go into its coffers, starving it of vital dollars.

Some people say Delgado is part of that problem. After the election she had worked with her longtime friend Guido Lombardi to create a network of Florida Republicans outside the formal campaign, which she believed had been taken over by RINOs—Republicans in Name Only. The Republican Party of Florida disavowed Delgado and her crew, claiming she was misusing the Trump name.

As casualties piled up in the civil war within the Florida GOP, it became clear to the renegades that they needed a heavyweight to intervene on their behalf.[7] Who better, they thought, than the president himself?

Delgado made her move at the March 10 fundraiser.

There was no time to say more than a few sentences before the president was whisked away to give his remarks on stage. Delgado simply told Trump to inquire with the party bigwigs whom she had briefed while waiting in line.

No one ever followed up on her warning. Delgado never got her signed photo. The campaign staff and Florida Republicans were upset that she would approach the president directly.

Delgado had miscalculated. She was thinking about the long-term health of the Republican Party. But Trump's club was becoming increasingly dependent not on bona fide Republicans but on the upstart promoters who were so skilled at exploiting Trump's cult of personality. After all, they were bringing in a lot of money that both the business and the campaign desperately needed.

Those who would threaten that are not warmly received.

THE FOUNDER OF the Trumpettes was one of those fake Republicans Delgado was trying to warn the president about, or at least so Delgado believed.

"Toni Holt Kramer—she is a trip," Delgado said.[8] "She saw an opportunity."

Since 2015 the Trumpettes had hosted luncheons and get-togethers in Palm Beach, but their first major party was planned for January 18, 2018, to celebrate the first anniversary of Trump's inauguration. They would host the event at Mar-a-Lago, of course. Everyone was excited.

The only problem was that the Trumpettes seemed to have little idea what they were doing.

So Annie Marie Delgado offered to help them get their act together.

"Toni is a fucking disaster," Delgado said acidly.[9]

First, the Trumpettes' event flyer had to be taken down because it didn't have the right disclaimer. Second, they hadn't secured sponsors to cover the cost of the catering and event space. Finally, in Delgado's opinion, the ticket price was way too low.[10] Kramer had set it at $250 per person.

Kramer said she wanted to make the event accessible to people who wouldn't normally be able to visit Mar-a-Lago.[11] Delgado told her that people wouldn't want to come if it seemed cheap. The price rose to $300.[12]

But true to her word, Kramer held tickets until interested parties could afford to pay. "I had to hold tickets for two weeks until the alimony check [cleared]," Kramer said. (By the third year, tickets to the annual Trumpettes' event would sell for $750 each.[13] Premium "ringside seating" went for $2,000.)

On the Trumpettes' big day, a swarm of more than nine hundred guests, most of them unused to the club's formalities, tried to bum-rush Eric Trump and his wife, Lara. They wanted pictures of the First Family. Delgado spent her time body blocking.

Eric and Lara mostly put up with it. The Trumpettes intended to give most—or maybe even all—of the gate to Mar-a-Lago.[14] The club needed the money. It had seen an exodus of events that year thanks to the controversial president.

"We had people in our lives that we thought were great friends that were nowhere to be found," Eric told the Trumpettes crowd.[15] "These are our true friends," he concluded, looking around at the room full of faces he had never seen before.

Aside from that, everything was perfect by the time the arch-conservative *Fox News* host Judge Jeanine Pirro began belting "Welcome to Mar-a-Lago!" from the stage in the grand ballroom.[16] (Unlike many in attendance, Pirro was no newcomer; she has been a Mar-a-Lago member since 1995.)

"It sure ain't no shithole!" Pirro cried to laughs and cheers from the crowd.[17]

Her comment was a reference to something Trump had said just a few days earlier. Frustrated by talks of protecting desperate refugees from places like Nigeria and Haiti, he had asked his staff, "Why are we having all these people from shithole countries come here?"[18]

Trump's remarks offended many. But not this new crowd at Mar-a-Lago. They loved him, and they loved being part of his world. Next year they'd come back to Mar-a-Lago for more.

By early 2019 Delgado was getting pissed.[19] But mostly she was worried.

The Trumpettes were planning a second party. It was bound to be more popular than the last. But in Delgado's opinion their events were doing nothing to get Trump re-elected. They were becoming a distraction. She knew political victories came from far less sexy things than bougie galas. Phone banks, flyers, polls, door knocking—that's what it takes to win.

Worse, Delgado suspected that the obsessive cult forming around Trump at Mar-a-Lago was especially susceptible to getting used by those with something to gain from the president. "Does Toni really know what she's doing? Absolutely not," Delgado said.[20] "Can she be taken advantage of? Absolutely."

Delgado had no idea whether that was happening. And she had no way to find out.

If the Trumpettes were registered as a political committee, Kramer would have to disclose who bought tickets to their events and what the group did with the money. Instead, Kramer filed documents in Florida to incorporate the Trumpettes as a nonprofit seeking tax-exempt status from the federal government.[21] A federal tax exemption would have prohibited the group from participating in political campaigns as well as making statements in favor of a political candidate. The status was never granted.[22] For the Trumpettes, that was a good thing. They are all about promoting Trump.

Just before their second Mar-a-Lago gala in 2019—the theme that year was "Country Comes to Mar-a-Lago"—Toni Holt Kramer got a phone call from a woman. The woman explained that she was calling on behalf of Eduardo Bolsonaro, the son of Brazilian president Jair Bolsonaro, known as the "Trump of the Tropics."[23] The younger Bolsonaro was himself a member of Brazil's Congress at the time.

"The president's son would like to come to the event," the woman told Kramer. "We want to buy tickets." And they wanted good seats.

Kramer liked the idea.

"Can I bring him up on stage?" she asked.

"Yes," came the response.

The Brazilians purchased three or four tickets, although Kramer wasn't exactly sure how the exchange worked. She assumed someone bought the tickets on behalf of Bolsonaro, whose father has been widely condemned for his hyper nationalism and violent statements against gays, women, and indigenous people. "It's a shame that the Brazilian cavalry wasn't as efficient as the Americans, who exterminated their Indians," Bolsonaro senior once said.[24] Trump considered him one of his closest allies in the Americas. Kramer was excited to host his son at Mar-a-Lago.

"Eduardo wanted to come because his father had been elected president and for the first time in probably eighteen years Brazil was getting out of this horrible, rotten, socialist environment where the only people doing well were the politicians, not the people," Kramer said. "Now all of a sudden, Bolsonaro wants to bring civilization [and] normalcy to Brazil."

People in cowboy hats descended on Mar-a-Lago on February 23, 2019. At the event Eduardo Bolsonaro brushed shoulders—and perhaps twirled lassos—with Eric Trump, actor Jon Voight, Judge Jeanine, and other power players in the Winter White House. He proudly posted the photos to Instagram.

When he took the stage to give a few remarks, Bolsonaro was effusive in his praise for Trump.[25] He told a story about someone who stopped him in the street to ask him about the 2016 election: If he were American, would he vote for Clinton or for Trump?

"I said, 'For Trump!'" he declared.

Bolsonaro told the cheering crowd the man had protested, saying Trump wanted to build a wall.

"And I answered him: I'm not going to the United States illegally."

The crowd went wild.

A few months later Trump sent a hand-written letter to Jair Bolsonaro praising his son's appointment as Brazilian ambassador to the United

States.[26] It was easy to wonder if Eduardo had earned that goodwill by pumping up a party at the president's private club.

Kramer was becoming a go-to for the global elite.

When Australian billionaire Gina Rinehart wanted to become a Mar-a-Lago member, Kramer endorsed her application. The mining magnate was Australia's second-richest person behind Anthony Pratt, who owned box-making factories in the American Midwest. Pratt had joined Mar-a-Lago in 2017 and eventually brought Trump on a well-publicized tour of his factory in Ohio, promising the president he would create more jobs.[27] When Trump slashed the corporate tax rate, Pratt's fortune soared by nearly $3 billion, increasing his lead on Rinehart for the title of richest Australian.[28]

"What an exciting weekend at Mar a Lago (The Winter White House), and a warm welcome to my newest Trumpette Gina Rinehart from Australia who has been visiting MAL," the Trumpettes' official Facebook page proclaimed.[29]

In Kramer's eyes, Rinehart was the perfect member.

"I will never, ever sign something I don't know or vouch for somebody I don't know," Kramer said.[30] "I don't want to put somebody in there who doesn't belong."

But the club had other priorities. Mar-a-Lago had thrown open its doors—and the party crashers were already inside.

10

"THE GIRL WHO OTHERS WOULD ENVY"

LI JUAN YANG HAD BEEN WAITING to throw a party at Mar-a-Lago all her life.

She just didn't know it.

Yang grew up poor in the 1970s in Harbin, an epicenter of industry in frigid northeastern China known for its "Ice and Snow" festival.[1] Now the nexus of Russian-Chinese trade, its name in the original Manchu suggests more humble roots: "a place for drying fishing nets." Yang had never heard of Mar-a-Lago. But, a relentless striver blessed with an entrepreneurial streak, she never stopped dreaming. Yang always wanted the best from life. She worked hard. Climbed every ladder she could. Moved to the United States after college. And became a US citizen.

On January 26, 2018, as she stood dressed in gold at the entrance to Mar-a-Lago's Donald J. Trump Grand Ballroom, she must have felt like a queen.

The charity gala that evening was sponsored by Elizabeth Trump Grau, the president's sister. But Yang was running the show. Her past had no place in the halls of old wealth. Most people called her "Cindy" now, a name she chose in homage to her favorite American supermodel, Cindy Crawford.[2] Mar-a-Lago's "Safari Night Ball" was her grand debut.

As guests in leopard print, zebra stripes, and Indiana Jones hats streamed into the club, Yang directed each to their assigned seats. Among them were a Palm Beach car salesman, a California real estate agent, a member of a biker club, and a Russian fugitive who had fled to Miami and was now trying his hand at journalism.[3]

Holding a flute of champagne, the exile turned to his assistant, who was recording him. "The most interesting thing," he said to the camera, "is that we met a lot of people here who speak Russian."

It certainly wasn't the usual crowd for a midseason charity gala in Palm Beach. And Cindy wasn't the usual kind of hostess. But sometimes stars align in the most unpredictable ways.

A march of white nationalists in Charlottesville, Virginia, the previous summer should never have thrown Palm Beach's social calendar into utter disarray. While terrifying, it should have been immaterial that hundreds of neo-Nazis were marching through streets a thousand miles away carrying torches and shouting, "Jews will not replace us." Even when a white supremacist drove a car into a cluster of counter-protestors, killing a young woman, it never seemed like the violence would change anything in this exclusive enclave of the country's richest people.

Then Donald Trump went off script.

He was at a Trump Tower press conference in August 2017 talking about infrastructure. But no one remembers that because after his prepared remarks, Trump began to defend the Charlottesville marchers, who included white supremacists like Richard Spencer and David Duke, the former grand wizard of the Ku Klux Klan.[4]

"You had some very bad people in that group, but you also had people that were very fine people, on both sides," Trump said.[5] "You had people in that group that were there to protest the taking down of, to them, a very, very important statue and the renaming of a park from Robert E. Lee to another name."

The neo-Nazis and Confederate sympathizers ended up handing Yang the opportunity of a lifetime.

Major charities whose annual galas were the lifeblood of Mar-a-Lago stopped holding events at the club.[6] The image-conscious charities had no choice but to pull out—or risk looking indifferent to racism.

"If you have a conscience, you're really condoning bad behavior by continuing to be there," Laurel Baker, executive director of the Palm Beach Chamber of Commerce, told *Town & Country*.[7] "Many say it's the dollars [raised at the events] that count. Yes. But the integrity of any organization rests on their sound decisions and stewardship. Personally, I do not feel that supporting [Trump], directly or indirectly, speaks well of any organization."

The American Red Cross ball? Canceled. The Cleveland Clinic's fundraising gala? Moved to the Breakers. Also out were the American Cancer Society, the Palm Beach Habilitation Center, and the Salvation Army.[8] All told, two-thirds of the major charities that had hosted events at Mar-a-Lago the previous year walked away.[9]

Trump's country clubs and hotels around the world took a 6 percent revenue hit from one year to the next.[10] Some of the financial gains he'd seen since becoming president evaporated. Mar-a-Lago was one of the biggest losers. The club's calendar emptied. But Palm Beach, just like nature, abhors a vacuum.

Yang was one of the first to fill it.

LIKE MANY IMMIGRANTS, Yang had made a life for herself in the United States by turning her intense work ethic into financial prosperity. She had a flare for finding nooks and crannies where there was money to be made.

After living in San Francisco, Yang moved to South Florida in the early 2000s. She liked the sun.[11] It was a place where she could reinvent herself. Yang began working in beauty spas, doing facials and nails. But she wanted to be her own boss.[12] By 2008 she had finally saved up enough money to open her own massage parlor.[13] Then she opened another. And another. She figured out a profitable and creative business model: after getting each spa off the ground, she could sell it (often to one of her best masseuses) and then use the proceeds from the sale to open a new spa. Flip, invest, and repeat. Within a few years she owned a chain of Asian massage parlors in South Florida called Tokyo Day Spa.

"She's one of the hardest workers I've ever met," said Woody McLane, a South Florida property broker who connects buyers and sellers of Asian spas.[14] "She opens a spa, starts it from scratch. She always finds places with cheap rent. That's one of the keys to making money."

Her parlors weren't exactly upscale. But they were generally located in the more genteel of Florida's legion of strip malls—the ones in nicer areas, with nicer stores, and nicer cars parked out front. Yang's flagship location in Palm Beach Gardens—a workaday mainland city ten miles northwest of Mar-a-Lago—had a pink exterior and tile roof. It was sandwiched between a dry cleaner and a yoga studio.

Yang recognized another niche too. The Chinese women who came to South Florida to work as massage therapists were almost exclusively recent immigrants who spoke little English.[15] The state's licensing exam was challenging even without the language barrier. Many of the women had no chance of passing—until Yang came along. She opened a massage school that offered classes in Mandarin, teaching students enough English to get through the exam. Yang herself had never mastered the language of her adopted home. It never stopped her.

In the intimate world of massage-parlor owners, Yang became something of a celebrity. "She was sort of—I'll use the word famous," McLane said.[16] "She was well known in the massage community. She was the girl that others would envy."

That didn't satisfy Yang.

Nothing was ever grand enough for Cindy Yang, who seemed determined to run from her humble roots as hard and fast as she could. She jumped out of airplanes, bragged she was fond of photographing eagles, and reveled in all life's challenges—the flashier, the better.[17] Everything she did went on social media as proof of her success.

"She likes to show off," Yang's mother told the *Miami Herald*.[18] "She likes to make people jealous."

Guiying Zhang worried about her daughter's ambition, frequently warning Yang that all the attention could only bring trouble.

Not one to be dissuaded, Yang set out to diversify her businesses. While maintaining her spa franchises, she branched out into the worlds of health care, education, and investment visas.

It didn't seem to matter to Yang what the venture was so long as there was money to be made or influence to be gained.[19] At one point she even billed herself as a talent agent who could help artists and their works "go global," including getting them a spot at Art Basel, the world-famous art fair in Miami Beach frequented by billionaires and royals.[20]

Despite having no background in science or technology, Yang traveled frequently from Florida to Silicon Valley, where she worked at DingDing TV, a tiny media company that promoted its ability to find funding for "robotics, 3D printing of human organs, deformable equipment, nano-fish, biological computers, bionic hands, reading emotions, wireless brain implantation," and other fantastical-sounding technologies.[21]

Around that time Yang turned to one of the best resources for ambitious Chinese Americans seeking to expand their businesses: the Chinese Communist Party. She started making connections with cultural and business organizations in South Florida that are closely linked to the Chinese government. A central plank of China's foreign policy depends on such "overseas" groups pushing Beijing's agenda abroad.[22] That doesn't mean everyone who participates is a die-hard communist.

"Many Chinese Americans do business here, and it is always better not being alone," said James Xuefeng Zhang, former president of a South Florida nonprofit dedicated to "strengthening ties between the local Chinese community and China."[23] Zhang got to know the eager Yang at parties and conferences. It was clear to him she wasn't motivated by ideology or political allegiance to the Chinese state. "She left us an impression that she was always seeking profits," he said.[24] Yang was just finding ways to know more people and make more money.

Her timing couldn't have been better.

Xi Jinping had taken power in China in 2012, determined to "rejuvenate" the nation.[25] Through one of the most ambitious global development plans the world has ever seen—the "Belt and Road Initiative"—Xi kickstarted China's economy and expanded its influence abroad. With a trillion-dollar investment plan, China began to build railroads, oil and gas pipelines, ports, highways, and fiber-optic networks in any country that would sign up.[26]

When Xi welcomed representatives from more than a hundred countries to a Belt and Road forum in Beijing, his core message mirrored Donald Trump's: He wanted to *Make China Great Again*, although his language was far loftier, with allusions to the Euphrates River, Confucianism, and Voltaire.

"The Belt and Road Initiative is rooted in the ancient Silk Road," Xi said.[27] "It focuses on the Asian, European, and African continents, but is also open to all other countries. All countries, from either Asia, Europe, Africa, or the Americas, can be international cooperation partners of the Belt and Road Initiative."

The Chinese push for relevance abroad relied on well-connected members of overseas Chinese communities. People like Cindy Yang.

"Merge with the local community, reward the local community, and contribute to the local community," Qiu Yuanping, director of the Chinese government office that handles diaspora affairs, said on a visit to the United States.[28] "The biggest beneficiaries of China and the US maintaining [a] good relationship are overseas Chinese."

Yang promoted Belt and Road from a high-rise apartment overlooking Miami's Biscayne Bay where she had started an offshoot of DingDing TV. The station's reach was negligible. But Yang was the master of making a dollar out of 15 cents. She used the station to bolster her credentials and became the vice president of the South Florida chapter of a nonprofit that "links the Communist Party of China and the Chinese government to the country's science and technology community."[29] Although people said Yang had to contribute money to get in, within a few years she received the group's Outstanding Service Award.[30] (Yang was later kicked out after the national organization said it discovered she was using its platform to make money.[31])

In 2015 Yang befriended a South Florida woman who worked for the foreign division of the Chinese government.[32] Together they founded a Florida-based nonprofit that hosted cultural exchanges between China and the United States, including a beauty pageant.[33] The events were organized in consultation with Chinese officials. They featured well-connected guests of honor like the businessman Shanjie Li, a former Chinese government advisor who had moved to Miami and helped a state-owned construction company invest $110 million into local real estate.[34] (The company described its plans to build waterfront luxury condo towers as part of Belt and Road.[35])

Yang was high on her new life.

She accompanied Chinese government officials on a tour of a Chinese warship docked in Florida, met Nobel Prize winners, and attended China's exclusive Boao Forum—the Davos of Asia—where she reported on Belt and Road initiatives in the healthcare industry.[36]

Yang was named vice president of the Florida Chapter of the Council for the Promotion of the Peaceful Reunification of China, which falls under the umbrella of the overseas division of the Chinese Communist Party.[37] The council, founded to oppose Taiwanese independence, "is a leading organization mobilizing international Chinese communities in support of Beijing's policies," a US congressional commission found.[38] (The party sent a letter congratulating the Florida chapter on its inauguration.)

When the consul general of China in Houston came to a Thanksgiving gathering in Florida in 2015, he greeted Yang: "We meet again."[39]

A MONTH AFTER MEETING the consul, Yang attended a breakfast event with a powerful politician of a different sort—Jeb Bush, the former Florida governor who was running for the Republican Party's 2016 presidential nomination.[40]

Her new contacts in South Florida's overseas Chinese associations had gotten her into American politics too.

In June 2015 they had partnered with a broader group of Chinese Americans to get out the vote for Bush. On social media the group called him a "moderate Republican" who appreciated Asian American support.[41] Yang brought more than two hundred people from South Florida's Asian American community to a Bush campaign rally, becoming one of the state's top GOP Asian American organizers.

Still, she sensed she didn't fit in. After attending a Palm Beach GOP meeting, she wrote on Facebook: "Need to learn more [about] the culture of the United States."[42] She had scarcely even voted since becoming an American citizen.[43] She wilted in any discussion of policy.[44] But she wasn't in it for the politics—no one in her family was political.[45]

"It was all because of the parties," her mother said.[46]

It was also all about the money.

And it soon became clear that Trump, not Jeb, was the real money-maker.

THROUGHOUT 2016 YANG supported Donald Trump's campaign.

She held banners on the street, encouraged Asian Americans to vote, and was delighted when the belligerent tycoon with whom she was becoming increasingly obsessed won the election.

She had been volunteering for a recently formed political group called the National Committee of Asian American Republicans, or the Asian GOP for short. In January 2017 Yang and the Asian GOP threw a ball at the Mayflower Hotel in DC to celebrate Trump's inauguration. Although Asian Americans skew Democratic, the Asian GOP focused on Trump's pro-business and anti-regulation messaging.

Yang had met the committee's executive director, Cliff Zhonggang Li, a Boca Raton tech entrepreneur with marginal political experience, at a Chinese cultural event in South Florida two years earlier.

Li immediately recognized Yang's talent: networking. When the Asian GOP had the chance to attend a high-level Trump fundraiser in New York City at the end of 2017, Li put Yang in charge of recruiting a guest list.[47] She spread the word on Chinese-language social media, tapping a growing market of Chinese who were interested in all things Trump. It worked.

Yang proudly took credit for more than a dozen attendees at the $2,700-a-head breakfast held in the swanky Manhattan restaurant Cipriani. "They're all my guests," she said as she gestured to the throng of mainland Chinese and Chinese American business people.[48]

In fact, word about the Cipriani event had soared far beyond Yang on Chinese social media. In total, nearly one hundred Chinese and Chinese Americans showed up.[49] The Chinese contingent was so large that even Trump noticed, joking to his American supporters that they better step up their donations or they'd lose "all the good seats."[50]

At least two of Yang's guests scored the ultimate prize: $50,000 signed photographs with the president.

The Asian GOP's success at the event was celebrated in Chinese state media.[51] But Cliff Li suspected something wasn't right. In his eyes, the fundraiser was "sort of messy," as he put it in his understated way.[52] Li was delighted to have Chinese Americans participating in politics. But he worried that some of the people at Cipriani weren't American citizens or green card holders.

That could be a problem. A big one.

Campaign finance law forbids foreign nationals from contributing to US political causes.[53] The law also bans people from donating to political candidates and committees in another person's name.[54]

To get a photograph with Trump at Cipriani, donors needed to kick in $50,000 to his GOP fundraising committee. But federal election records show that Yang's two guests who received photos with Trump didn't pay a dime. One of the men would later explain that a friend had given him the $50,000 ticket as a gift—and with it, a nearly priceless grip-and-grin.[55] (He wouldn't name the friend.)

So who paid $100,000 for the photos with Trump? It's unclear.

But before the event Cindy Yang and three of her associates at the Asian GOP together contributed more than $135,000 to Trump Victory, the president's joint fundraising committee with the RNC.[56] One of the donors told the *Miami Herald* she didn't remember making a $25,000 donation listed under her name and address.

Cliff Li had stressed to Yang that she had to follow fundraising rules, although he acknowledges he never watched her closely. He thought she understood. He had even taken her to a campaign finance training session. But after Cipriani he wasn't so sure. He couldn't have his group involved in a scandal. So he decided that from then on the Asian GOP would have a strict policy: no more foreign nationals could come to political events as the group's guests.

Soon after the rule was implemented, Yang quit.[57] She was breaking out on her own. She didn't need Cliff Li or the Asian GOP anymore. They'd already given her a leg up. Over the previous two years, as Yang had built contacts in South Florida's GOP, she snagged photos with every politician she could find, building her brand as someone well connected and influential.

To get this far, she'd become a quintessential photo bomber.

"She looks for people that she thinks the president knows and hangs out at their table so she can take a picture while the president is there so it looks like she knows him," said society columnist Shannon Donnelly. "She hovers around until he gets nearby and hops into the picture or tries to get an introduction."

Donnelly met Yang—sort of—at a Mar-a-Lago Christmas dinner in 2017.[58] Trump had been over at Donnelly's table talking golf with her son moments before Yang swooped in. "All the sudden this woman comes over to me and starts talking to me like she knows me," said Donnelly, who couldn't really make out what Yang was saying. "I just ignored her, and she walked away."

Yang knew those photos were a money maker. She used them to legitimize her newest business—GY US Investments, a Florida company that promised clients the chance to "take pictures with the president."[59]

Established ten days after the Cipriani event, GY US Investments was billed as a consulting company for Chinese businesspeople hoping to branch out into the United States.[60] But it was really just a tour operator. And Yang had her sights set on one destination: Mar-a-Lago.

She was going to corner the market.

She just needed the keys.

WHEN YANG HEARD that a small charity needed help selling tickets to a 2018 "Safari Night" fundraising gala at Mar-a-Lago, she jumped into action.

The charity was run by Terry Bomar, a Palm Beach County pastor who had been friends with Elizabeth Trump Grau since 2003 when his family's art gallery sold her some pieces. Though the charity had largely gone dormant in recent years, the president's sister suggested Bomar hold an event at Mar-a-Lago. After Charlottesville, the calendar was looking pretty bare, after all. Trump Grau even agreed to cosponsor the party with her husband. It seemed a worthy cause: Young Adventurers mentored young people, helping their careers and sending them on trips abroad. It also sponsored a school in Kenya.

Bomar agreed to put on the ball. He didn't like how people reacted to Trump's comments on Charlottesville—"the media twists things," he believes—and he thought the big charities were wrong to pull out. There was still a bright side.

"It opened an opportunity for little charities like us," Bomar said.[61]

He couldn't pull off the gala alone.

The pastor had met Cindy Yang through the Asian GOP. While he had a hard time understanding her English, he could tell one thing: the woman had ambition and drive. She wanted to buy a table, maybe more than one, which Bomar had priced at $5,000 apiece. She went all in with her support, saying she could even plan an exchange trip to China for the Young Adventurers' kids, all expenses paid. She also asked Bomar if Trump would show up. But a lot of people had asked that question, and the pastor didn't think anything of it.

Yang quickly became the driving force behind the event, using it to launch the Mar-a-Lago division of her Trump tourism business.

Taking to her social media network, Yang spread the word about Safari Night far and wide. A savvy saleswoman, she tweaked the description of the event to appeal more to her prospective clients. Young Adventurers became a footnote. With Yang as an impromptu impresario, Safari Night transformed into something far grander and more attractive to members of China's business class: a chance to meet the president's sister.[62] On WeChat, China's dominant social media platform, individual tickets were marked up from the standard $600 that Young Adventurers was asking to $1,000 from Yang and her associates.[63] VIP packages that promised two nights at Mar-a-Lago were priced at $10,000.[64]

Forty people RSVP'd to Yang's invitation to the club.[65] They weren't there to support the charity. They were there for Trump. And they had paid good money to get in.

Among Yang's Safari Night guests was Xianqin Qu, the leader of the Florida chapter of the Council for the Promotion of the Peaceful Reunification of China, who had helped Yang organize a South Florida welcoming party for Xi's 2017 visit to the club.[66]

"I was very surprised by the number of Chinese Americans there," said another guest, Xinyue "Daniel" Lou, a Chinese American businessman who traveled from New York City to attend Safari Night.[67]

Lou had seen an advertisement on WeChat and thought the cost was reasonable. How often, after all, did one get the chance to party inside the home of a president? He immediately saw the value of Yang's business.

"The reason Mar-a-Lago all the sudden became so impressive is that President Xi flew over and had a meeting with President Trump there," he said. "That made it into an attractive destination. All the Chinese people want to take a trip there."

Safari Night was a smash, raising $50,000 for Young Adventurers.

A Chinese dance troupe provided entertainment for the four hundred guests, while a local artist painted portraits of Albert Einstein and Melania Trump in real time as partygoers bid on the works. Models recruited by a woman who once ran a Russian mail-order-bride service glided between tables showing off their ball gowns, engaging in small talk, and handing out business cards. (One teenage model later said she felt like *she* was being sold, not the clothes.[68]) Enthralled with the safari-chic theme, guests posed with cardboard cutouts of African wildlife. Trump Grau wore leopard print; Terry Bomar donned an Indiana Jones hat, showing off a cheetah-spotted vest under his tuxedo.

Yang spent the night networking.

"She speaks really horrible English, but she would talk to everybody," said one member of South Florida's Chinese American community.[69] Yang didn't dance. She didn't drink. She was there doing what she had always done: "looking for rich people."

Safari Night marked a new era at the elite club. While Mar-a-Lago had always flouted some of the conventions of polite society, the ladies of Palm Beach remained its principal aristocracy. But after Charlottesville, the doors opened to anyone who could pay. A new class moved in.

Safari Night's most successful promoter, massage-parlor queen Yang suddenly held the keys to Mar-a-Lago.

"She was the gatekeeper," the person who knew her said. "It was prestigious."

11

"PRINCE" CHARLES

FOR YANG'S NEW BUSINESS, the best part of Safari Night was how much Prince Charles enjoyed the party.

At Mar-a-Lago the prince wore a floral, dark red Mao jacket.

He wasn't the heir to the British throne but rather a bald and stocky Chinese travel agent named Li Weitian, who often went by Charles Lee, or Dr. Charles, or sometimes "Prince" Charles.

Lee ran a group called the United Nations Chinese Friendship Association, which in reality had nothing to do with the United Nations. He also had no relationship with two prominent Chinese American politicians listed on his website as board members. (Staffers for Representatives Grace Meng and Judy Chu said their bosses had never heard of Lee or his group.[1])

What Lee really did was use the UN brand to package trips for Chinese business people who wanted to visit seats of power and meet important people in the United States and around the world.

The blistering rise of China as an economic power had created a new class of Chinese tourists with cash in their pockets and dual loyalties in their hearts—half capitalist-style entrepreneurs, half Chinese Party Communists. Their primary currency: photographs with the global elite, leveraged as proof of their status and influence. They used the photos to attract investors.[2]

The Chinese government encourages this practice. Lee advertised his services as part of Xi Jinping's "civilian diplomacy" program, although again there was no indication of any actual connection between Lee and the government.[3]

He offered his clients the chance to receive awards and honorary ambassadorships, essentially pieces of paper with semi-official-sounding language and Lee's signature. He once gave what the media dubbed a "hoax" UN peace prize to a member of Myanmar's military junta.[4]

Lee had once promoted trips to the United States centered around President Barack Obama, with stops in New York, Philadelphia, and Washington, DC.[5] But Obama did not own an estate open to the public. There were far fewer opportunities to get close to him. Gaining access to Trump, however, was easy—especially after Lee connected with Cindy Yang.

At Yang's invitation, Lee attended Safari Night to scout Mar-a-Lago as a destination for his clients. He called the club a "sacred place."[6]

"The first time I met Charles was Safari Night," said a member of South Florida's Chinese American community.[7] "Cindy invited him. He said he would have his clients come, but he needed to know what it looks like."

Lee liked what he saw.[8]

On his website he raved about his experience: the club, its grandeur, the beautiful models, the thrill of taking a photo with the president's sister. He was already pitching an upcoming Mar-a-Lago event to his clients as part of an eight-day travel package priced at $13,500 that included trips to Wall Street, Harvard, the United Nations, and West Point.[9]

"I know he was advertising a lot of stuff. Some in China. Some in Japan. Some in England. Everywhere," said Xiaoqi Wang, an organizer for the Asian GOP who attended Safari Night.[10] "I thought, 'This guy probably works with a lot of people.'"

Over the next year Lee would distribute Yang's advertisements and recruit more than a dozen Chinese guests for at least four more Mar-a-Lago galas Yang promoted. The offer was always the same: buy tickets to the event and get a chance to rub shoulders with Trump or his family.

Using her photos of Mar-a-Lago from Safari Night, Yang advertised her access to Trump's "second White House."[11] She claimed to be a member of "the president's club."[12] GY US Investments, Yang's new company, boasted that she had set up a "presidential round table meeting and presidential dinner" for clients who had received a "group photo with the president."[13] She was operating on a tried-and-tested model, with a Palm Beach twist.

"Cindy was following the new Chinese immigrant playbook. They try to get in with whoever is in power. In 1996 it was Clinton. Now it's Trump," said a former GOP political operative.[14] "It's about creating some kind of notoriety so she can say, 'I know famous American politicians' and promise the same to other people."

But those who know her said Yang didn't actually have the kind of access or influence she was promising clients in 2018.

"All she could do was get them into a ball or gala and hope the president would come," said Terry Bomar, the pastor behind Safari Night.[15] (Bomar had no idea Yang was using Mar-a-Lago charities like his as a business opportunity. "She seemed to be very sincere," he said.[16])

High-level CEOs and executives didn't need someone like Yang to open doors for them. "She's using this to attract your third-, fourth-, [and] fifth-tier Chinese businesspeople," the former GOP operative said.

Ultimately, Yang delivered on the one thing those clients cared about— photos that made them look important.

In her client's eyes, getting a shot with the president was best. But photos in the president's home with members of his family and other high-level politicians would do too.

More than even the White House, Mar-a-Lago became the crown jewel of China's new Trump tourism industry.

"These rich people have been everywhere, seven-star hotels, everywhere. But they've never been to the president's house," said someone familiar with Yang's business.[17]

"You have money, but you can't buy class," the person said. "That's what Mar-a-Lago is: class."

DEMAND FOR ACCESS to Mar-a-Lago was so high that it didn't matter what the event was, so long as tickets were available. Yang experienced no shortage of supply. The club's post-Charlottesville newcomers were eager to sell her tables.

Among the first to sell to her was Steven Alembik, a Republican activist and die-hard Trumper known for sporting a custom-made stars-and-stripes blazer. (He's also remembered for once calling Barack Obama a "f******* Muslim n*****."[18]) Even before Charlottesville, Alembik had been planning an event to commemorate the forty-fifth anniversary of the 1972 Munich attacks on the Israeli Olympic team.[19] The idea came to him, he said, after the suicide bombing at South Florida pop star Ariana Grande's concert in Manchester, England, in 2017. Alembik's brainchild, held to benefit a pro-Israel charity called the Truth About Israel, was originally scheduled to take place at the Boca Raton Resort & Club.

Mar-a-Lago had been booked on February 25, 2018, for an Israeli disaster-relief organization's fundraiser.[20] But the group canceled after the president's remarks on Charlottesville. Alembik pounced.

"I picked up the phone, I call Mar-a-Lago, they think I'm calling to cancel some other gala or some event, and I said no. I'd like to come here and show our support for the president of the United States," Alembik said at the time.[21]

He called the charities that pulled out "spineless."

Alembik got to work selling tickets, dangling the hope that Trump would show up.[22]

In fact, all he could do was hope and pray that the president might be in town that weekend—and would deign to stop by.

Cindy Yang and Charles Lee seized the opening presented by Alembik's event.

In advertisements Lee described the evening as a "dinner" with Trump and said his clients would receive a group photo with the president.[23]

Other promoters picked up on the event too. On Chinese social media and blog posts a flyer circulated that featured a headshot of Trump and advertised a black-tie, invitation-only event at Mar-a-Lago the same night as the Truth About Israel gala.[24] "Because this event is a charity dinner," one ad read, "the price of taking a photo with the president is lower than usual!"[25]

A Chinese cryptocurrency platform purporting to be "the world's first transaction platform to buy and sell the time of celebrities" advertised the event as a private dinner with US politicians and business people that would give attendees the chance to shake hands with the president and snap a photo with him.[26]

When the big day rolled around, the mainland Chinese tourist contingent numbered upward of a hundred, more than a quarter of the total guests. Some said there were as many as 250 Trump tourists in attendance. They were decidedly not there to learn the truth about Israel.

"To the Chinese, Mar-a-Lago is like the Taj Mahal," one bemused attendee told Shiny Sheet society columnist Shannon Donnelly.[27] "They want to see it."

Though Mar-a-Lago was no stranger to the bizarre bordering on absurd, Alembik's Truth About Israel event stood out. A Chinese Michael Jackson impersonator roamed the crowd. The pro-Trump social media stars Diamond and Silk fangirled over the impersonator. "Pinch me," one of the women said to Paulette Martin, the event's official photographer.[28] "Michael Jackson! I need my picture with him!"

From the moment the doors opened, the event was something of a disaster.[29]

The observant Jews who attended to support Israel found that hors d'oeuvres served around the pool included unkosher items like coconut shrimp.[30] Many of the Chinese visitors couldn't speak English and struggled to communicate with the Palm Beach ladies stationed at the door. When a guest offered to write her name out for a confused check-in attendant, she could only spell it in Chinese characters.

Making matters worse, there was no obvious seating chart, leading to a mad dash for tables.

When headliners like future Florida governor Ron DeSantis and GOP congressman Brian Mast mounted the stage for the serious portion of the evening, the Chinese had no clue what the impassioned, pro-Israel speechifiers were saying. Instead of listening, the overseas guests chatted amongst themselves, looked at their phones, and took photographs. "It was so pointless," a Mar-a-Lago staffer said. Guests repeatedly approached staff, asking where the president was and how they could meet him.[31]

One woman used her phone to show a Mar-a-Lago staffer videos of her daughter singing. She wanted to find out how her little girl could perform for Trump. Other guests tried to pass out electronics to employees as gifts, hoping it might grease the wheels for a presidential introduction. As far as the staffers could tell, the gadgets were largely junk. They didn't turn on. "I tried to decline, but they insisted I accept them because they thought I could help them get access to Trump," one staffer said.[32] "Their English was so limited. I tried to explain that I couldn't help."

Unlike the guests, organizers knew Trump wasn't coming before the event even began.

On Chinese social media a screenshot circulated that appeared to show a conversation between Alembik and one of the Chinese middlemen promoting the event.

"About 30 minutes ago, I was notified of a change in the President's schedule," read the message from Alembik.[33] "He will not be in attendance on Sunday. We are looking at some possible alternatives. Will keep you apprised."

"What the fuck," one guest who traveled to Palm Beach for the event wrote in a blog post.[34]

The Chinese cryptocurrency platform claimed the president's schedule had been affected by a shooting, likely referencing the massacre of schoolchildren and teachers that occurred at South Florida's Marjory Stoneman Douglas High School earlier that month.[35] But that wasn't the real reason. Trump had long been scheduled to be in Washington hosting the annual Governor's Ball.[36] He had never planned to attend Alembik's gala.

"The event was such a mess," said a Chinese American guest who bought tickets because he was led to believe the president would appear.[37] "People were cheated."

Charles Lee had to scramble to keep his clients happy.

"The biggest regret of the banquet was that President Trump failed to attend," Lee wrote in a recap of the Truth About Israel gala.[38]

Luckily, he had a backup plan: a high-dollar fundraiser set for the following weekend at Mar-a-Lago to raise money for the president's reelection.

"The National Committee of the Republican Party of the United States apologized to all the representatives attending [the Truth About Israel event]! And immediately sent an invitation letter to take remedial measures: Inviting all delegates to the banquet [at Mar-a-Lago] on March 3, 2018," Lee wrote in his recap. (The RNC had no part in Truth About Israel, nor did it take any remedial action for the president's absence.[39])

There was just one catch—Chinese nationals like Lee and his overseas guests couldn't legally buy tickets. Federal campaign finance law states that only US citizens or green card holders can donate to a US political campaign. Tickets to the March 3 event were a political donation. That didn't stop Lee from using an RNC flyer to advertise the event online—with the official prices haphazardly scratched off.[40]

The only way for Lee and his guests to attend Trump's fundraiser without breaking the law would be if an American citizen or green card holder gifted them thousands of dollars' worth of tickets.

THE DAY BEFORE the March 3 fundraiser, GOP activist Annie Marie Delgado got a call from a friend.[41]

The friend said she had gotten a request for six tickets—and the people wanted to pay cash.

That made Delgado nervous. She wanted to know where the money came from.

The friend wasn't sure but said the people asking were from China.

Delgado responded with a lecture on campaign finance law and a strict warning: "Stop right there."

12

SGT. PEPPER'S LONELY HEARTS CLUB BAND

THE PRESIDENT'S RE-ELECTION campaign was rolling out a new fundraising strategy, and the Mar-a-Lago luncheon on March 3, 2018, was part of its launch party.[1]

The Republican National Committee was using the event as a reboot amid a growing crisis for Trump's administration.[2] Mar-a-Lago was becoming a choice venue for its fundraisers. At the $2,700-per-plate event, the president could rake in money for his campaign while simultaneously ensuring a profit for his suffering business.[3]

Win-win.

Everything was shaping up perfectly. Except the president was late to his own party.[4]

He was tweeting. As Trump digitally fumed about trade deficits and the "crazy" mainstream media, hundreds of Republican donors milled around Mar-a-Lago's Donald J. Trump Grand Ballroom.

Kris Hager was getting very hungry.[5] The Gold Star dad had been asked to say a prayer to kick off the speakers' portion of the event. (Hager's oldest son, Staff Sergeant Joshua Hager, had been killed while serving as an Army Ranger in Iraq more than a decade earlier.[6]) Not knowing when he was going to be called on stage to give the invocation—and not wanting to be caught with his mouth full—Hager kept turning away waiters offering platters of food and glasses of wine. He ended up eating at

McDonald's on his way home. He didn't care. He was just honored to be at Mar-a-Lago.

Unlike Hagar, most of the other guests were grateful for the delay. Trump's tardiness gave them the opportunity to ruthlessly network in the new epicenter of American power.

Guests at the Winter White House claw their way up the political ladder in the same way minor-league socialites had always embellished their way to relevance in the tiny town's country club scene: by being seen with the right people. Back in Mar-a-Lago's earlier days, that meant being pictured with the right people in the society pages. Now it means tagging the right people in your Facebook photos. During the Trump administration the first hours of most Mar-a-Lago events are dominated by people hunting for the politically connected.

How one gets to Mar-a-Lago in the first place? Well, that remains largely the same. Know someone who knows someone. Pay a lot of money. Or follow the instructions in the little black book. In a symbiotic relationship as old as time, young men fresh out of college and hungry for connections latch onto the club's aging socialites. The men get event tickets, while the women enjoy handsome escorts to brag about to their friends.

A montage of the people milling around the grand ballroom waiting for Trump on March 3 would have looked something like the album cover of the Beatles' *Sgt. Pepper's Lonely Hearts Club Band*, with its assortment of random and oddly distorted faces inexplicably clustered together around a group of self-important celebrities.

It was a who's-who of the new South Florida establishment.

As the fundraiser kicked off, RNC chairwoman Ronna McDaniel and Trump's new campaign manager, Brad Parscale, walked around taking photos with guests.

Parscale, plucked from the staff of the Trump Organization's digital marketing team, had served as the social media coordinator for Trump's 2016 campaign. The day before the fundraiser Parscale had founded a digital media company that would eventually take in nearly $1 million from a pro-Trump PAC.[7] He knew the value of establishing himself as a respected player in the Florida crowd. By that time, everyone in the MAGA world understood how important it was to have allies at Mar-a-Lago. Parscale would even relocate his family from San Antonio to South Florida—right in the center of the action.[8]

Pastor Mark Burns won the MVP for networking that weekend, appearing in what felt like every single photo posted to social media. Burns had traveled all the way from South Carolina in hopes that a visit to Trump's Winter White House would give a much-needed boost to his campaign for Congress. He proudly posted a photo of himself meeting Republican donor and Florida sugar baron José "Pepe" Fanjul, among many, many others.[9]

Cindy Yang also snagged a shot with the pastor. Yang saw Burns talking with a woman she knew and, in her usual style, approached the duo. "Cindy came over and interrupted the conversation and said, 'I raise money for President Trump, I have all these businesses,'" said the woman Burns had been talking to when Yang butted in. "She was trying to make herself feel important."

Burns also got acquainted with a hefty man wearing traditional Chinese clothing. In front of a Trump-Pence backdrop, they snapped a photo shaking hands that Burns later posted to Facebook.

"Great discussing bringing Jobs to the SC 4th District, Greenville & Spartanburg, SC with Chinese Businessmen today. President Trump is bringing Jobs back to the US," Burns wrote in his post.[10]

But the man Burns was shaking hands with wasn't a powerful Chinese industrialist or someone who had any real interest in bringing jobs to South Carolina.

It was Prince Charles.

Charles Lee and his Chinese guests had somehow gotten into the party, although there was no record in federal elections disclosures of them buying tickets. Who paid their way—and whether anyone broke the law to get them in—remains unclear.

As for the hapless Burns, he would soon be knocked out of the race with just 2.5 percent of the vote.[11]

THE PRESIDENT WAS LATE to the fundraiser but apparently didn't care. He was having a terrible week.

The Saturday event had been advertised as a dinner party, but it had to be moved to lunch after Trump decided he wanted to attend the Gridiron Club Dinner in DC that night instead. The change meant Trump barely had time for his normal game of golf—a much-needed moment of self-care. The *Washington Post* was calling the previous seven days the "darkest" yet for his administration.[12]

It had been a week of truly unrelenting bad news.

White House communications director Hope Hicks—who had served as something like Trump's in-house therapist—had resigned that week, a day after giving eight hours of testimony in front of the House Intelligence Committee in which she admitted to telling white lies for the administration.[13] Trump's son-in-law Jared Kushner had lost his top-level security clearance amid concerns over possible conflicts of interest regarding his business deals abroad.[14] Trump later had to overrule intelligence officials to get him reinstated.[15]

The president had also chosen that week to throw a few sucker punches. They didn't all land.

First, he'd hit US trading partners with tariffs on steel and aluminum, raising fears of a trade war.[16] The announcement was so unexpected and ill-advised that it soon drove his top economic advisor to quit.[17]

Trump had also been trying to deal with fallout from the Parkland massacre, in which seventeen people were shot and killed at a school near his Palm Beach home, but he couldn't quite get it right. He had suggested that the government take guns away from potentially dangerous people, infuriating his base and the National Rifle Association.[18]

To add insult to injury during this week from hell, several foreign countries seemed to be mocking him. Earlier in the week Russian president Vladimir Putin had released a propaganda video boasting the strength of a new cruise missile.[19] In the video a mock missile trajectory showed the warhead landing on the southern tip of Florida.

It seemed a barely veiled threat to Mar-a-Lago.

"No one in the world has anything similar," Putin said. "It can attack any target, through the North or South Pole, it is a powerful weapon and no missile defense system will be able to withstand."

Finally, the new owner of a seventy-story tower in Panama City decided to remove the Trump name from the facade, sparking a feud that turned physically violent as the owner attempted to force his way into the Trump Organization's offices in the building. In response to the violence, Panamanian authorities opened an investigation. Although Trump wasn't running the day-to-day operations of his company, he still owned it, and so the government of a Central American nation began investigating the business of the president of the United States.[20]

White House staff whispered to each other in concern as they noted the president had become increasingly isolated and volatile. Trump's friends had taken to trading off calling him to check in.[21]

The morning of the Saturday fundraiser, Trump barely had time for golf at his West Palm Beach club—his hundredth visit to one of his own golf clubs since becoming president.[22] He left the course with just two hours to spare before his scheduled remarks.

As the motorcade sped him back, he passed fans waving signs that read, "Make America Great Again" and billboards that read, "Make America Horny Again," advertising an upcoming strip-show tour featuring Stormy Daniels, Trump's alleged onetime mistress who received $130,000 in hush money arranged by the president's personal attorney, Michael Cohen.[23] And Cohen, who had once said he would take a bullet for Trump, was about to begin cracking under the weight of a federal investigation.[24]

Trump started tweeting to blow off steam as soon as he arrived back at his suite from golf. "The United States has an $800 Billion Dollar Yearly Trade Deficit because of our 'very stupid' trade deals and policies," he wrote.[25] "Our jobs and wealth are being given to other countries that have taken advantage of us for years. They laugh at what fools our leaders have been. No more!"

Then he went downstairs and gave a speech to his Republican donors. He mentioned Xi Jinping, who had recently amended China's constitution to allow himself to maintain power indefinitely.

"He's now president for life. President for life. No, he's great," Trump said.[26] "And look, he was able to do that. I think it's great. Maybe we'll have to give that a shot someday."

The crowd cheered. They loved this president.

"I am not into politics, but I support strong people who strive for success," one woman in the crowd posted on Instagram.[27]

The comments eventually leaked to the media, sparking a new round of Trump bashing. Even without the political blowback for celebrating authoritarianism, it might have been better for Trump to stay up in his room tweeting that day. Among the crowd were three people who, more than a year later, would each cause their own kind of damage to the president's image.

LIKE MANY OTHERS, Igor Fruman used Mar-a-Lago like a currency.[28]

On March 3 Fruman sported a lightly window-paned navy blazer and arrived at the president's club with one thing in mind: pot.

Fruman hoped to buy one of Florida's new medical marijuana licenses and flex some muscle in Congress on cannabis policy.[29] Mar-a-Lago would be his trump card. When he and his partner Lev Parnas scored a meeting with Miami Republican congressman Carlos Curbelo in the weeks after the event, they played up the connection.[30]

Parnas told Curbelo how well connected the duo was in Washington and that they knew Trump personally from his club. The Ukrainian American was wearing alligator shoes, a gray blazer, and a white shirt open to mid-chest—all the better to see the lucky horseshoe dangling from his gold chain.

"When Trump would see us, he would call us 'my boys,'" Parnas said to the *Washington Post*.[31] "Me and Igor together? It's not something you'd forget."

Parnas told Curbelo about a dinner with the president at Mar-a-Lago the two had planned for the coming Friday—coincidentally, 4/20.[32] Throughout the meeting Fruman stayed quiet. That was more his style.

It would have been typical of their braggadocio to embellish. Parnas especially was notorious for taking a kernel of truth and pretending it was the whole cob. Years before he got into politics, he tried to sucker a New Jersey man into investing in a film deal by setting up a dinner with Jack Nicholson. The dinner happened—it's not clear exactly how Parnas knew the Hollywood star—and the investor bit, sinking $350,000 into the doomed project, called *Anatomy of an Assassin*.[33]

Like Hansel and Gretel, Parnas and Fruman had left a trail of debts and other bad deals behind them.[34] Curbelo's staff clearly hadn't bothered to do much research on the curious pair. If they had, they might have discovered that Parnas, a former stockbroker who came to the United States from Ukraine as a young child, had worked for three separate securities firms expelled from the industry by American regulators.[35] He had also been sued repeatedly. He seemed to have such a tin ear for public relations that he founded a business called Fraud Guarantee, although it was later suggested that he chose the name to push down negative Google results for

"Parnas" and the word "fraud."[36] Fruman, born in Belarus, reportedly had connections in the seedy underworld of Odessa, the port city in Ukraine.[37]

Their Florida marijuana deal never happened. The duo couldn't prove they had the cash.[38]

"Mr. Parnas is a con man, he is a crook," the New Jersey investor's wife told the *Miami Herald*.[39] "He conned us from day one."

At Mar-a-Lago the pair fit right in.

As it turns out, it appears Parnas wasn't embellishing his connections to the club when he spoke to Curbelo. There is ample proof. Parnas seated next to Don Jr. in the club's Library Bar.[40] A video of him introducing a former Ukrainian official to Trump.[41] Another of him and Trump chatting privately at an intimate donors' meeting.[42]

At the March 3 RNC fundraiser Fruman kept a lower profile. That was important, especially in politics. Too much attention would make the "buzzards descend," as a colleague once warned them.[43]

Fruman's alligator-shoe-wearing partner was nowhere to be seen. But another future associate was hanging out at the club that weekend. Former New York City mayor Rudy Giuliani had taken the stage at the RNC's spring retreat the night before. Giuliani told the crowd about coming to Mar-a-Lago for Trump's 2005 wedding to Melania. Then he took the opportunity to throw a jab at one of his favorite punching bags. "Hillary was also here," Giuliani said.[44] "And she actually fit through the door."

The crowd gasped. His wife glowered. Even Trump hedged. "I'm just glad I didn't say it," the president told the audience.[45]

A month later Giuliani became the president's personal lawyer. He also grew close with the two Ukrainians.[46] Parnas named the former mayor godfather to his son.[47] He and Giuliani smoked cigars together.[48] They went to George H. W. Bush's state funeral.[49] Giuliani was even supposed to become the face of Fraud Guarantee, or so an investor who paid him $500,000 thought.[50] The commercials never happened.

Parnas and Fruman leaned on their relationship with the president's lawyer when they met with Ukrainian officials to pitch a pipeline project that would carry natural gas from Poland to Ukraine.[51] Giuliani was a potential investor, they said. (He later denied it.)

They also used Global Energy Producers, the Delaware company they'd set up for the pipeline deal, to buy their way closer to Trump. In May 2018 the company made a $325,000 donation to a pro-Trump super PAC.[52]

Such largesse was ultimately what sank the pair. But it was their work in Ukraine that would nearly sink the president.

The pipeline project was a pipe dream.

In fact, Parnas and Fruman spent most of their time abroad in 2018 and 2019 working with Giuliani to pressure Ukraine's government into publicly announcing an investigation of Hunter Biden, the son of Trump's most likely 2020 oppoentn, Democratic front-runner Joe Biden. Parnas, Fruman, and Giuliani believed, without much in the way of evidence, that Hunter Biden's work for a Ukrainian energy company had been corrupt—and that daddy had saved his little boy by having Ukraine's top prosecutor removed.[53] (Biden *did* work to have the prosecutor removed in 2016 as part of an anticorruption effort supported by US allies in Europe. There's no evidence that helped his son in any way.[54])

The trio scored meetings with Ukrainian officials—Giuliani was the president's attorney, after all—and told them that Trump wouldn't be satisfied until he had his investigation. No investigation? No Mike Pence at the inauguration of Ukraine's new leader.[55] And no more US military aid as the country battled a Russian invasion. Giuliani and his two sidekicks even said they could help dig up the dirt. But the Ukrainian government wouldn't play ball.

Trump gave the order to suspend military aid.[56] Then, on July 25, 2019, he picked up the phone and asked Ukrainian president Volodymyr Zelenskiy for a favor.

"There's a lot of talk about Biden's son," Trump said on the call, "that Biden stopped the prosecution and a lot of people want to find out about that so whatever you can do with the Attorney General would be great. Biden went around bragging that he stopped the prosecution so if you can look into it. . . . It sounds horrible to me."[57]

In August a CIA officer working at the White House filed an anonymous complaint about the efforts in Ukraine, claiming "that the President of the United States is using the power of his office to solicit interference from a foreign country in the 2020 US election."[58] The whistleblower mentioned the bizarre back-channel diplomacy of two unnamed Giuliani "associates."[59] When congressional Democrats got their hands on the complaint the next month, Parnas and Fruman became household names. They hadn't exactly been inconspicuous in Ukraine.

Nor had they been careful in America. In October 2019, federal prosecutors indicted Parnas and Fruman.[60] It all came back to pot. Prosecutors said the two men had tried to worm foreign money into US elections to buy favor with politicians and grease the wheels for their marijuana deals. As for the $325,000 donation tied to their pipeline company, prosecutors said it violated the straw donor ban. The funds came not from Global Energy Producers, as indicated on the donation paperwork, but from a loan Fruman got for a Miami-area condo. He and Parnas made the donation through Global Energy Producers, instead of their own names, to buy the company some credibility in DC—and also to avoid tipping off creditors that they had money.[61] They pleaded not guilty.

Trump told the American people he didn't know those two Ukrainian "gentlemen" and called Parnas a "con man" and a "groupie."[62] Fruman might have been content to slink off. But Parnas was outraged. Every photo, every video, every conversation he had with the president he blasted out to the public, including a thirty-seven-minute-long video secretly taken at Mar-a-Lago and a recording of Trump saying he wanted to get rid of the US ambassador to Ukraine.

As for his Ukrainian wheeling-and-dealing, Parnas claimed Trump gave him a "James Bond mission."[63]

"The president knew everything that was going on," Parnas said.[64]

A wealth of evidence presented in Congress suggested that was indeed the case.

On December 18 the House of Representatives impeached Trump, although he survived a removal trial in the Senate.

Giuliani somehow skated through, despite embarrassments such as testimony revealing that the former US ambassador to the European Union had once complained that Rudy always "fucks everything up."[65]

Trump publicly tried to distance himself from his own lawyer, saying the former mayor had "other clients, other than me."[66] But Giuliani was still welcome in his home. Shortly after the impeachment, Giuliani was seen at Mar-a-Lago living it up at a Studio 54–themed party. Having shed his suit jacket, Giuliani leaned back on a padded bench, happily playing around on his phone.[67]

Although Trump only said a few words to him that night, it must have been nice to feel back home again at the president's club.

THE 2018 RNC SPRING FUNDRAISER proved to be a cluster of headaches for Trump.

Though she was not involved in the impeachment, Cindy Yang's presence at the club brought about one of the biggest scandals the Winter White House would ever see. It also prompted another federal investigation into money received by Trump's campaign.

On March 3, 2018, Yang stood directly next to the president of the United States as a photographer snapped a picture of them in front of a blue curtain. Yang was wearing a dark silver dress. She flashed a gleeful smile.[68]

Her triumphal moment had not come easy—or cheap. The RNC had capped individual contributions at $5,400 for the event. That meant Yang had to recruit contributions from others to buy her grand prize. She had scraped and clawed and fought her way to put together the $50,000 needed to stand with the president for a photo. In the days leading up to the fundraiser, an unlikely group of people connected by just one thing—Cindy Yang—maxed out their contributions to Trump.[69]

Bingbing Peranio was sitting at her desk at Yang's Tokyo Day Spa, where she worked as a receptionist, when Yang approached her shortly before the Mar-a-Lago event.[70] Yang wanted to help her fill out a $5,400 check for Trump. (Peranio would refuse to answer when the *New York Times* asked if Yang had reimbursed her for the donation, which would be illegal.)

In addition to Peranio, Yang's elderly mother and father, who live in a small townhouse in an obscure part of Palm Beach County, each gave $5,400. So did Yang's husband.

Another $5,400 came from a twenty-something-year-old woman who listed her occupation as a "facial instructor" at Yang's Tokyo Beauty & Massage School.

Also donating the $5,400 maximum: the owner of another day spa who was friends with Yang, a South Florida massage therapist, an investor in GY US Investments, and a woman listed as a director of one of Yang's spas.

All told, it was at least $54,000, including $5,400 from Yang herself.

Yang spent the weekend of the RNC fundraisers showing off her be-jeweled MAGA purse and trying to get into snapshots with as many peo-ple as she could. She got the one photograph she really needed, signed by the president himself.

The ladies of Mar-a-Lago cheered.

"Love this," wrote a member of the Trumpettes when Yang posted her official photo with the president to Facebook.[71] "Congratulations my friend!"

Yang was finally part of the in-crowd.

By this point she had married and transferred many of her spas into her parents' and new husband's names as she poured all her energy into what she called her "new life."[72]

"I'm pursuing a sense of accomplishment," Yang wrote in a profile of herself.[73] "I'm a low-key person doing a high-key job and trying to write a brilliant chapter in my future resume."

She started planning a move to the Virginia suburbs of Washington, DC, to fully launch her political consulting business. She put her spas on the market, although her ambitious pricing meant she had few takers.[74]

In September 2018 she received the most exciting gift of her life. It was a letter from the White House.[75]

"To: Ms. Li Juan Yang, Thank you for your friendship and dedication to our cause. Leaders like you in Florida are the key to fulfilling our bold agenda to Make America Great Again!"

The note was signed in blue sharpie: Donald J. Trump.

She was also personally invited to a Lunar New Year celebration at the White House, although Trump wasn't there.[76]

As it turned out, Yang probably should have listened to her mother. All of the politics, the fame, and glory—however limited—could only bring trouble.

For Yang, trouble came in the form of a $79 blow job, given without her knowledge, to a man she didn't know, at a Florida spa she didn't own. Even her mother couldn't have seen *that* coming.

13

SNOW ON THE GROUND

SNOW WAS SEEN ON THE GROUNDS of Mar-a-Lago over Christmas in 2018.

So was Snow's owner.

A perky white Pomeranian, Snow was happily prancing around the club's grassy backyard one afternoon in late December, a tiny pink tongue poking out in an open-mouthed doggy smile. On the other end of Snow's studded blue leash was one of China's highest-profile dissidents—who also happened to be one of its most wanted men.

Guo Wengui wore dark sunglasses, black pants that were slightly too baggy for his frame, and a gray suit jacket closed at the top two buttons.

Behind him was a giant inflatable rat sporting a blonde comb-over and red tie. The rodent was perched in the back of a fishing boat. Its likeness to the baron of the estate was undeniable. *The Clash* blared from the boat's speakers: "I fought the law and the law won."

The message wasn't intended for the man and his dog but for the Don of Mar-a-Lago. Since 2017 anti-Trump activist Claude Taylor had dedicated himself to trolling the president in the most public of ways. Up to his usual mischief, Taylor had traveled from Washington, DC, to South Florida, where he chartered a boat to take him and his Twitter-famous, twelve-foot inflatable Trump rat up the shallow waters of the Intracoastal Waterway to the president's house.[1] The giant balloon had the body and face of a rat with the hair and orange-tinted skin tone of Donald Trump. The rat also wears the too-long red tie favored by the president.

Taylor and the rat showed up at Mar-a-Lago on December 30, 2018, the ninth day of what would be the longest partial-government shutdown in American history, as Trump and the Democrats battled over his demand for funding for a border wall.[2]

The Rat Boat captain cut the engine when Taylor and his cargo were forty feet or so off the property's sea wall. They looked across acres of perfectly manicured grass illuminated by mid-afternoon sun.

By this point the Rat Boat was close enough that Mar-a-Lago's unsecured Wi-Fi popped up on Taylor's phone. He connected and immediately received a barrage of promotions for stays at other Trump-branded hotels and golf courses.

The president himself was not at the club that day. The shutdown had left him pouting in DC over Christmas while most of his family relaxed in their South Florida home. That meant security was especially lax. The machine gun–mounted Coast Guard boats that normally patrolled the intracoastal waterways, chasing away rubberneckers on paddle boards and jet skis, were still at the harbor. No one came to eject Taylor from the property's edge, at least not right away. He was snapping photos from beside his rat balloon when he noticed a man accompanied by a woman in a pink shirt and straw hat walking a Pomeranian. The couple came directly toward him. The woman had her phone out pointed in his direction.

A little while later a photo was sent to Taylor's phone, transferred via the shared Wi-Fi. The picture was a close-up of a Chinese man in a gray suit jacket and dark glasses walking Snow by the sea wall. Taylor was in the photo too, standing to the left of the spoof rat, holding his phone with two hands, poised to take a picture.

Taylor assumed the photo was sent to him by the woman in pink. It was the perfect inverse of the photo he had just snapped of her.

Then his phone chimed again. It was more pictures of the man wearing the same gray-and-black outfit. In one, he was sitting inside the club where Donald Trump and Xi Jinping had taken photos together during the official state visit the year before. In another, Guo stood holding a copy of the *Palm Beach Post*.[3]

Bingo! Taylor thought. *Contact from the inside.*

Why he was contacted? There was never any explanation. But Taylor used his "resistance" Twitter network to identify Guo, a billionaire

Chinese real estate developer wanted in his home country for myriad alleged crimes, including sexual assault, fraud, and bribery.[4] Guo had fled China a few years earlier to live in a $70 million New York penthouse, saying that the government had fabricated the charges in retaliation for his public criticism of the Communist Party.[5] He spent most of his time bashing China's oppressive regime and government corruption. He often folded his critiques into energetic workout videos he posted to social media from his penthouse. Sometimes his tiny white dog would make an appearance. Every time his content was taken offline—and it happened often—it seemed like further proof of Chinese government retaliation.

Just before Xi Jinping's 2017 visit to Mar-a-Lago, Guo tweeted a photo of himself standing on the grounds with the club's managing director, prompting fears he might try to disrupt the summit and spark an international incident.[6] In the end, Guo stayed away. A month later four Chinese secret agents visited Guo in his New York apartment and told him to give up his antigovernment activities in exchange for clemency.[7] Guo said no deal. Then he applied for political asylum in the United States. "My home country wants to harm me, by any means necessary," Guo said.[8] (His petition is still pending.)

Floating in the waters off Mar-a-Lago, Taylor speculated as to why he'd been sent Guo's photos. "He wants as many people as possible to know he is a [Mar-a-Lago] member in good standing," Taylor said.

Guo, also known as Miles Kwok, would not comment on Taylor's assertion, nor on any other aspect of his life, including when exactly he joined Mar-a-Lago. But it seems like joinig the club had nothing to do with Trump's presidency. Guo was already a member long before anyone thought Trump was a real contender. In a February 26, 2015, application to buy his penthouse at the Sherry-Netherland Hotel, the Chinese billionaire listed a Mar-a-Lago membership among his credentials.[9] (Guo also boasted a letter of recommendation from former British prime minister Tony Blair.[10])

Though it may not have been the reason he bought his way into the elite club, Guo's membership had helped endear him to the president.

In 2017 Trump had received a request from the Chinese government to deport Guo. According to the *Wall Street Journal*, the request had been hand delivered by longtime Trump associate and Republican National Committee finance chairman Steve Wynn, a casino magnate with business interests in Macau.[11] (Wynn denied it.) Trump was said to be amenable to the request. In a meeting with top advisors, Trump had reportedly declared there was at least one "Chinese criminal" he knew he needed to deport.

"Where's the letter that Steve brought?" Trump called out to his secretary.[12] "We need to get this criminal out of the country."

It's not clear whether Trump knew who Guo was or anything about his case. Aides tried to talk the president out of it because they thought Guo offered leverage against Beijing. So they told Trump that Guo was a member of Mar-a-Lago, according to the *Journal*.[13] The maneuver seems to have worked. Trump dropped the subject.

It was not exactly how his administration treated the far less well-connected masses of refugees fleeing violence in Central America and the Middle East.

Lucky for him, Guo had unwittingly stumbled through the side door in Trump's wall.

It was Mar-a-Lago's front gate.

GUO SEEMED TO FIND a kindred spirit in Trump when the anti-China hardliner unexpectedly won the presidency.

Guo also found a new best friend.

Stephen K. Bannon and the eccentric Chinese billionaire grew close after Trump's chief strategist unceremoniously left the administration in August 2017.[14] (Bannon and Jared Kushner did not get along, and Trump was a family-first kind of guy.)

Guo and Bannon bonded over their mutual loathing of communist China. They could often be found together arm-in-arm making YouTube videos about the regime like long-lost brothers. Bannon was even given his own channel on Guo's media website.

But Guo's dissident bona fides were eventually called into question.

Known for his litigious streak, Guo became entangled in a nasty lawsuit after falling out with an American research firm he had supposedly hired to uncover intelligence on a group of Chinese government sympathizers in the United States. In 2018 a Hong Kong company associated with Guo sued the research firm in New York federal court over a $1 million payment.[15] The legal complaint said the firm failed to deliver the goods. The research firm turned on Guo and accused him in a countersuit of secretly working for China—essentially painting him as a double agent.[16]

"Guo was not the dissident he claimed to be," lawyers for the research firm wrote in a court filing.[17] "Instead, Guo Wengui was, and is, a dissident-hunter, propagandist, and agent in the service of the People's Republic of China and the Chinese Communist Party."

Guo's attorney responded that the claim "utterly lacks credibility."[18]

The attorney said the firm was "abusing the litigation privilege to slander Mr. Guo." If Guo really did work for China, he said, why did Xi's government freeze his assets there?

Guo had wanted the firm to dig up dirt on a list of Chinese nationals living in the United States—described only as "fish" in a contract.[19] The firm was hired after several meetings at Guo's ritzy apartment in Manhattan.

There seemed to be no reason the researchers wouldn't deliver. Their impressive track record included investigations on behalf of Republican politicians, a Middle Eastern prince, and a member of the Russian opposition.[20] The firm had deep connections in DC and was headed by the widow of a former GOP senator from Wyoming. But it failed to provide the investigation on the "fish," according to the lawsuit filed by the Hong Kong company associated with Guo. Instead of high-quality original material, the researchers were accused of providing only publicly available information.

In its counterclaim against Guo and the company, the research firm said those fish should never have been on the line. The people Guo wanted investigated were classified by the US government as "records protected" people, the firm said, meaning they "were foreigners who were either assisting the US government on law enforcement or national security cases, were under federal investigation for criminal activity, or were potentially to come under investigation."[21] The researchers worried that uncovering the information might be against the law.

The countersuit also claimed Guo had pledged his loyalty to Xi Jinping, had lied about being arrested during the Tiananmen Square massacre in 1989, had ties to state security services, and had sued or threatened to sue Chinese dissidents living in the United States. They said he used Bannon to promote his image and enhance his ties to the Trump administration.

"He lied about his identity as a dissident," the firm's lawyers said.[22] "Guo was artful. A Chinese intelligence veteran, he quickly gained access to—and, alarmingly, the loyalty and services of—the country's top China hawk, Stephen K. Bannon."

While a judge dismissed the research firm's counterclaim against Guo as an individual, the lawsuit between the two companies rages on—and with it the allegation that Guo is secretly working for China.[23]

THERE'S NO EVIDENCE that Guo used his 2018 holiday stay at Mar-a-Lago to talk with anyone in the administration or Trump family, and it's unclear what exactly he hoped to accomplish with the trip. Perhaps he just wanted a nice holiday in the sun.

Eventually Claude Taylor's Rat Boat caused a kerfuffle at the water's edge next to Mar-a-Lago. A staffer saw the bizarre craft and called the club's private security contractor. A slimmed-down Secret Service detail was there too, protecting the president's family while they celebrated the New Year. Federal agents and club staff approached the water, stood on the sea wall, and gave the Rat Boat "the hairy eyeball," in Taylor's words.[24] They had no boats of their own and couldn't chase him off. After a couple of hours Taylor motored away.

It wasn't the only time Taylor witnessed something strange at the club. The next time he brought the Rat Boat back to Mar-a-Lago, security staffers who walked down to give him the stink eye were suddenly called away when someone drove up to a side entrance and started shouting about a member of the president's family.[25]

When Secret Service isn't around, club security is frequently overwhelmed by the number of people trying to breach the perimeter of the president's home. The club simply becomes a "ghost town" security-wise when Trump isn't there, one former staffer said.[26]

Budgets at Mar-a-Lago are always tightly managed. The Trump Organization doesn't even hire enough guards to assign one to each potential access point on the massive property. And the ones they do hire aren't armed. Unlike most Palm Beach country clubs, Mar-a-Lago hasn't made it a practice to pay off-duty police officers for security.

"They really are that stupid and that cheap," said an employee familiar with the organizational set-up.[27] "Nobody gives a shit."

For Trump, turning Mar-a-Lago into a secure, high-tech compound like the White House would be bad for business.

"The president doesn't want his members to be patted down or have to walk through a metal detector," said Shannon Donnelly.[28] "He doesn't want to make them think that they're walking into anything other than a lovely private club which just happens to have a little apartment where the president lives when he's in town."

Fred Rustmann, the club member and former CIA officer, mentioned in an offhand comment that it is perfectly permissible to bring a gun into the club when the president isn't there—and it would even be possible to hide the weapon for later use.[29]

"They could tape it under a table or something like that," he said, although he wasn't particularly concerned. But many others don't seem to share Rustmann's perspective on the club's laissez-faire approach to security.

"There could be a terrorist attack," Donnelly said.[30] "Everyone worries about that."

WHILE GUO TRAIPSED AROUND Mar-a-Lago, President Trump was lonely. Amid the government shutdown that would prove to be a thirty-five-day stalemate, Trump canceled his entire annual trip to South Florida—the only time the president spent Christmas at the White House.

"I am all alone (poor me) in the White House waiting for the Democrats to come back and make a deal on desperately needed Border Security," he wrote on Twitter.[31]

Trump's family still made the trip south to partake in festivities. As eight hundred thousand federal workers went without pay, including airport employees tasked with seeing people through holiday travel, taxpayers footed part of the bill for the Trump family vacation. On December 19 the Secret Service paid a South Florida party supplier $54,020 for tent rental at Mar-a-Lago.[32] The tents were part of the Secret Service's perim-

eter around the club set up when any members of the president's immediate family are home.[33]

Don Jr. was in town celebrating his birthday (New Year's Eve) with
his new girlfriend. Melania seemed to be having a grand time as well.
She posted a rare selfie and posed for photos with a Trumpette as well as
Charlie Kirk, the conservative activist.

Trump's absence over the 2018 holiday season was bad news for
Cindy Yang. She had sold tickets to the club's New Year's Eve party, and
her guests wanted to meet the president. Among them was Chinese ac-
tress Sun Ye, who bought her ticket through Prince Charles. Sun wanted
a picture with Trump to bolster her image in China and abroad and said
she stayed with Yang while in South Florida. With the president unable
to attend, she ended up trading down for a picture with Don Jr.

"I wanted to see the president of the United States, and although I
didn't meet him, I met his family," Sun told the *New York Times*.[34] "It
made me feel like I achieved my dream."

Charles Lee later spun the disaster into a success online, saying that
Trump had sent his family in his stead (though really the First Family had
planned to attend all along). For Sun, her package trip to Mar-a-Lago also
came with a certificate from Lee's "US President Trump Economic Cooperation and Development Committee Inc."[35] The paper deemed her a
"US-China Friendship Ambassador"—whatever that is—for her outstanding contribution to "civil friendly diplomacy" between the two nations.

While Sun snapped her shot with Don Jr., hundreds of guests milled
around sipping champagne and lining up for photos with any member of
the Trump family they could find.

For the privilege of ringing in 2019 at the Winter White House, the
club raised prices to their highest levels ever, excluding its once-in-a-
millennium Y2K party. Members forked over $650 to attend. Their guests
paid $1,000.[36] That was a bump from the member price of $600 the year
before and $525 the year before that.[37]

As 2018 waned, the crowd started its countdown.[38] Golden confetti
blasted onto the gold-hatted heads of the crowd.

Cindy Yang posted a dozen photos on Facebook the next day wishing
a happy New Year to all of her friends.

It would be.

Until the FBI got involved.

14

"FRIENDLY, CHEERFUL ORIENTAL LADIES"

ROBERT KRAFT FELT like getting a massage.

It was the eve of the 2019 AFC championship, and his team, the New England Patriots, were playing. He needed to loosen up.

So his friend, Peter Bernon—the milk-and-plastics mogul whom he had brought to dinner at Mar-a-Lago with Trump and Japanese prime minister Shinzo Abe—picked up Kraft from his waterfront apartment in Palm Beach. On January 19, 2019, he drove Kraft to an Asian-themed day spa in the small town of Jupiter twenty miles north. Bernon parked his 2014 white Bentley outside and waited for his friend to finish.[1]

Inside a private room at the Orchids of Asia Day Spa, the Patriots owner undressed, lay down on a massage bed completely nude, and pulled a sheet partway over his body.[2] At 4:49 P.M. the spa's manager and another employee entered and began massaging Kraft. After twenty-three minutes, he rolled over onto his back. The lights went out. When they came back on one of the women was giving the billionaire a hand job. Two minutes later she wiped down his penis with a white towel. Kraft handed the women cash. They hugged him, and he left.

Cindy Yang couldn't know it, but those few minutes would destroy her burgeoning new life at Mar-a-Lago.

Yang had once owned Orchids of Asia. She opened it in 2009 under a different name: Tokyo Day Spa. True to her business model, Yang got the spa off the ground and flipped it in 2012. Under new ownership, nothing much changed except the name. "Same staff, services, and pricing," one happy customer wrote in a 2013 online review of Orchids of Asia.[3] "A great atmosphere, and friendly, cheerful Oriental ladies. Marvelous services with authentic Asian Massage!"

After selling the Jupiter spa, Yang had nothing more to do with it. She moved on with her life, opening new spas and flipping them too. She had started pulling out of the massage business altogether by the time a state health inspector visited Orchids of Asia in 2018.

The health inspector wasn't there just to make sure the place was clean. A Jupiter police detective had asked her to keep an eye on Orchids of Asia. One county north of Palm Beach, the Martin County Sheriff's Office was working a wide-ranging human trafficking investigation into spas and massage parlors. Because of apparent financial links between the Martin County spas and Orchids of Asia, sheriff's detectives brought the Jupiter Police Department into the case. Orchids of Asia was one of at least eight Florida spas that had triggered the suspicions of police. (None of the other spas had ever been owned by Yang, and she was never part of the investigation.)

At Orchids of Asia the health inspector found beds with sheets and pillows, a refrigerator full of food and condiments, and dressers packed with clothes and medicine.[4] They were all indications that women were living there. To police, those were warning signs of human trafficking. Using "sneak-and-peak" warrants designed to fight terrorism, the cops secretly installed surveillance cameras in the massage rooms of Orchids of Asia as well as other spas.

And so it was completely by chance that police were watching Kraft's happy ending. The cops were watching the next day too, when Kraft came back and received oral sex, again paying cash.[5]

Unaware of the peeping toms, Kraft happily relayed his experience to a friend. "You won't believe what happened to me," he told the friend, who chided him for accepting a "rub-and-tug," according to *Vanity Fair*.[6] But the billionaire insisted that he had made a genuine connection with the two spa workers.

After getting the blow job, Kraft flew to Kansas City to watch the Pats knock the Chiefs out of the NFL playoffs.

TWO WEEKS LATER Donald Trump cheered the Patriots to a Super Bowl victory surrounded by adoring fans at Trump International Golf Club in West Palm Beach. Cindy Yang was in the crowd.

It was her first Super Bowl, and she was excited.[7] Trump's annual Super Bowl party always follows a certain pattern, mixing the lowbrow with the high-priced. Cheerleaders from a local university. Tables covered with football-themed party favors. A steak and lobster buffet.[8]

Dressed in a red hoodie, Yang spent the party hanging around Carol Brophy, the event coordinator for the Trumpettes. Yang documented the whole experience, posting everything to Facebook and tagging Brophy: pictures of brownies cut into the shape of footballs, a video of the national anthem, a photo with Don King. She even managed to capture video of the moment Trump had the crowd weigh in on his 2020 campaign slogan.

"What do you like better? Make America Great Again or Keep America Great?" Trump asked.[9]

The crowd voiced its preference.

"Keep America Great," someone said.

"Yeah, I think so," the president replied.

"You're already doing it," the woman exclaimed. Trump agreed.

Sometime in the middle of the game Yang got the opportunity of a lifetime. A candid moment with the president. She whipped out her cell phone, held it aloft, and quickly snapped a photo.

It wasn't a very good selfie. Yang's head seemed to be creeping into the shot from the lower-left corner, blocking much of Brophy's face with her own—but she'd at least kept the president fully in the shot. Her new crowd at Mar-a-Lago fawned over it. They were jealous of Cindy Yang, and they told her as much. "Love this photo of the 3 of you!" a Trumpette wrote on Facebook.[10]

Soon Yang posted the photo on her company's webpage as more evidence of her ability to get close to the Trumps.

"Founder watched the NFL finals with the President and first lady at Trump's golf club," the website for GY US Investments declared.[11] "The founder posed for a selfie with President Donald Trump."

A few weeks later Yang's phone rang. It was a reporter from the *Miami Herald*.

ON FEBRUARY 22, 2019, the hammer dropped on Robert Kraft.

Authorities from Jupiter to Orlando raided the Asian spas they'd been investigating. They arrested at least eight women accused of managing a ring of prostitution and charged hundreds of alleged johns.[12]

One of the johns was Kraft. He was charged with two misdemeanor counts of soliciting prostitution for his alleged escapades at Orchids of Asia. Authorities justified the sweep by claiming Kraft and the others had abetted a far more serious evil. They said the madams had confiscated some of the women's passports and forced them to work in the sex trade.

"Human trafficking is evil in our midst," Palm Beach state attorney Dave Aronberg said at a press conference heralding the investigation.[13] "Modern-day slavery . . . [can] happen anywhere, including in the peaceful community of Jupiter, Florida."

"It's very safe to say without any hyperbole that this is the tip of the iceberg," said Martin County Sheriff William Snyder, who criticized many of the johns for being married or in relationships.[14]

If there *was* an iceberg, no one ever saw below the water line. Police were not able to bring direct charges of human trafficking against the parlor owners, largely focusing on lower-level crimes due to a lack of evidence. It seemed they had spent more time videoing the johns than interviewing alleged victims and building a comprehensive case.[15]

"There is zero evidence of human trafficking in this case," an attorney for Kraft told the *Wall Street Journal*.[16] "The state attorney should carefully review how the evidence was obtained in this case. It's the right thing to do."

A lower-court judge threw out the video evidence of hand jobs and oral sex on civil liberties grounds. The judge pointed out that police had also taped clients who were just getting regular massages and doing nothing wrong. (The state appealed.[17])

It seemed like Kraft's name would be cleared. But that wouldn't help Cindy Yang.

YANG DIDN'T UNDERSTAND why reporters from the *Miami Herald* kept calling her.

They had been to her spa locations and to her and her parents' homes.

"We don't do anything illegal," Yang said when the newspaper finally managed to reach her by phone on March 6, 2019.[18] "We don't do any problem things."

She thought they were calling about Orchids of Asia, the spa she had sold in 2012. She thought they were just calling about Robert Kraft.

"I sold those locations a long time ago," Yang said.

But it wasn't Orchids of Asia that so intrigued reporters. Nor was it her other spa where police officers had investigated possible sex work during the years when Yang ran the operation.[19] No one can own a chain of massage parlors—no matter how on the up-and-up—and completely avoid association with the sale of sex. Yang was no exception. Police reports and internet reviews suggest that sex had been offered at several Tokyo Day Spas while Yang and her family still owned them. Reporters asked about those allegations, but that wasn't really what they were calling about.

What reporters found so fascinating about Yang were all the photos she had posted online: rallies, charity galas, and political fundraisers with Sarah Palin, Senator Rick Scott, Florida governor Ron DeSantis, RNC chairwoman Ronna McDaniel, *Fox News* host Jesse Watters, Transportation Secretary Elaine Chao, Representative Matt Gaetz, to name just a few. The ones that caught their eyes most? Yang's two photos with the president of the United States—one an official portrait, the other a blurry selfie. The *Herald* had discovered the photos while researching the past and present owners of the spa Kraft patronized. Reporters were baffled by how a modest spa owner had forged so many connections with the nation's most powerful people. How did she know Donald Trump?

"I don't know the president," Yang insisted on the phone.[20] "I just come to some events. There's nothing special."

"If you don't know the president, then why does your website say you can introduce people to him?" one of the reporters asked.

"Please," she said. "I don't want any story."

When the article came out two days later, the lead photo showed Yang's Super Bowl selfie with Trump. The cosmic coincidence of the moment—Yang watching Kraft's team at the president's golf club after he had been caught on video doing the dirty at a spa she used to own—led the *Herald* story to go viral.

The White House said Trump didn't know Yang, a statement that was by all accounts accurate.[21] "I don't know her," the president affirmed to reporters.[22] "I don't know who she is. Who is that?"

The founder of the Trumpettes said the same.[23] So did every other Mar-a-Lago member and club-goer who could be reached. Suddenly everyone had come down with a case of Cindy Yang amnesia.

Brophy, the other woman in the selfie, said Yang was pulling the trick for which she had become notorious at Mar-a-Lago: bursting into the president's space and trying to get noticed. "While a dear friend of mine was taking a picture of me as I was speaking with the president, Cindy Yang swooped in and photobombed," Brophy told the *Herald*.[24]

Within hours national outlets started converging on Yang. Her Trump tourism business illustrated all the ways Trump and a legion of Mar-a-Lago grifters were using his presidency to profit.

Top congressional Democrats called on the FBI to launch criminal and counterintelligence investigations into her conduct.

"Although Ms. Yang's activities may only be those of an unscrupulous actor allegedly selling access to politicians for profit, her activities also could permit adversary governments or their agents access to these same politicians to acquire potential material for blackmail or other even more nefarious purposes," the lawmakers wrote in a March 15 letter.[25] "These allegations raise serious counterintelligence concerns. China has frequently used non-traditional intelligence collectors and businesspersons to compromise targets."

Yang hired a public relations crisis manager to do damage control. The woman she chose for the job, a conservative media commentator and former Mrs. Florida, was once accused in civil court of threatening her husband's ex-wife with a Louboutin stiletto heel. Yang's new hire would also plead guilty to stealing her dying mother's Social Security checks.[26]

The spokeswoman wanted her client to tell her story. But Yang just wanted everyone to go away. "I only talked to the president two sentences," she told a local CBS affiliate in a rare interview.[27] "'Hi, Mr. President,'... 'Can I take a picture with you?'"

Yang denied any wrongdoing, said she had no contact with China's government, and insisted that she wasn't selling access to Trump. She said she had never even had a private conversation with the president.

"I'm Chinese. I'm Republican," Yang told *NBC News* in her only national television appearance.[28] "That's the reason the Democrats want to check me."

"I love Americans. I love our president. I don't do anything wrong," she added.

Yang's new life was rapidly unraveling. The South Florida groups linked with China's government disavowed Yang, as members across the country worried that federal authorities might start knocking on their doors.

Within a few months the FBI would open a public corruption investigation into the contributions Yang had bundled together for the privilege of taking a photo with Trump at the March 3, 2018, fundraiser.[29] They began interviewing Yang's Chinese American associates. Local Republican activists complained the investigation had a chilling effect on the Chinese American community's still-nascent support for the GOP.

Subpoenas also went out to Bingbing Peranio and other potential straw donors. Federal prosecutors demanded financial records from Mar-a-Lago and Trump Victory, although Yang—not they—were the target of the probe.[30] Investigators suspected that Yang was the true source of the funds, not her family and employees, opening her up to potential charges for breaking campaign finance laws.

"The FBI has spoken to at least ten people, most of them Chinese," said Yang's realtor, Kerry Kensington, who frequently went to Mar-a-Lago events with Yang.[31] "I know I cooperated. I don't know about the others."

Overnight Cindy Yang became persona non grata at the president's club.

The timing couldn't have been worse. On March 30 Yang was set to unveil her event of the year: a "forum" between members of the president's family and Chinese businesspeople that she was promoting online. In reality, the conference was Safari Night 2019. Elizabeth Trump Grau was hosting the gala for the second year running to benefit Terry Bomar's youth charity.

Charles Lee was clearly planning on Safari Night 2.0 being even better than the previous year. Lee increased the price for travel packages to

$20,000, compared to $13,500 the year before. His company advertised the event as "a forum on economic and trade collaboration and exchanges at President Trump's private club at Mar-a-Lago."[32]

Yang's consulting business also advertised the event as a "conference for international leadership." The participation of Trump Grau was prominently displayed in Yang's online flyers. Her ads never mentioned a Safari Night to benefit young children.

"It is the first time for Chinese to play the leading role within Mar-a-Lago," Yang's advertisement proclaimed.

Before the Kraft news broke, Terry Bomar had called Yang to complain about the flyer featuring Trump Grau. Although Bomar didn't know what the Chinese characters said, he didn't want Trump Grau to feel like she was being used.

After the *Herald* story about Yang's selfie, Bomar realized his event was doomed. He called Yang.

"I know why you're calling," she said before the pastor could get a word in.

"I don't have much choice," he replied.[33]

"I won't come to any part of it," Yang said, volunteering to skip the event entirely.

It was too late for that.

Bomar called up Mar-a-Lago and said they needed to call off Safari Night, costing him a $15,000 deposit. (He said he knew the club was going to cancel the event anyway.) He gave up the $50,000 he hoped to raise. The twenty-five students and six orphans living at the school in Kenya supported by his charity wouldn't be getting a new van or building after all. "That's who's getting hurt," he said.

Within a month Yang disappeared from public view. She took down her Facebook page and the website for GY US Investments. She stopped returning calls from friends. On WeChat she changed her username to "I'm Innocent" and stopped posting. She sold her house in Wellington, saying she was moving to California, as far away from Florida as she could get.

Charles Lee also took down the web pages where he had promoted the event. He told a reporter he was in Europe and defended his business as a public service.[34]

"Everything we do is for free. Our purpose is to help the government by promoting these events. We're a nonprofit organization," he said.[35]

"What we're trying to do is to promote the friendship between China and the United States."

Then he hung up.

But not everyone was so quick to retreat.

Yujing Zhang, a Shanghai businesswoman who had seen Yang's Safari Night flyer, was about to gate-crash Mar-a-Lago in the most spectacular fashion.

15

A WOMAN CALLED VERONICA

IT WAS THE LAST WEEKEND of March 2019, and President Trump and his family were cruising to Palm Beach on Air Force One as a Secret Service "protective zone" was being erected around Mar-a-Lago in preparation for their arrival.

This presidential drill had become routine, with road blocks, restricted access signs, and marine patrols. Taking their stations were squads of Palm Beach County Sheriff's Office deputies on taxpayer-funded overtime and Secret Service agents in charge of keeping Trump's Winter White House safe during his visits.

At the first security checkpoint, housed under a canvas tent in a parking lot across the street from the club, a large white sign with red-and-black lettering greeted visitors with a less-than-welcoming message: "UNITED STATES SECRET SERVICE RESTRICTED AREA. NOTICE: PHOTO ID REQUIRED."[1]

"You are entering a 'Restricted Building or Grounds,' as defined in Title 18, United States Code, Section 1752. Persons entering without lawful authority are subject to arrest and prosecution," the sign read.

"All vehicles and personnel entering or leaving the premises are subject to search. The following items are PROHIBITED: FIREARMS, EXPLOSIVES, KNIVES, MACE/PEPPER SPRAY, DRONES & OTHER UNMANNED AIRCRAFT, WEAPONS OF ANY KIND & ANY OTHER ITEM DETERMINED TO BE POTENTIAL SAFETY HAZARDS."

It was nearly 80 degrees at high noon when a young Asian woman dressed in a gray evening gown slipped out of her taxi and walked up to this security checkpoint.[2] The woman's dress would have been appropriate for an evening gala, but it was preposterous in the middle of the day. If she was aware of her fashion faux pas, no one knew it. She was similarly unfazed by the ominous sign and the gauntlet of federal agents and Mar-a-Lago security staffers in the parking lot. The agents and staff may have been taken aback by her evening wear, but it wasn't the first bizarre costume they'd ever seen while working the gate at Mar-a-Lago. What she was wearing wasn't their business.

The only requirement for entry was an invitation. By the rules that govern security at the president's club, federal agents have no control over who is on the guest list.[3]

At Mar-a-Lago a guest with a history of violent crimes wouldn't be flagged or turned away by federal agents. (Mike Tyson was wandering the pool deck taking pictures with fans at almost exactly the same time Zhang arrived at the front of the club.) Nor, theoretically, would agents know if someone arrived who was on a terrorist watchlist. Warning signs of a possible agent from another nation also wouldn't be flagged because the Secret Service does not background check club guests.[4]

At the outer perimeter the agents' only job is to make sure each guest has a valid ID that matches a name on the club guest list. Only staff and people scheduled for official, private meetings with the president undergo routine enhanced background screenings. It's unclear whether the Secret Service ever background checks club members.

Trump was out golfing in West Palm Beach when the woman in the gray dress walked up to his home, although his family was still inside, and he had a fundraiser scheduled at the club that night. As the woman approached, a Secret Service agent asked for her identification.[5]

Yujing Zhang pulled out two pieces of ID from the People's Republic of China: an expired passport that included a still-active ten-year visa for traveling in the United States, and another passport that was good through 2027. The documents showed that Zhang lived in Shanghai, China's largest city, and was making her fifth visit to the United States since 2016, all apparently short business trips.

But Yujing Zhang wasn't the name she had used when she tried to visit the club the day before.

Zhang had hired a cab to take her from Palm Beach's iconic Colony Hotel, where she had been terrorizing staff with her demanding disposition, to scope out Mar-a-Lago.[6] When the driver asked if she had an invitation to enter the historic property, she said no. So instead he gave her a tour of the wealthy island enclave. As he looked in the rearview mirror, he could see her talking on her cell phone and taking pictures. When she asked for a receipt, Zhang told the driver her name was "Veronica."[7]

By the time Zhang approached the Secret Service checkpoint outside the club the next day she had ditched the pseudonym.

She presented her passports to the Secret Service agent manning the checkpoint and said in strongly accented English that she was going to the pool. The agent asked her no questions.

As is standard practice at the Winter White House, the Secret Service agent turned to Mar-a-Lago staff to check whether Zhang's name was on the club's list of members and guests. At first, no one could verify that it was. A staffer called a manager at Mar-a-Lago's Beach Club, who said Zhang was the last name of a member. The staffer asked Zhang if that member was her father. "What do you mean by 'dad'?" she responded.

Terrified of offending billionaire members, club staff don't like to push the question of whether someone belongs at Mar-a-Lago.[8] The general rule: "If you look like you belong, you're in," said one staffer.[9] Billionaires don't take too kindly to having their friends and family hassled.

Believing that Zhang might be a relative of the member, club staff told Secret Service that the eccentric young woman should be allowed to enter Mar-a-Lago.

"She's good to go," they told the agent.[10] "She's on the list."

No one seemed to consider that Zhang is one of the three most common surnames in China, a country of 1.4 billion people.[11]

Zhang's foray into Trump's club exposed a huge and glaring weakness in presidential security.[12]

"At Mar-a-Lago the Secret Service agents have to depend on the club's security staff to check on members and guests to see who is coming and going; they don't have control over the list or the information on it," said a US law enforcement official who is familiar with security at Trump's club.[13] "The agents have to ask Mar-a-Lago's staff for access to it. They are hindered by that lack of control, which is unprecedented in the history of the United States."

"All the Secret Service cares about is identifying visitors, protecting the president, and making sure no guns or bombs get into Mar-a-Lago," the official added.

At the White House it's inconceivable that people would be let in willy-nilly. But at the Winter White House they come and go as they please. The president makes money off everyone who walks through the gates.

The last thing he wants is his members feeling caged in by security.

BY ALL ACCOUNTS Yujing Zhang was painfully ordinary growing up.[14] She was shy and liked watching American TV. *Grey's Anatomy* and *Prison Break* were her favorites. She always dreamed of traveling, maybe to Europe, but she never really had the opportunity. Her father was a taxi mechanic. Her mother had passed away just a few years after Zhang graduated college, right around the time she left her first job.

She had worked in a low-level position at an international securities firm in Shanghai, where she struggled to make deadlines. She had a tendency to procrastinate. What twenty-something doesn't? Just as often as her millennial habits, it was Zhang's modest resources that held her back. All too often her worn-out laptop would refuse to turn on, leaving her further behind schedule and feeling smaller than ever.

"She was pretty introverted in her personality," said a man who dated Zhang briefly around that time.

He was eleven years her senior and setting up a hedge fund when Zhang reached out to him over social media in 2013 to ask for business advice. She wanted to start a company of her own, she told him, though she had no plan other than doing something related to finance. They went on a few dates.

Zhang had been excited about the romance at the time. She wanted commitment, a *real* boyfriend, she said.

The man wasn't interested. Zhang had told him that her father liked to read the *Shanghai Morning Post*, a tabloid. That was a "paper read by ordinary Shanghai people," the man said. "In all, she gave the impression of being a very ordinary girl, in every respect: ordinary looks, ordinary family, and an ordinary education. Everything was ordinary."

The two quickly fell out of touch.

Perhaps it was the constant rejections and failures that instilled Zhang with a stubborn, irrepressible drive to succeed, even when circumstance and common sense seemed to dictate otherwise.

Within a few years of being snubbed by the elitist hedge funder, Zhang, then in her late twenties, had somehow transformed herself from a disorganized young woman into a successful financier who drove a BMW and owned a pricey apartment in Shanghai, China's banking capital.[15]

But she still didn't have status—and that's exactly the kind of thing that a trip to Mar-a-Lago could buy her.

"I think she just really wanted to succeed," her ex-boyfriend said.[16] "The more ordinary things are in your family, the more shortcuts you have to take."

Zhang had bought a ticket to an event at Mar-a-Lago through Charles Lee on February 19, 2019.[17] He sent her a flyer that advertised "International Leadership Achievement Awards" and the chance "to develop an international vision, to build a broad network of contacts, and to expand business opportunities."[18] Beneath the promises of grandeur was the name of the promoter: Cindy.[19] It all sounded good to Zhang. She paid Dr. Charles $20,000 for a seven-day package tour that included stops in South Florida and New York.[20] At Mar-a-Lago she would join elites from Taiwan, Hong Kong, Macau, Australia, and Europe to discuss US-China economic relations—or so she thought.

Zhang especially wanted to meet Donald and Ivanka Trump, who she mistakenly believed was hosting the evening. She thought she could use Mar-a-Lago to recruit clients for her financial business. She wanted to snap photos in the center of power.

But on March 18 Charles Lee told Zhang that there was a problem with her dream trip.

"Eh, here is the thing—I just got an email," Lee told Zhang.[21] "I read an email, an email saying that in Trump's estate—it says that the event on 3/30 may be canceled."

On March 26, one day after Zhang celebrated her thirty-third birthday, Lee confirmed the bad news. It was official.[22] "Hey Gorgeous," Lee said.[23] "The event at Trump's estate, it's been put on hold for now. We can forget about it."

The event had been canceled after the *Miami Herald* published stories on Cindy Yang and her access peddling at Mar-a-Lago. If Lee knew the specifics, he didn't tell Zhang.

As a consolation, he tried to pitch his client a financial gathering with Warren Buffett.[24] It would cost $20,000 to go, but $60,000 if she wanted a photo with the celebrated investor. Lee also had tickets to an event with power couple Bill and Hillary Clinton.

Zhang was not interested. Why would she want to meet a *former* secretary of state? For her, it was Trump or bust.

"Forget it," she told Lee the next day. "Just get a refund then. Wire it straight to my account. I'm not going. Need the money urgently."

"It's okay," Lee responded. "Just send me your account number."

But twenty-four hours after she said she wasn't going, Zhang walked up to a ticket agent, suitcase in hand, and paid $2,057—cash—to catch the next flight from Shanghai to Florida.[25]

Zhang woke up to Palm Beach sunshine on the morning of March 30—and a voice message from Charles Lee.

She had asked him the night before to call Mar-a-Lago and find out why the summit had been canceled.

"Gorgeous," he said. "Regarding Trump's event, this is what happened . . . They accused Trump of colluding with Russia."

He rambled on about Democrats and the media.

"They talk this and that and a bunch of nonsense about all of Trump's events, saying that those events are sponsored by foreigners and something about election interference," Lee explained. "In order to minimize the nonsense, they canceled his events for the time being."

But from her $773 room at the Colony Hotel, the luxury boutique where celebrities like Meryl Streep unwind with pool-side mimosas, the situation didn't sound that bad. She messaged Lee back at 8:53 A.M. "We are not involved in politics," she said.

By mid-morning she was thinking about real estate—and the president.

"I was thinking that since Trump himself was in [the] real estate business . . . perhaps we could have something to talk about. Don't you agree?" she asked Lee. What did politics have to do with her business plans? "Some small business collaboration shouldn't be a problem," she added as she started getting ready for her day.

She pulled on her gray evening gown, just like all the ladies of Mar-a-Lago wore in their Instagram photos from the club. She grabbed her purse and began stuffing it with electronics: a MacBook Air laptop, a 500-gigabyte hard drive, three iPhones, an iPad, a Google Pixel smart-phone, and a small SanDisk thumb drive.[26] It was as if she'd swept the contents of an entire shelf at Radio Shack into her bag. But she didn't pack the wad of cash, $8,000 in US and Chinese currency, that she'd carried with her from Shanghai. She also left behind an ID that gave her name as Veronica. She grabbed her two passports instead.

Just before noon Charles Lee rang again.

"I got it, Gorgeous," he said. "But Trump's event is canceled for the time being." He said he'd let her know if there were other opportunities. He'd make all the arrangements.

"Right, right, right," Zhang replied.

Then she hailed a cab and told the driver to take her to Mar-a-Lago.

IT TOOK ZHANG just a few minutes to clear the club's exterior ring of se-curity after Mar-a-Lago staff told the Secret Service that she was a mem-ber's daughter and therefore allowed to use the pool.

A valet in a golf cart drove her from the parking lot to a second secu-rity checkpoint near the entrance of the historic mansion's ornate lobby. They passed three Secret Service agents in marked bulletproof vests and another restricted access sign. Zhang hopped off the golf cart and paused to read yet another restricted access sign before proceeding through a metal detector manned by Secret Service. By this point the message should have been clear: *Invited guests only.*

During the screening the agents found her cell phones and all the other electronics.[27] But her equipment—and the sheer number of de-vices—did not set off any alarms. None of it violated Secret Service se-curity protocols as weapons, bombs, or hazardous chemicals would have done. They waved her through.

Zhang entered Mar-a-Lago the way all visitors do—through the main reception area. It was only at this point—once she had made it past the

government security that protects the president of the United States—
that Zhang became the target of suspicion.

Mar-a-Lago receptionist Ariela Grumaz was sure she had never seen
the woman in gray before.[28] Like all club staff, Grumaz was trained to
remember the faces of members and frequent guests.

As soon as Zhang walked in, her opulent ball gown caught Grumaz's
eye. Zhang was shooting video with her phone. That was technically for-
bidden, although the rule was usually only enforced when the president
was around. Still, to Grumaz, who had worked for two years as a receptionist at the club, the woman's behavior was a dead giveaway that she
didn't belong. For one thing, she didn't even stop at the receptionist's
desk to say hello, as many members and guests who knew the ropes did.

Grumaz confronted Zhang. Politely, of course. She couldn't risk offending the woman in case she turned out to be a legitimate guest.

"Ma'am, sorry, do you have an appointment?" Grumaz asked Zhang in
English with a hint of an Eastern European accent.[29] Zhang approached
her desk. She didn't mention going to the pool or being related to a Mar-
a-Lago member. Instead, she asked the receptionist to wait a moment as
she searched for something on her iPhone. Zhang showed Grumaz an
image of a document written in Chinese. It was her invitation to Cindy
Yang's summit. Grumaz couldn't read it.

Going far beyond what the Secret Service and club security did outside, Grumaz pressed Zhang for more information. It wasn't easy. Zhang
kept going on about attending an event for Chinese Americans. She
called it a "United Nations Friendship gathering." Grumaz didn't have a
clue what she was talking about. There was no such event on the calendar
for that Saturday evening. The only public event that had been scheduled
was Safari Night, and that had been canceled weeks earlier.

Then the receptionist asked a simple question—what was the strange
woman's name? Zhang replied, but Grumaz didn't know how to spell
what she said, so she tried to write the name as it sounded. The receptionist was growing increasingly frustrated as she attempted to pin Zhang
down on why she was there. Lunch? Dinner? An appointment with a
member? What exactly?

Struggling for words, Zhang just kept trying to show Grumaz the invitation written in Chinese characters on her iPhone.

At her wit's end, the receptionist tried calling the club's general manager for help, but there was no answer. "Wait here," Grumaz told Zhang.[30]

She asked a Secret Service agent to keep an eye on Zhang while she walked over to the manager's office. She was worried about the increasingly skittish visitor wandering through the club unsupervised. Grumaz and the manager checked the list of events for the month on his computer and found nothing about a United Nations Friendship event between China and the United States. They also checked to see if Zhang's name was on the guest list for any event scheduled that evening. There was no match. They checked to see if her name popped up on a membership or guest list or some other list granting her access to the president's home. Again, nothing.

Yujing Zhang was not supposed to be at Mar-a-Lago.

Grumaz returned to her desk and quickly noticed that the intruder had vanished.[31] The receptionist glanced over at the Secret Service agent who was supposed to be watching Zhang. He was waiting outside the ladies' room, where Zhang had apparently taken refuge.

Grumaz sought out another agent.

"Something is weird," she told Special Agent Samuel Ivanovich.[32] "I don't know how she got on the premises. I need your help."

Young and eager, Ivanovich tried to take control of the situation. The rookie agent had graduated from college six years earlier and spent the beginning of his law enforcement career working as a police officer in the village of Evendale, Ohio, population 2,859. But he was confident and well spoken and joined the Secret Service in 2017. Still, his clean-shaven baby face wasn't exactly intimidating, and it was only his second month working in the agency's West Palm Beach office.

When the Chinese woman emerged from the restroom, Ivanovich approached. Zhang told him in English that she had come to Mar-a-Lago to attend a United Nations Friendship event and arrived early to see the property and take pictures. She showed him the Chinese-language invitation on her iPhone. "I cannot read it," Ivanovich said. She pulled the screen away and rushed off to the ladies' room again.[33]

Minutes passed. Zhang didn't come out. Ivanovich and the other agent waited outside, growing increasingly uneasy.

"Do you want me to go inside and get her?" Grumaz asked the agents. They agreed it was a good idea. As soon as she stepped into the hallway leading to the ladies' room, Grumaz saw Zhang texting on her iPhone. She was pacing back and forth.

It was clear Zhang wasn't using the facilities.

"Ma'am, can you please step outside?" Grumaz asked her with a politeness that would never have been afforded to an obvious intruder at the actual White House. A federal agent may not have been so respectful to Zhang, who was—for all the US government knew—sending photos of the club's layout to a foreign government or terrorist group. But Grumaz was just a receptionist.

She tried to calm the woman down: "Nothing is going to happen to you."[34]

Then she escorted Zhang back to the lobby, where Ivanovich and other Secret Service agents were waiting. The woman seemed unperturbed by the imposing force of federal agents surrounding her. Grumaz, sitting back down at her desk, was struck by Zhang's demeanor. She seemed so cool and under control. Was she oblivious to the gravity of what was happening? Or just exceptionally accustomed to pressure?

Ivanovich towered over the petite woman.

"You are not allowed on the premises," he told Zhang.[35] She grew upset after the agents started going through her electronics but agreed to talk with them further. She had an invitation, she insisted. Ivanovich brought her to the Secret Service's office in West Palm Beach for questioning.

JUST ACROSS THE Intracoastal Waterway—and a world apart from Mar-a-Lago—Zhang was placed under arrest.

Secret Service agents gave her a Miranda warning in English and asked her to sign a document waiving her right to remain silent or to have an attorney present.

Ivanovich asked Zhang several times if she understood English.

"English, yes," Zhang responded.[36]

Just in case, Ivanovich enlisted the help of another agent from the Los Angeles office who was fluent in Mandarin and had been assigned to help with presidential security that weekend.

Ivanovich challenged Zhang about why she had come to Mar-a-Lago and offered apparently false explanations about wanting to use the pool and being related to a member. Zhang said she hadn't lied to anyone and blamed a language barrier. She insisted that she had never even mentioned the pool. And she said she thought Zhang, the name of the Mar-a-Lago member, was the person running the United Nations Friendship event. She never told anyone she was his daughter, she added.

Agents were baffled when Zhang said a Chinese friend by the name of Charles had sold her a package to travel all the way from Shanghai to Palm Beach to attend this United Nations event.[37] She had hoped, she said, to talk with the president and his family about Chinese American economic relations.

The agents were sure Zhang was lying. They noted how fluent her English seemed, ruling out in their minds any lost-in-translation mishaps. And the club had no UN summits on the calendar that night, they knew. But the agents didn't know anything about the Chinese cottage industry bringing droves of tourists to Mar-a-Lago. They didn't know about how Charles Lee had pitched the youth charity gala to Zhang. They never asked to see those messages. There was no one by the name of "Charles" on her phone, and that was enough for them. They didn't know to look for Li Weitian, Charles Lee's real name. And they never asked the Mandarin-speaking agent to translate the invitation that Zhang had been thrusting in their faces all day.

At around 10 P.M. on March 30 Zhang was taken into federal custody on charges of making false statements to a federal officer and entering a restricted property. More charges might still come.[38] Agents thought there would be no trouble, considering the facts of the case. Zhang, they thought, was a liar.

And there was a more disturbing possibility: Was this strange woman a spy for the Chinese? Was she planning to use her devices to infiltrate Mar-a-Lago's network and collect information on the president?

Suspicions mounted when agents realized Zhang had carried one of her phones in a Faraday bag—the kind of purse used to block electronic signals.[39] When they searched her hotel room later on, they found nine USB drives, five SIM cards, and the thick wad of hundred-dollar bills she'd left behind. But what struck them most was her "signal detector," a portable device that can detect radio waves, magnetic fields, and hidden-camera equipment.

When one of Ivanovich's colleagues took Zhang's thumb drive and inserted it into a computer to see what was on it, the device began installing files. The agent quickly shut down the computer in order to protect it from being corrupted. Federal prosecutors would say in court the thumb drive seemed to contain malware—software that aims to disrupt, damage, or gain unauthorized access to a computer system.

What if the thumb drive had been inserted into a computer at Mar-a-Lago? Zhang had gotten very close to at least one computer in her brief moment at the club, where even the wireless network is unsecured. (Trump is notoriously cheap when it comes to information technology.[40])

China's foreign policy is fueled by economic espionage—business-people collecting information through the normal course of their days.

"Mar-a-Lago, because it's associated with the president, represents a unique collection target. Anyone would want to have a foot in the door," said Nicholas Eftimiades, a former intelligence officer and author of the book *Chinese Intelligence Operations*.[41]

Zhang certainly did not act like a typical Chinese spy, Eftimiades said. She hadn't followed the normal "hands-off" approach of a trained intelligence officer. She'd walked right in the front door and gotten caught almost immediately. But that didn't rule out the possibility that she made the trip on behalf of the Chinese government.

China wanted Mar-a-Lago and wanted it bad. For three months the US Attorney's Office in Miami and the FBI had been secretly probing potential Chinese espionage in South Florida—and at the president's club.[42]

"Maybe [Zhang] was amateur hour," Eftimiades speculated. "But eventually they're going to get it if they keep throwing bodies at it."

At trial the US government seemed determined to use Zhang's case to send a message to the Chinese government: stay away from the Winter White House or face the full might of American law.

But as the Secret Service agents placed Zhang in handcuffs on March 30, they had no idea that this open-and-shut case was about to blow up in their faces. They had been sloppy, from conducting her interview in English despite having an interpreter available, to listing Zhang's passports as coming from Taiwan rather than China in her charging document.

(Ivanovich wrote the "Republic of China" rather than the "People's Republic of China.")

And it definitely would have helped if agents had recorded the interview with Zhang. But the interview room Ivanovich chose was wired only for video recording, not audio, something he didn't realize.

It was just one more entry on a long list of things the Secret Service agents didn't know.

16

"SOMETHING NEFARIOUS"

YUJING ZHANG SPENT the night locked up in the Palm Beach County jail.[1]

She was without a country, without a family, and without a lawyer. And she really needed a lawyer.

Two days later she appeared in federal court for the first time. Zhang stood before Judge William Matthewman, a former defense attorney and police officer with a cordial manner.

Matthewman calmly explained Zhang's rights and the government's allegations along with the maximum penalties. He said that she was being charged with making false statements to a federal officer, a felony, and with entering or remaining in a restricted building or grounds, a misdemeanor.[2] He told Zhang that the US Attorney's Office was seeking to keep her locked up through her trial because the government considered her an "extreme flight risk" to China.

Prosecutors emphasized just how little was known about Zhang, saying there were "security implications" to her case.[3] Among their primary concerns was her thumb drive, which they said had been loaded with "malicious malware." Just two days after the hearing the *Miami Herald* would break the news that Zhang's case had been folded into the ongoing Chinese espionage investigation.[4]

For her part, Zhang was measured and thoughtful, standing before the judge in prison clothes and speaking mainly through a Mandarin interpreter but also sometimes in English. She asked sophisticated questions about whether she could be released on bond and how she could obtain an attorney.

"You're obviously very intelligent because your questions are excellent for a defendant in this situation," Matthewman remarked.[5]

Zhang pleaded not guilty.

She chose to keep the federal public defenders who had been assigned to her case. They hired interpreters and contacted her family back in China. Losing could mean spending her next five years in prison.

Still, it seemed from Zhang's unruffled demeanor that she had not yet grasped her new reality. The full weight of a foreign justice system was about to come crashing down on this young woman who had once loved watching *Prison Break* as a teenager in Shanghai.

FEDERAL PROSECUTORS NEVER publicly said Zhang was a spy.

But they weren't hiding their suspicions.

The government lawyers painted her as a woman who "lies to everyone she encounters." They questioned all the electronic devices and cash found in her hotel room. But they didn't have much more to go on than that. "There are a lot of questions that remain to be answered, but at this point we are not alleging in the criminal filing that she is involved in espionage," Assistant US Attorney Rolando Garcia told Matthewman.[6]

The judge had questions: "The government continues to investigate whether or not the defendant was engaged in espionage or spying, would that be accurate?"

"Yes, sir," Garcia replied.

As Zhang's case seemed to morph into a spy thriller, it prompted new questions about Cindy Yang, whose tourism business had nearly given Zhang access to Mar-a-Lago. Yang said she had no idea who Zhang was. That didn't matter. If China's government wanted to see how far an agent could penetrate the president's private club, secretly sending someone on a Trump tour was a pretty good starting point. (Yang also said she didn't know Charles Lee, who said the same about her.)

Zhang's public defenders were adamant their client had a reasonable explanation for being at Mar-a-Lago. They brought proof for the judge—a document from China showing that Zhang had wired $20,000 to an entity called the Beijing Peace and Friendship Management Consulting Co., Ltd., which Charles Lee had used to process payments for tickets to Mar-a-Lago events.[7] The public defenders said the receipt was for a trip to attend a March 30 event at Mar-a-Lago. "Twenty thousand dollars to attend an event at Mar-a-Lago, is that what you're saying?" an astonished Matthewman asked.[8]

Zhang's lawyer, Robert Adler, explained the Trump tourism industry that had sprung up around the club.

"So in other words, Judge, these exhibits we believe establish and will establish that she came here innocently after paying a fee to . . . go to an event that she thought was scheduled at Mar-a-Lago," Adler said.[9] In communications with Lee, "she was informed that she could go to the event early in order to basically just acquaint herself with the Mar-a-Lago grounds prior to the event."

This was all news to prosecutors, who were caught flat footed.

Adler then produced photos Lee had used to promote his organization on various websites. There was one photo of Lee with a US congressman, another of him with former California governor Arnold Schwarzenegger, another of himself purporting to be the secretary general of a Chinese UN group in New York, and yet another of him posing with models. It was classic Prince Charles.

"This seems to be a man who was promoting himself, that if you wanted to contact personally anyone of importance in the United States that he was the go-to guy," Adler told the judge.

The assistant public defender said Zhang showed up to attend the charity event with good intentions, only to have a language barrier blow a minor misunderstanding into a life-changing catastrophe.[10]

For a moment it seemed Zhang might walk free.

But in the days that followed prosecutors and agents, forced to confront the fact that "Charles" really did exist, dug up the messages from Zhang's iPhone showing that Lee had told her on March 26 that the Mar-a-Lago gala was off.[11] That was two days before she left China. The trail of messages blew a gaping hole in her defense. It seemed like she was a liar again.

With that evidence, it wasn't surprising when Matthewman ordered that Zhang be held in pretrial detention. The judge cited the number of electronic devices in her possession and noted she had the financial resources to leave the country and no family ties to the United States. (The US government has no extradition treaty with China.)

"It does appear to the court that Ms. Zhang was up to something nefarious," Matthewman said, leading to a wave of damning headlines.[12]

Zhang could be going away for a long time.

PUBLICLY, THE CHINESE GOVERNMENT all but ignored Zhang's case. There was little indication it planned to help her out of her bind.

China's consulate in Houston, which handles issues for Chinese citizens based around the southern United States and Puerto Rico, told reporters that it had provided consular services to Zhang but refused to elaborate.[13]

While she was being held in the county jail, Zhang started receiving calls from Houston.[14]

There is no record of what was said, but someone who answered the phone at the consulate later told reporters that they were simply concerned about Zhang's well-being. At least six calls were exchanged between Zhang and the consulate in her first month behind bars. And at least one private attorney visited her in jail—much to the chagrin of the public defenders representing her.[15] It's not clear if it was the prisoner—or someone else—who extended that invitation to step on their toes.

As the months wore on, the once-composed Zhang began to grow more and more bizarre—to the point that many observers questioned whether she had been sane to begin with. The woman who sat straight during initial hearings, taking notes on a yellow legal pad and asking questions that suggested a level of intelligence,was gone. By June, Zhang slumped in her chair. She no longer spoke in English, and when the judge would ask her a question through a court-appointed translator, she sometimes appeared not to understand what was being said in her native language either. Sometimes she would just stare and smile at the judge, nodding her head to answer questions rather than speaking out loud as she had been instructed over and over again.

The federal judge presiding over her trial, Roy Altman, had been patient at first. But after hours of repeating himself, Altman accused Zhang of trying to "play games with the court."

Zhang was irrational. She stopped trusting everyone, even breaking off contact with her public defenders. A family friend said it was because she believed her attorneys would go to the press and bring more unwanted attention. She started to show other signs of paranoia too, including once asking the judge for the full names of everyone in the courtroom for "security" reasons. She never elaborated on what she meant. Alarmed by her comments and the shift in her behavior, Altman asked if she was being threatened. Zhang said no.

At one hearing a *Miami Herald* reporter overheard one of Zhang's public defenders beseeching her to cooperate with them. Zhang had been ignoring them for weeks.

"We would like to meet with you to talk to you more," the attorney said to her stubborn client.[16] "What you tell us is private."

But once the hearing started, Zhang stood up and suddenly told the judge she wanted to represent herself.

"I don't need the attorneys, thank you," she said through an interpreter.[17]

Everyone was confused. Maybe she *had* gone crazy.

"Do you want to represent yourself or do you want a lawyer?" Altman asked, seeking clarity.

"Today, I don't want the attorney," Zhang replied.

Altman, a star litigator whom Trump had just appointed to the bench at the precocious age of thirty-six, told her that's not how it works.

"I don't need an attorney," Zhang replied.

Altman said she "really, really did" and that representing herself was a "very bad decision."[18]

"I have read some [legal] books," Zhang told him.

"A trained lawyer would defend you much better than you could represent yourself," Altman replied. "I strongly urge you *not* to represent yourself. . . . I've been a lawyer for a very long time."

"I still don't want to communicate with the attorneys," Zhang said. "There are a lot of reasons." She said the courtroom wasn't the right place to explain. Altman offered to seal the court and transcripts so she could talk freely. "I think still I cannot discuss about it," she said.

The public defenders asked for a psychiatric evaluation. Zhang wouldn't cooperate, but a review of her mental health history showed no red flags. Altman ultimately agreed that Zhang was mentally competent to represent herself.

Back in jail her behavior became still more erratic.

On June 27, 2019, a real estate investor named Clayton Davis got a jailhouse collect call.[19]

On the other end of the line was Zhang.

"I need money," she said. "I know you from Palm Beach."

Davis had never spoken with her in his life. But he did advertise in South Florida newspapers, so he speculated that Zhang had seen his name in one of the listings.

He could barely understand what she was saying.

What a nutcase, he thought to himself, hanging up and blocking the number.

Over the next few weeks Zhang would make dozens of calls to bail bondsmen and real estate agents.

None of them had any clue what she wanted. And there was certainly nothing they could do for her. Zhang had been denied bail for months.

"She was asking me what happens next as if she didn't know," said Francine Adderley, a bail bondswoman in West Palm Beach.[20] "I'm almost positive she called everybody on the list just trying to figure out something."

WHILE ZHANG SEEMED to be losing it, federal prosecutors were still digging into the question of whether she was a spy.

Michael Sherwin, a former naval intelligence officer who worked in the national-security section of the US Attorney's Office in Miami, was running the probe into potential Chinese espionage in South Florida. Within two weeks of Zhang's arrest Sherwin took over her case.

In June he asked Judge Altman for permission to file "classified information" under seal.[21] If Altman agreed, the evidence would be presented during closed-door meetings in his chambers, and not even Zhang, much less the public, would ever get to see it.

Sherwin asked that the sensitive evidence be sealed under Section 4 of the Classified Information Procedures Act. While the evidence could have simply been information about Mar-a-Lago's security protocols, legal experts speculated that the government might have proof Zhang was working for the Chinese government.[22]

What had started as a trespass case was now looking far graver.

Altman agreed to the government's request. The judge wrote that public disclosure of the information could "cause serious damage to the national security of the United States." Adding to his reasoning: "none of the classified information is exculpatory."[23] In other words, it wouldn't help Zhang's defense.

ON SEPTEMBER 9, 2019, about fifty people were summoned for jury duty in the case of the *United States of America v. Yujing Zhang* in Fort Lauderdale's federal courthouse, a brutalist, concrete structure on the city's main thoroughfare.

When Zhang entered Altman's courtroom, the judge was instantly taken aback that she was wearing a brown inmate's uniform instead of her civilian clothes.[24] Altman said he did not want potential jurors to see her dressed that way. Prison garb could prejudice the jury against her. Altman asked why she wasn't wearing her regular clothes.

Zhang, clearly mortified and speaking through an interpreter, told Altman that the jail hadn't provided her with any clean "undergarments" that day.

"You have no undergarments in your cell?" he asked.

"No," said Zhang, who was being held in a Broward County jail facility.

She refused to elaborate about why she preferred her jail clothes, saying she wasn't comfortable speaking in front of the court—in other words, in front of men. She seemed embarrassed to say the truth out loud: without a bra, her nipples would show through the gold-and-rose-hued silk blouse that had been provided from her suitcase.[25] Instead, she said she didn't understand the judge's English. A frustrated Altman told her to listen to her Mandarin interpreter or else "we could be here for a year."

Finally, Zhang agreed to change, obviously humiliated. (The day's headlines would all be about her lack of underwear.)

Then the judge introduced her to the prospective jurors. Out of nowhere she replied that she thought the trial had been canceled.

"You are obviously unprepared to proceed," Altman rebuked her. He "strongly recommended" that she go to trial with the assistant federal public defender by her side.

"I don't think so," she told the judge, and jury selection began.

Donald Trump was not in the courtroom. Nor was the president standing trial or in any way directly involved in Zhang's case. But he was certainly on the minds of some of the jury candidates chosen from the voter rolls of Broward County, a bastion of hardcore Democrats.

A few openly said they didn't like Trump or his politics.

Altman asked them if their attitudes toward the president would affect their ability to fairly evaluate evidence against Zhang.

"Trump is in my head," one prospective juror told the judge. "He drives me crazy."

Another seemed a bit less judgmental.

"Aside from my feelings about Trump, I will be fair," one woman told Altman.

"And your feelings about him?" he asked.

"Negative," she replied.

As Altman proceeded to explain jury selection rules to Zhang, the judge told her for the umpteenth time that she would be better served if she allowed a public defender to at least sit next to her so she could ask the attorney for procedural help if she needed it. This time Zhang took the judge up on his recommendation.

"She has much [more] experience than me," Zhang said in English, "so that would be helpful."

With the trial finally underway, Sherwin started off by telling the jury that Zhang had lied multiple times in order to get into Mar-a-Lago.[26]

"In no way was this defendant authorized to be there," Sherwin said.

Zhang's opening statement was less than a minute long.

"Good afternoon, grand jury," she intoned awkwardly.[27] "What I want to say . . . I don't believe I did anything wrong. And thank you, USA."

Throughout the two-day trial Zhang would have chances to mount a defense. An experienced attorney would surely have poked holes in the prosecution's case. For instance, when the taxi driver who drove Zhang to Mar-a-Lago the day before Safari Night was called to testify, he said he wasn't sure if the woman sitting at the defense table was the same one who had ridden in his cab. "Maybe," he said. "I'm not sure."

Zhang failed to pounce. Nor did she speak up as prosecutors called a series of witnesses—from Secret Service agents to Mar-a-Lago's receptionist—to testify against her.

Zhang called no witnesses of her own, leaving the prosecution as the only voice in the room.

"She said she was there for a United Nations friendship event. Well, that was a clear lie," Garcia, the prosecutor, told the jurors in a closing statement.[28] "She was bound and determined to get on that property. . . . She lied to everybody to get on that property."

A public defender would have pointed out that she'd followed every protocol. She went through the security checkpoints. She provided valid ID. The Secret Service, following the advice of club staff, had let her in and then she told a club receptionist exactly why she was there. In fact, Zhang's lawyers did make that argument months before she fired them.

"The only thing that Ms. Zhang did was give a very common Chinese name, with no claims whatsoever that she was there as a member [or] family member, and it was decided that she be allowed in," one of her public defenders had said at an earlier hearing.[29] "So I don't understand how this could support a trespass charge where she was allowed in after making no type of direct misrepresentation, where apparently it must be either a misunderstanding or failure to follow up of the security staff."

Three months after Zhang's trial another Chinese tourist would wander onto the grounds of Mar-a-Lago and be arrested for trespassing.[30] (Trump wasn't in Florida at the time.) Unlike Zhang, the woman agreed to let public defenders represent her. Their main argument: the club was so porous that the woman, who spoke almost no English, didn't understand it was private property and thought she was allowed to be there. "It was an open gate that was very pretty," the woman said in state court through a Mandarin interpreter.[31] A jury acquitted her of trespassing.[32]

Zhang had fired the only people who could have made a similar argument on her behalf. And so Garcia went on unchallenged.

"She lies to everyone she encounters," the prosecutor repeated.[33] "She tries to lie her way in to say she's going to the pool."

He argued she was more than just a fame-obsessed businesswoman hoping to meet the president and brought up her purse full of electronics.

"That suggests she isn't some misguided tourist," Garcia said. "She had an agenda to be on that property."

But the allegation that Zhang might be a spy? It never came up directly. She hadn't been charged with espionage, only trespassing and lying. Still, it was hard to imagine the idea hadn't crept into the jury's mind.

"I do think I did nothing wrong," Zhang told jurors in closing.[34] She doubled down on what she'd always said: "I did no lying."

The jury deliberated for four-and-a-half hours, with some wondering whether Zhang could really be guilty of trespassing. It seemed like she was just headstrong and confused. Others said they didn't really care if she posed a possible threat to Trump and his family. But in the end, the group of twelve convicted her unanimously on both counts. It did seem that she had been told the event was canceled. She'd even asked for a refund. And they didn't have any evidence to acquit her, thanks to Zhang's refusal to mount a defense. As the guilty verdicts were read aloud in the courtroom on September 11, 2019, Zhang showed no reaction. She was taken back to jail.

Her sentencing hearing was held just before Thanksgiving. Prosecutors urged the judge to send Zhang to prison for one and a half years, casting her as an unrepentant and chronic liar.[35]

It was only then that Zhang seemed to wake from her months-long stupor. She stood up and criticized the prosecutors for how they portrayed her at trial by implying she was "up to something nefarious," as the magistrate judge once said. Zhang said they had misrepresented the facts. She said she never lied to the Secret Service about why she was visiting Mar-a-Lago.

"I already said I come to meet the president and his family and make friends," Zhang said, startling more than one person in the courtroom.[36]

"You wanted to come to make friends with the president and his family?" Altman asked in bewilderment.

Zhang chuckled and said yes.

Finally Zhang was talking and Altman had questions. "Why did you have the signal detection device?" he asked, referring to the contraption found in her hotel room that could pick up hidden cameras.

"I'm just cautious . . . because I'm a female . . . for my security," Zhang answered.

As for the "malicious malware" the feds accused her of bringing into the president's estate, prosecutors had already acknowledged it was likely a false positive. They said the government had never fully been able to reproduce what happened the first time agents plugged her infamous thumb drive into a computer.

In the end Altman cut Zhang a break, sentencing her to time served. By then she'd been in jail for eight months.

She was transferred to federal immigration authorities and held at a detention center for deportation to China.[37]

But that would not be the end of *l'affaire Zhang.*

Although she had no legal status in the United States, Zhang challenged her so-called removal order rather than simply accept her return to Shanghai.

What would make someone want to stay in a foreign country as a felon with no family, friends, or job?

Perhaps she was facing something worse back home.

In the summer of 2019 federal law enforcement officials briefed Trump about possible Chinese spying at his estate.[38]

If he was worried by what they told him, Trump never expressed it publicly. The coming Palm Beach social season was ramping up to be one of the best yet, with a full calendar of charity galas and political fundraisers. Trump and his Mar-a-Lago cohort had dollar signs in their eyes.

Security remained an afterthought.

Although most club members seemed to brush off Yujing Zhang's intrusion as a bizarre fluke, a few did seem to stop coming out of fears for their safety. And some employees were growing increasingly uneasy about working at the Winter White House, which they'd always been told was one of the safest places in the world.

"We're a target whether the president is home or not," one employee said.[39] "The more people he pisses off, the more of a target we become."

As 2019 drew to a close, Mar-a-Lago remained largely accessible even to nonmembers during events and galas. At one luncheon held in the

Grand Ballroom in December, checking in appeared to be optional. No one showed ID. The proper attire—Palm Beach chic—was still enough to gain access to the president's home, at least when he wasn't there.

A few new security measures *had* been implemented before the upcoming high season. Staff now carry ID badges so security can easily identify them as employees with permission to walk the grounds.

And, for the first time, the Secret Service held two mandatory information sessions for club employees in the lead-up to the high season.[40] In a small room in the main building three Secret Service agents from the Miami office told the staff to be wary of strangers who might offer them favors in exchange for information on the president and his friends. They warned that foreign intelligence agencies might target staffers with large debts and offer to pay them off in exchange for small favors. Once you agree to one thing, no matter how small, agents cautioned, they can force you to keep going.

If approached, staff were instructed to call the Secret Service or club security. Agents passed out business cards.

This would have been a typical briefing for federal employees who dealt with anything even remotely related to national security. Now it was being offered to servers and receptionists at the president's private club, most of whom are foreign guest workers on short-term visas. The Secret Service presentation felt complicated and technical.

One staffer went up to an agent to offer a bit of perspective on what he saw as a much more immediate threat.

"Literally anyone could walk in," the employee said.[41] "Anyone."

Epilogue

PANDEMIC AT THE DISCO

ON THE EVENING of March 7, 2020, the chairwoman of the president's re-election committee was shaking her booty in Mar-a-Lago's Gold and White ballroom surrounded by DC politicians, top administration officials, right-wing media pundits, all four of Trump's adult children, and the president himself. The only person missing was the First Lady.

As Kimberly Guilfoyle motioned for the crowd to surround her on the dance floor and "back that ass up," she didn't know there was a party crasher in their midst.[1] She didn't know that a dangerous intruder had already infiltrated the castle where she and her boyfriend, Donald Trump Jr., felt most safe. She didn't know that the bespectacled man standing just feet away as the president of Brazil raised a proverbial glass in her honor had brought this unwanted guest into Trump's gilded home.[2]

The man probably didn't know it either. It would be days before anyone realized what had happened, although by March 7 everyone at Guilfoyle's birthday party should have seen it coming.

Under the cover of an informally organized international summit and a "Party in the USA," the king of modern viruses was invading the halls of American power, forcing everyone—even the lord of the realm himself—to a knee.

A novel coronavirus broke out in central China in mid-December 2019. It mercilessly attacked the lungs of its victims, claiming the lives of thousands, including a doctor who was arrested by the Chinese government after informing the public of the new disease.[3] The World Health

Organization named the killer COVID-19—the coronavirus disease of 2019.

By February the Centers for Disease Control and Prevention announced a pandemic was likely in the United States.[4] Advisors warned Trump that hundreds of thousands of Americans could die.[5] But the president didn't seem to be listening. He was most concerned about the damage that rapid containment measures would do to the economy—and, consequently, to his ratings. Re-election was at stake. He looked for other things to talk about.

Over President's Day weekend, right around the time Italy went into emergency lockdown, a member of Mar-a-Lago presented Trump with an intriguing letter.[6] It contained a request from a Brazilian financier asking to set up an "informal visit" between Trump and Brazilian president Jair Bolsonaro at the "Southern White House" on March 7.

Trump decided that was a good plan. He and Bolsonaro had lots to talk about: immigration, security, trade, the "gift" Trump had given his Brazilian counterpart by not imposing metal tariffs.[7] Pressed for time, the summit was orchestrated not by State Department officials but by special interests and members of the president's club who paid little heed to red tape. "If we had gone through official channels, the meeting probably wouldn't have happened," the Brazilian financier told the *Miami Herald*.[8]

Concerns about the virus were officially brushed off by the White House.

"The American people deserve to know that the risk of contracting the coronavirus to the average American remains low," Vice President Mike Pence said while meeting with cruise industry executives in Fort Lauderdale just before the Bolsonaro summit.[9]

"It is safe for healthy Americans to travel," Pence said. "The American people can continue to go about their business." (The next day the CDC issued a statement warning people to avoid cruises.[10])

For his part, Trump felt invincible at his court.

"I'm not concerned at all," he said while standing outside Mar-a-Lago with Bolsonaro on March 7.[11] "No, I'm not. No, we've done a great job."

Within a week the president would declare a national emergency.

Not everyone in Trump's circle was so naive. On the day of the summit *Fox News* host Tucker Carlson made his first and only visit to the club on a mission to pull Trump aside and warn him about the virus that he believed "could be a massive problem in the United States."[12]

Carlson understood the reasons Trump and his White House were disinclined to acknowledge the impending crisis. He also knew the time for political hedging was long over. The pundit hated the idea of backdooring anything. He didn't want to be seen as *that guy*, another nonexpert whispering into the president's ear. But he had done his research, and he was worried. Very worried. And although Trump watched his show, Carlson wasn't sure that was enough to get this particular message across. He knew the best place to influence the president was at his club.

"I felt—and my wife strongly felt—that I had a moral obligation to try and be helpful in whatever way possible," Carlson told *Vanity Fair*.[13]

He asked the Secret Service to sneak him into the club so no one could see what he was doing. He spoke with the president for two hours. Pence also joined them for a time.

"I just want to make it clear this is totally real," Carlson said to the president. "People you know are going to get it."

It was already too late. Days later the bespectacled Brazilian press secretary who stood feet from Trump at Guilfoyle's fifty-first birthday party tested positive for COVID-19.[14] So did a senior Brazilian diplomat who also attended the Mar-a-Lago summit.

Thousands of people were potentially exposed to the contagion by guests at the club that weekend. Miami mayor Francis Suarez tested positive after meeting the Brazilian emissaries in Miami.[15] Congressman Matt Gaetz, who was at Guilfoyle's party, went into self-quarantine.[16] At least one person from Orlando who attended a campaign fundraiser hosted by Guilfoyle at the club the following day contracted the disease.[17] Many who were exposed flew home to New York and DC.

Despite his odds of contracting the disease, Trump initially refused to get tested. (He later did, saying the result was negative.[18])

Many Mar-a-Lago members were in a similar state of denial. A rumor circulated that the best way to stay healthy was to blast one's face with hot air from a hairdryer.[19]

Comforted by snake oil and loath to end the party season early, many Palm Beachers continued to go out to restaurants and clubs. When the news started sounding especially bad for Florida, some fired their housekeepers, fearing that the immigrants might bring the bug into their homes.

"I vacuumed for the first time today," a Mar-a-Lago member bragged in mid-March.[20] "I quite enjoyed it." Many kept going out.

What Palm Beachers didn't yet understand was that the virus didn't care how much money they had or about their superior upbringing or their connections or the color of their skin.

"The people at Mar-a-Lago are like the first class on the Titanic," a club staffer said in late March.[21] All that was missing were violins playing as the ship went down. "The world is going to shit in a handbag, and they're enjoying themselves?"

Facing the novel coronavirus, Trump was Napoleon at Waterloo. Overstretched and outmatched.

Mar-a-Lago stayed open until the bitter end. As charities started canceling galas, the club's restaurant and pool still welcomed members and guests. Then the restaurant closed, even as the tennis courts stayed open. Within two weeks of Trump brushing off the outbreak, the Winter White House caved to the inevitable. On March 20 members were informed that the club was closing indefinitely.[22]

Across Trump's businesses, more than fifteen hundred employees were laid off as a result of COVID-19 emergency closures.[23] By early April the Trump Organization was losing $1 million per day.[24] It didn't matter. Mar-a-Lago wouldn't reopen that season.

As this book goes to print, hospitals in Brooklyn and Detroit are stacking bodies.[25] Travelers who followed Pence's March 7 advice are dying on board cruise ships as port after port deny them entry, including the one in Fort Lauderdale where he'd played down the dangers.[26] And as Florida's death toll nears one thousand, more people have died of coronavirus in Palm Beach than almost any other county in the state.[27]

People had long predicted a terrible demise for Mar-a-Lago. Most Floridians just thought it would be a hurricane.

In the end, it wasn't that. It wasn't the emoluments lawsuits or the endless stream of trespassers that shuttered the club in the months leading up to the 2020 election.

It was a pandemic.

NOTES

PROLOGUE. INTRUDER AT THE WHITE HOUSE

1. Professor F. Blair Reeves, *Mar-a-Lago: Historic American Buildings Survey*, Office of Archeology and Historic Preservation, National Park Service, Department of the Interior (Spring 1967), 5, 12, 20, http://lcweb2.loc.gov/master/pnp/habshaer/fl/fl0100/fl0181/data/fl0181data.pdf.

2. Interview with Jeff Greene, October 4, 2019.

3. Interviews with former Mar-a-Lago staff members.

4. Interview with a former Mar-a-Lago member.

5. US Government Accountability Office, "Presidential Security: Vetting of Individuals and Secure Areas at Mar-a-Lago," January 2019, www.gao.gov/assets/700/696549.pdf.

6. Greene, November 4, 2019.

7. Rahel Gebreyes, "Mike Tyson Just Endorsed Donald Trump," *HuffPost*, October 26, 2015, https://www.huffpost.com/entry/mike-tyson-endorses-donald-trump-2016_n_562e8853e4b00aa54a4aba46.

8. Declaration of Domicile, Donald J. Trump, Palm Beach County Clerk's Office, CFN 2019 036427:1 (October 4, 2019).

9. Interview with a senior federal law enforcement official.

10. Liz Johnstone, "Tracking President Trump's Visits to Trump Properties," *NBC News*, October 22, 2019, www.nbcnews.com/politics/donald-trump/how-much-time-trump-spending-trump-properties-n753366.

11. Interview with one current and one former Mar-a-Lago employee.

12. Interviews with a second federal law enforcement official .

13. Police calls for service, January 10, 2020, Palm Beach Police.

14. *State of Florida v. Kelly Ann Weidman*, 50 S, No. 4 (Fla. 15th Cir. January 21, 2017).

15. *United States of America v. Mark Lindblom*, 18 F, No. 16, PACER (S.D. Fla. 2019).

16. Jane Musgrave, "College Freshman Slipped into Mar-a-Lago While Trump Was in Town," *Palm Beach Post*, May, 28, 2019, www.palmbeachpost.com/news/20190528/college-freshman-slipped-into-mar-a-lago-while-trump-was-in-town.

17. Greene, October 4, 2019.

18. US Government Accountability Office, "Presidential Security," www.gao.gov/assets/700/696549.pdf.

19. *United States of America v. Yujing Zhang*, trial testimony, Secret Service Agent Samuel Ivanovich, case no. 19-cr-80056, PACER (S.D. Florida, April 8, 2019).

20. Ibid.

21. Greene, October 4, 2019.

22. Interview with a Mar-a-Lago staff member.

23. Donald Trump, "Remarks by President Trump and Prime Minister Abe of Japan Before Bilateral Meeting," *The White House*, April 17, 2018, www.whitehouse.gov /briefings-statements/remarks-president-trump-prime-minister-abe-japan-bilateral -meeting-mar-a-lago-fl/.

24. Thousands of internal federal government emails collected through a Freedom of Information Act request by *Property of the People*, published online by *ProPublica*, April 29, 2019, www.documentcloud.org/documents/5982879-State-Department-Mar -a-Lago-Spending-Records.html#document/p33/a498206.

CHAPTER 1. KISSING THE RING

1. Interview with Guido Lombardi, July 11, 2019.

2. Ronald Kessler, *The Season: Inside Palm Beach and America's Richest Society* (New York: HarperTough, 1999).

3. Certificate of Marriage for Lombardi and Lahainer lists the groom's place of birth as Switzerland (Palm Beach, FL, 2000).

4. Lombardi, July 11, 2019.

5. Lombardi, July 4, 2019.

6. Professor F. Blair Reeves, *Mar-a-Lago: Historic American Buildings Survey*, Office of Archeology and Historic Preservation, National Park Service, Department of the Interior (Spring 1967), http://lcweb2.loc.gov/master/pnp/habshaer/fl/fl0100/fl0181 /data/fl0181data.pdf.

7. Ibid.

8. Interview with a former Mar-a-Lago staff member.

9. Interviews with former Mar-a-Lago staff members.

10. Interview with Ronald Kessler, December 30, 2019.

11. Lloyd Grove, "Is Chris Ruddy the One Person to Make Trump Sound Sane?," *Daily Beast*, January 13, 2018, www.thedailybeast.com/is-chris-ruddy-the-one-person -to-make-trump-sound-sane; and Isaac Arnsdorf, "The Shadow Rulers of the VA," *ProPublica*, August 7, 2018, www.propublica.org/article/ike-perlmutter-bruce-moskowitz -marc-sherman-shadow-rulers-of-the-va.

12. Doug Kyed, "Why Robert Kraft Will Support Donald Trump Despite Political Differences," *New England Sports Network*, May 3, 2017, https://nesn.com/2017/05 /why-robert-kraft-will-support-donald-trump-despite-political-differences/.

13. Nicholas Vinocur, "Donald Trump's European Fixer . . . Is His Neighbor," *Politico*, December 5, 2016, www.politico.eu/article/trumps-ambassador-europe-far -right-news-lombardi/.

14. Reeves, *Mar-a-Lago*.

15. Julie Brown, "Cops Worked to Put Serial Sex Abuser in Prison. Prosecutors Worked to Cut Him a Break," *Miami Herald*, November 28, 2018, www.miami herald.com/news/local/article214210674.html.

16. The authors viewed a membership list showing that Epstein's account had been closed.

17. Lombardi, July 11, 2019.

18. David A. Fahrenthold, Beth Reinhard, and Kimberly Kindy, "Trump Called Epstein a 'Terrific Guy' Who Enjoyed 'Younger' Women Before Denying Relationship with Him," *Washington Post*, July 8, 2019, www.washingtonpost.com/politics /trump-called-epstein-a-terrific-guy-before-denying-relationship-with-him/2019/07/08 /a01e0f00-a1be-11e9-bd56-eac6bb02d01d_story.html.

19. James Hendicott, "Donald Trump: Michael Jackson Lost His Confidence Due to 'Bad, Bad, Bad Facial Surgery'," *NME*, February 19, 2016, nme.com/news/music /michael-jackson-11-1198588.

20. National Park Service, "National Historic Landmarks," Updated: February 21, 2020, www.nps.gov/subjects/nationalhistoriclandmarks/list-of-nhls-by-state.htm.

21. Ellyn Ferguson, "Trump Takes Possession of Mar-a-Lago," *Miami Herald*, December 29, 1985, www.miamiherald.com/news/politics-government/election/donald -trump/article132286214.html.

22. Tom Winter, "Trump Bankruptcy Math Doesn't Add Up," *NBC News*, June 24, 2016, www.nbcnews.com/news/us-news/trump-bankruptcy-math-doesn-t -add-n598376.

23. Ronald Kessler, "The Anatomy of a Trump Decision," *Washington Times*, April 26, 2017, www.washingtontimes.com/news/2017/apr/26/trump-decisions-show-there -is-more-than-chaos-in-w/.

24. Jacqueline Bueno, "Trump's Palm Beach Club Roils the Old Social Order," *Wall Street Journal*, April 30, 1997, www.wsj.com/articles/SB862335923489989500.

25. Trump Organization (@trump) "#FryDay never looked so good," Instagram photo, May 10, 2019, www.instagram.com/p/BxSyvzalqkB/.

26. Laura Litinsky, "The Mar-a-Lago Club," *Florida Design* 15, no. 4, www.maralago club.com/files/Florida%20Design%20Magazine-%20Donald%20Trump_s%20 Mar%20a%20Lago.pdf.

27. Christine Stapleton and Carolyn DiPaolo, "Trump in Palm Beach: A Look Back at New Year's Eve at Mar-a-Lago," *Palm Beach Post*, December 28 2019, www.palm beachpost.com/news/trump-palm-beach-look-back-new-year-eve-mar-lago/GKEmRN bGFPXFXJc7XeaJ3K/.

28. Kimberly Chrisman-Campbell, "How Gold Went from Godly to Gaudy," *Atlantic*, December 2, 2016, www.theatlantic.com/entertainment/archive/2016/12/the-midas -touch-gold-trump-gouthiere/509036/.

29. Interview with Fred Rustmann, December 6, 2019.

30. Stapleton and DiPaolo, "Trump in Palm Beach."

31. Rustmann, December 6, 2019.

32. George Bennett, "Trump in Palm Beach: Rare Golf Outing with Jack Nicklaus, Tiger Woods," *Palm Beach Post*, February 2, 2019, www.palmbeachpost.com /news/20190202/trump-in-palm-beach-rare-golf-outing-with-jack-nicklaus-tiger -woods.

33. Antonio Fins, "Trump in Palm Beach: Rush Limbaugh Appears to Be at Lunch with President," *Palm Beach Post*, December 22, 2019.

34. Interview with Jeff Greene, November 4, 2019.

35. Interview with a Mar-a-Lago staff member.

36. Interview with a former Mar-a-Lago staff member.

37. Interview with a Mar-a-Lago staff member.

38. Interview with a former Mar-a-Lago staff member.

39. Ibid.

40. Lombardi, July 11, 2019.

41. Interview with a former Mar-a-Lago staff member.

42. Interviews with two former Mar-a-Lago staff members.

43. Lombardi, July 11, 2019.

44. Interview with a former Mar-a-Lago staff member.

45. Greene, November 4, 2019.

46. Interview with three sources familiar with Mar-a-Lago operations.

47. Interview with a former Mar-a-Lago staff member.

48. Interviews with two sources who frequent the club.

49. Interview with Valentina Deva, October 31, 2019.

50. Interviews with two former Mar-a-Lago staff members.

51. Rustmann, December 6, 2019.

52. Interview with a Mar-a-Lago member.

53. Lombardi, July 11, 2019.

54. Agence France-Presse, "Mongolia Invites North Korean Leader Kim Jong-un to Visit Capital," *South China Morning Post*, October 16, 2018, www.scmp.com/news /asia/east-asia/article/2168846/mongolia-invites-north-korean-leader-kim-jong-un -visit-capital.

55. Isabella Steger, "When It Comes to North Korean Diplomacy, Keep an Eye on Mongolia," *Quartz*, October 19, 2018, www.qz.com/1429643/could-mongolia-host-the -next-summit-between-donald-trump-and-north-korea-leader-kim-jong-un/.

56. Edward Cavanough, "Trump, Kim, Mongolia? A Dream Fades in the Switzerland of Asia," *South China Morning Post*, May 6, 2018, www.scmp.com/week-asia /geopolitics/article/2144777/trump-kim-mongolia-dream-fades-switzerland-asia.

57. Chris Kaplonski, "Prelude to Violence: Show Trials and State Power in 1930s Mongolia," *American Ethnologist* 35, no. 2 (May 2008), www.chriskaplonski.com /downloads/PreludeToViolence.pdf.

58. Lombardi, July 11, 2019.

59. Photograph provided to the authors by Guido Lombardi shows Donald Trump, Mongolian diplomat, and Lombardi on the terrace at Mar-a-Lago.

60. Photograph provided to the authors by Guido Lombardi shows Koch in a discussion with the Mongolian emissaries.

61. Lombardi, July 11, 2019.

62. Photograph provided to the authors by Guido Lombardi show him standing in front of a statue of Genghis Khan during a personal trip to Ulaanbaatar.

63. Terrence Edwards, "Former Martial Arts Star Battulga Wins Mongolian Presidential Election," Reuters, July 8, 2017, www.reuters.com/article/us-mongolia-election /former-martial-arts-star-battulga-wins-mongolian-presidential-election-idUSKBN19 T05Z.

64. Matthew Campbell and Terrence Edwards, "Mongolia's Khaltmaa Battulga, the Other Populist President with a Business Background and Ties to Putin," *South China*

Morning Post, October 4, 2019, www.scmp.com/magazines/post-magazine/long-reads/article/3031376/mongolias-khaltmaa-battulga-other-populist.

65. Matthew Campbell and Terrence Edwards, "Mongolia's President Is a Genghis Khan-Idolizing Trump of the Steppe," *Bloomberg*, September 26, 2019, www.bloomberg.com/news/features/2019-09-26/mongolia-s-president-is-the-trump-of-east-asia.

66. Cavanough, "Trump, Kim, Mongolia?"

67. Ibid.

68. Hannah Ellis-Petersen and Kate Lyons, "Vietnam Summit: Donald Trump and Kim Jong-un Meet in Hanoi—As It Happened," *Guardian*, February 27, 2019, www.theguardian.com/world/live/2019/feb/27/donald-trump-kim-jong-un-summit-vietnam-north-korea-hanoi-live?

69. Lisa Gutierrez, "'Great Spiritual Awakening': Pastors Lay Hands on Donald Trump in the Oval Office," *Kansas City Star*, July 12, 2017, www.kansascity.com/news/nation-world/article160904779.html.

CHAPTER 2. BETTER THAN SEX

1. Ronald Kessler, *The Season: Inside Palm Beach and America's Richest Society* (New York: HarperTough, 1999).

2. Interview with Guido Lombardi, July 11, 2019.

3. Russ Buettner and Charles V. Bagli, "How Donald Trump Bankrupted His Atlantic City Casinos, but Still Earned Millions," *New York Times*, June 11, 2016, www.nytimes.com/2016/06/12/nyregion/donald-trump-atlantic-city.html.

4. Kessler, *The Season*.

5. "Frank Lahainer (1904–1995)," updated December 28, 2016, www.findagrave.com/memorial/174617877/frank-lahainer.

6. Lombardi, July 11, 2019.

7. Clintonlibrary 42, "Pres. Clinton at Natl. Italian-American Foundation Dinner (1994)," YouTube, November 19, 2018, www.youtube.com/watch?v=jtX-Sg18hKU.

8. National Italian American Foundation, "NIAF Mourns the Passing of Supreme Court Justice Antonin Scalia," news release, February 13, 2016, www.niaf.org/niaf_event/niaf-mourns-the-passing-of-supreme-court-justice-antonin-scalia/.

9. Alexander Stille, "How Matteo Salvini Pulled Italy to the Far Right," *Guardian*, August 9, 2018, www.theguardian.com/news/2018/aug/09/how-matteo-salvini-pulled-italy-to-the-far-right.

10. Alessio Perrone, "A Different League—How Italy's Far-Right Lega Nord Let Go of Its Roots to Govern," *Delayed Gratification*, May 31, 2018, www.slow-journalism.com/delayed-gratification-magazine/a-different-league-how-italys-far-right-lega-nord-let-go-of-its-roots-to-govern.

11. Roberto Saviano, "Fascism Is Back in Italy and It's Paralysing the Political System," *Guardian*, February 10, 2019, www.theguardian.com/commentisfree/2018/feb/11/fascism-is-back-in-italy-and-its-paralysing-politics.

12. Daniele Albertazzi, Arianna Giovannini, and Antonella Seddone "'No Regionalism Please, We Are *Leghisti*!' The Transformation of the Italian Lega Nord Under the Leadership of Matteo Salvini," *Regional & Federal Studies* 28, no. 5 (2018): 645–671, doi: 10.1080/13597566.2018.1512977.

13. Crispian Balmer, "Italy's League Leaves Northern Bastions, Bangs Anti-Migrant Drum," *Reuters*, February 9, 2018, www.reuters.com/article/us-italy-election-league /italys-league-leaves-northern-bastions-bangs-anti-migrant-drum-idUSKBN1FT1Q9.

14. Alessandro Franzi, "L'amico italiano di Trump? Un tempo inneggiava alla Padania," *Linkiesta*, January 21, 2017, www.linkiesta.it/it/article/2017/01/21/lamico -italiano-di-trump-un-tempo-inneggiava-alla-padania/33007/; and according to filings maintained by the Florida Department of State's Division of Corporate Records on Amici Leganord, Inc.

15. Lombardi, July 4, 2019.

16. Certificate of marriage for Lombardy and Lahainer (Palm Beach, FL, 2000).

17. Roberto Maroni (@RobertoMaroni_), "Con Donald Trump a New York, qual- che anno," Twitter, May 21, 2016.

18. Guidogeorge Lombardi, "Mar a lago D Trump and George Lombardi Com- pressed," May 3, 2016, YouTube, www.youtube.com/watch?v=9ik9Iy3J24w.

19. "Anti-Muslim," Southern Poverty Law Center, www.splcenter.org/fighting-hate /extremist-files/ideology/anti-muslim.

20. Lombardi, "Mar a lago D Trump and George Lombardi Compressed."

21. Lombardi, July 11, 2019.

22. Jim Yardley and Gaia Pianigiani, "Italian Court Upholds Berlusconi's Acquit- tal in Sex Case," *New York Times*, March 11, 2015, www.nytimes.com/2015/03/12/world /europe/italian-court-upholds-berlusconis-acquittal-in-sex-parties-case.html.

23. Bianca Soldani, "Inside the Corruption Investigations That Rocked Italy to Its Core," *SBS News*, September 28, 2016, www.sbs.com.au/news/inside-the-corrup- tion-investigations-that-rocked-italy-to-its-core.

24. Ewen MacAskill, "Donald Trump Bows Out of 2012 US Presidential Election Race," *Guardian*, May 16, 2011, www.theguardian.com/world/2011/may/16/donald -trump-us-presidential-race.

25. Lombardi, July 4, 2019.

26. Joshua Gillin, "Bush Says Trump Was a Democrat Longer Than a Republican 'In the Last Decade," *Politifact*, August 24, 2015, www.politifact.com/factchecks/2015 /aug/24/jeb-bush/bush-says-trump-was-democrat-longer-republican-las/.

27. Interview with Pam Wohlschlegel, December 16, 2019.

28. Alex Leary, "That Time Donald Trump Met the Tea Party in Florida and Saw the Path to 2016," *Tampa Bay Times*, September 10, 2016, www.tampabay.com/news /politics/stateroundup/that-time-donald-trump-met-the-tea-party-in-florida-and-saw -the-path-to/2292984

29. Wohlschlegel, December 16, 2019.

30. Ibid.

31. "Speech: Donald Trump Attends a Tea Party Rally in Boca Raton, FL," C-SPAN, YouTube, April 16, 2011, www.youtube.com/watch?v=P5UiVPI23bM.

32. Laura Davison and Andrew M. Harris, "How Trump's Tax Returns Could Become Public," *Bloomberg*, November 25, 2018, www.washingtonpost.com/business /how-trumps-tax-returns-could-become-public/2019/12/12/b919e37a-1d2f-11ea-977a -15a6710ed6da_story.html.

33. Karen Tumulty, "How Donald Trump Came Up with 'Make America Great Again,'" *Washington Post*, January 18, 2017, www.washingtonpost.com/politics/how

-donald-trump-came-up-with-make-america-great-again/2017/01/17/fb6acf5e-dbf7
-11e6-ad42-f3375f271c9c_story.html.

34. Leary, "That Time Donald Trump Met the Tea Party in Florida and Saw the Path to 2016."

35. Rebekah Monson, "Trump Picks Up the Tab for Boca Raton Tea Party Rally," *South Florida Sun Sentinel*, June 22, 2011, www.sun-sentinel.com/sfl-mtblog-2011-06 -trump_picks_up_the_tab_for_tea-story.html.

36. Lombardi, July 4, 2019.

37. Leary, "That Time Donald Trump Met the Tea Party in Florida and Saw the Path to 2016."

38. Alan Silverleib, "Obama Releases Original Long-Form Birth Certificate," CNN, April 27, 2011, www.cnn.com/2011/POLITICS/04/27/obama.birth.certificate/index .html.

39. "President Obama at the 2011 White House Correspondents' Dinner," C-SPAN, YouTube, April 30, 2011, www.youtube.com/watch?v=n9mzJhvC-8E.

40. "Donald Trump Joins Allen West at Tea Party Rally in Boca Raton," *Crowley Political Report*, April 14, 2011, www.crowleypoliticalreport.com/2011/04/donald -trump-joins-allen-west-at-tea-party-rally-in-boca-raton.html.

41. News Service of Florida, "Retiring GOP Operative Mac Stipanovich Says Trump 'Sensed the Rot' in Republican Party and Took Control of It," *Orlando Sentinel,* December 24, 2019, www.orlandosentinel.com/politics/os-ne-mac-stipanovich-republican -20191224-tz7bjps56jazbcwb3ficlnacqa-story.html.

42. Interview with Maycol and Lilian, December 4, 2019.

43. Interview with Phil Gordon, May 12, 2017.

44. Philip Bump, "Trump Returns to Phoenix, the Place His Campaign Truly Began," *Washington Post*, August 22, 2017, www.washingtonpost.com/news/politics /wp/2017/08/22/trump-returns-to-phoenix-the-place-his-campaign-truly-began/.

45. The authors' analysis of data from the US Department of Labor's Public Job Registry.

46. Ken Bensinger, Jeremy Singer-Vine, and Jessica Garrison, "Trump Says Mar-A-Lago Can't Find US Workers to Hire. New Documents Show Dozens Applied," *BuzzFeed*, April 26, 2019, www.buzzfeednews.com/article/kenbensinger/mar-a-lago -rejected-dozens-of-americans-in-favor-of-foreign.

47. Analysis by the Center for Responsive Politics, www.opensecrets.org/orgs/re cips.php?id=D000000186&cycle=2016&state=&party=&chamber=&sort=A&page=1.

48. Interview with Harry Hurt III, December 17, 2019.

49. Ibid.

50. Robert Costa and Anne Gearan, "Donald Trump Talked Politics with Bill Clinton Weeks Before Launching 2016 Bid," *Washington Post*, August 5, 2015, www .washingtonpost.com/politics/bill-clinton-called-donald-trump-ahead-of-republicans -2016-launch/2015/08/05/e2b30bb8-3ae3-11e5-b3ac-8a79bc44e5e2_story.html.

51. Interview with Rodney Howard-Browne, October 29, 2019.

52. Derek Kravitz, "How Taxpayers Covered a $1,000 Liquor Bill for Trump Staffers (and More) at Trump's Club," *ProPublica*, May 1, 2019, www.propublica.org/article /trump-inc-podcast-taxpayers-covered-liquor-bill-for-trump-staffers-and-more-mar-a -lago.

53. River School of Government (@rsgovernment), "The Mar-a-Lago Club (Pictured: Pastor Kenneth Howard-Browne and President of the River Bible Institutes)," Instagram, April 20, 2019.

54. "The American Pro-Israel PAC," accessed January 4, 2020, https://apip.org/.

55. Christine Stapleton, "Where Did Pro-Israel PAC Go After Mar-a-Lago? No One Seems to Know," *Palm Beach Post*, September 27, 2019, www.palmbeachpost .com/news/20190927/where-did-pro-israel-pac-go-after-mar-a-lago-no-one-seems-to -know.

56. Lachlan Markay, "God Declares Swamp Drained at Mar-a-Lago Super PAC Fundraiser," *Daily Beast*, December 6, 2018, www.thedailybeast.com/god-declares -swamp-drained-at-mar-a-lago-super-pac-fundraiser.

57. Letter to American Pro-Israel PAC, Federal Election Commission, August 15, 2019, www.docquery.fec.gov/pdf/736/201908150300045736/201908150300045736.pdf; Letter to American Pro-Israel PAC, Federal Election Commission, February 19, 2020, www.docquery.fec.gov/pdf/239/202002190300057239/202002190300057239.pdf.

58. A program for the event lists Guido Lombardi as welcoming guests.

59. Interview with Edwin Sepulveda, October 1, 2019.

60. Lombardi, July 11, 2019.

61. Yondon Otgonbayar (@OtgonbayarY), "US National Security Adviser Amb. John Bolton visits Mongolia," Twitter, June. 30, 2019, https://twitter.com/OtgonbayarY /status/1145287555409047552?s=20.

62. Hayes Brown, "Enough Jokes, You Guys, John Bolton Clearly Wanted to Be in Mongolia," *Buzzfeed*, July 1, 2019, www.buzzfeednews.com/article/hayesbrown/john -bolton-mongolia-north-korea.

63. Natasha Turak, "Trump Becomes First Sitting US President in History to Cross Border into North Korea," CNBC, June 30, 2019, www.cnbc.com/2019/06/30/rtrs -190630-trump-kim-quotes-dmz-eu.html.

64. Philip Rucker and Karen Tumulty, "Donald Trump Is Holding a Government Casting Call. He's Seeking 'the Look,'" *Washington Post*, December 22, 2016, www .washingtonpost.com/politics/donald-trump-is-holding-a-government-casting-call-hes -seeking-the-look/2016/12/21/703ae8a4-c795-11e6-bf4b-2c064d32a4bf_story.html?.

65. John Bolton, "The Legal Case for Striking North Korea First," *Wall Street Journal*, February 28, 2018, www.wsj.com/articles/the-legal-case-for-striking-north-korea -first-1519862374.

66. Jonathan Lemire, Zeke Miller, and Deb Riechmann, "Inside Bolton's Exit: Mongolia, a Mustache, a Tweet," Associated Press, September 11, 2019, www.apnews .com/b4abacafde4d4e4cbed26a6d33ddf279.

67. MNB World, "Minister of Foreign Affairs Reported the Conclusion of U.S. National Security Advisor John Bolton's Visit," Facebook, July 3, 2019, www.facebook .com/watch/?v=1100408876820456.

68. Lauren Egan, "Trump Names Horse Gifted by Mongolian President: 'Victory'," *NBC News*, July 31, 2019, www.nbcnews.com/politics/donald-trump/trump -settles-name-horse-gifted-mongolian-president-victory-n1037386.

69. Siobhán O'Grady, "The Trump Administration and Mongolia Are Getting Cozy. Here's Why," *Washington Post*, August 8, 2019, www.washingtonpost.com /world/2019/08/08/trump-administration-mongolia-are-getting-cozy-heres-why.

70. Jake Pearson and Anand Tumurtogoo, "Donald Trump Jr. Went to Mongolia, Got Special Treatment from the Government and Killed an Endangered Sheep," *ProPublica*, December 11, 2019, www.propublica.org/article/trump-inc-podcast -donald-trump-jr-went-to-mongolia-got-special-treatment-from-the-government-and -killed-an-endangered-sheep.

71. Batchimeg B., "Foreign Affairs Minister Meets US President Donald Trump," *Montsame*, September 27, 2019, www.montsame.mn/en/read/201937.

CHAPTER 3. KING OF THE SWAMP

1. James B. Stewart and Jesse Drucker, "Milken Had Key Allies in Pardon Bid: Trump's Inner Circle," *New York Times*, March 1, 2020, www.nytimes.com/2020/03/01 /business/michael-milken-trump-pardon.html.

2. Michael Strauss, "Trump Nets Namesake Tourney Win for Charity," *Palm Beach Daily News*, February 27, 2001, www.thegivingtrump.com/donald-trump-hosts-the-4th -annual-cap-cure-pro-am-tennis-benefit-raised-2-5-million-for-prostate-cancer/.

3. Interview with Fred Rustamann, December 6, 2019.

4. A series of interviews with a Mar-a-Lago staff member.

5. "Australian Open 2014: Novak Djokovic into Round Four," BBC News, January 17, 2014, www.bbc.com/sport/tennis/25771715.

6. "Malaria," Florida Department of Health, www.floridahealth.gov/diseases-and -conditions/mosquito-borne-diseases/_documents/guidebook-chapter-eight.pdf.

7. "Elimination of Malaria in the United States (1947–1951)," CDC, updated July 23, 2018, www.cdc.gov/malaria/about/history/elimination_us.html.

8. John Kelly, "What's with All Trump's Talk About 'Draining the Swamp'?" *Slate*, October 26, 2016, www.slate.com/human-interest/2016/10/why-do-trump-and-his -supports-keep-talking-about-draining-the-swamp.html.

9. Winfield P. Gaylord, "Letter to the Editor," *Daily Northwestern*, October 10, 1903, www.newspapers.com/clip/42737754/drain-the-swamp-1903/.

10. Peter Overby, "Trump's Efforts to 'Drain the Swamp' Lagging Behind His Campaign Rhetoric," NPR, www.npr.org/2017/04/26/525551816/trumps-efforts-to-drain -the-swamp-lagging-behind-his-campaign-rhetoric.

11. Ted Widmer, "Draining the Swamp," *New Yorker*, January 19, 2017, www.new yorker.com/news/news-desk/draining-the-swamp.

12. Donald Trump (@realdonaldtrump), "Hillary is the most corrupt person to ever run for the presidency of the United States. #DrainTheSwamp," Twitter, October 18, 2016, https://twitter.com/realdonaldtrump/status/788538743950938112?lang=en.

13. "Transcript of the August 6, 2015, Republican Presidential Debate," Rev, updated July 25, 2019, www.rev.com/blog/first-2015-republican-primary-Debate-transcript -classic-debates-from-2016-election-cycle.

14. Nick Gass, "Trump Has Spent Years Courting Hillary and Other Dems," *Politico*, June 16, 2015, www.politico.com/story/2015/06/donald-trump-donations-democrats -hillary-clinton-119071.

15. Erin Dooley, "Donald Trump Says His Money Drew Hillary Clinton to His Wedding," *ABC News*, August 7, 2015, https://abcnews.go.com/Politics/trump-money -drew-hillary-clinton-wedding/story?id=32936868.

16. Kathryn Watson, "'You All Just Got a Lot Richer,' Trump Tells Friends, Referencing Tax Overhaul," *CBS News*, December 24, 2017, www.cbsnews.com/news/trump-mar-a-lago-christmas-trip/.

17. Thomas Graham, "The First Developers," in *The History of Florida*, ed. Michael Gannon (Gainesville: University Press of Florida, 2013).

18. Joe Knetsch, "Hamilton Disston and the Development of Florida," *Sunland Tribune* 24, no. 3 (2018), https://defendersofcrookedlake.com/document/Hamilton-Disston-and-the-Development-of-Florida.pdf.

19. Graham, "The First Developers."

20. Frederick Davis, "The Disston Land Purchase," *Florida Historical Quarterly* 17, no. 3 (January 1939): 200–210.

21. Laurence Leamer, *Mar-a-Lago: Inside the Gates of Power at Donald Trump's Presidential Palace* (New York: Flatiron Books, 2019).

22. Nancy Rubin, *American Empress: The Life and Times of Marjorie Merriweather Post* (New York: iUniverse Star, 2004).

23. Ibid.

24. David Foxley, "The Kennedy Winter White House Is Updated with the Unexpected," *Architectural Digest*, December 11, 2017, www.architecturaldigest.com/story/kennedy-winter-white-house-palm-beach.

25. Don Snider, "Party Time at Mar-a-Lago," *South Florida Sun Sentinel*, June 18, 1995, www.sun-sentinel.com/news/fl-xpm-1995-06-18-9506220187-story.html.

26. Quit claim deed between the United States of America and the Marjorie Merriweather Post Foundation, Palm Beach County Property Appraiser, March 23, 1981.

27. Julie Eagle, "Trump Closes on Mar-a-Lago," *South Florida Sun Sentinel*, December 28, 1985, www.sun-sentinel.com/news/fl-xpm-1985-12-28-8503010217-story.html.

28. Kristine Phillips, "The Story of Donald Trump's Grandfather, Who Came to the U.S. as an Unaccompanied Minor," *Washington Post*, July 12, 2018, www.washingtonpost.com/news/retropolis/wp/2018/06/27/the-story-of-donald-trumps-grandfather-who-came-to-the-u-s-as-an-unaccompanied-minor/.

29. Donald Trump and Kate Bohner, *Trump: The Art of the Comeback* (New York: Times Books, 1997), 61–62.

30. Ibid.

31. Eagle, "Trump Closes on Mar-a-Lago."

32. Michael Kranish, "A Fierce Will to Win Pushed Donald Trump to the Top," *Washington Post*, January 19, 2017, www.washingtonpost.com/politics/a-fierce-will-to-win-pushed-donald-trump-to-the-top/2017/01/17/6b36c2ce-c628-11e6-8bee-54e800ef2a63_story.html.

33. Ibid.

34. Jonathan Mahler and Steve Eder, "'No Vacancies' for Blacks: How Donald Trump Got His Start, and Was First Accused of Bias," *New York Times*, August 27, 2019, www.nytimes.com/2016/08/28/us/politics/donald-trump-housing-race.html.

35. Michael Kranish and Robert O'Harrow Jr., "Inside the Government's Racial Bias Case Against Donald Trump's Company, and How He Fought It," *Washington Post*, January 23, 2016, www.washingtonpost.com/politics/inside-the-governments-racial-bias-case-against-donald-trumps-company-and-how-he-fought-it/2016/01/23/fb90163e-bfbe-11e5-bcda-62a36b394160_story.html.

36. Dan Mangan, "FBI Releases Files on President Trump's Late Lawyer, Roy Cohn," CNBC, September 27, 2019, www.cnbc.com/2019/09/27/fbi-releases-file-on -trumps-late-lawyer-roy-cohn.html.

37. Kranish, "A Fierce Will to Win Pushed Donald Trump to the Top."

38. Mahler and Eder, "'No Vacancies' for Blacks.'"

39. "Decades-Old Housing Discrimination Case Plagues Donald Trump," NPR, September 29, 2016, www.npr.org/2016/09/29/495955920/donald-trump-Plagued-by -decades-old-housing-discrimination-case; and David Corn, "Here's Another Time a Trump Company Was Sued for Discriminating Against Black People," *Mother Jones*, October 25, 2016, www.motherjones.com/politics/2016/10/another-housing -discrimination-lawsuit-donald-trump/.

40. Joe Palazzolo and Michael Rothfeld, *The Fixers: The Bottom-Feeders, Crooked Lawyers, Gossipmongers, and Porn Stars Who Created the 45th President* (New York: Random House, 2020).

41. Jason M. Breslow, "The Frontline Interview: Barbara Res," PBS, September 27, 2016, www.pbs.org/wgbh/frontline/article/the-frontline-interview-barbara-res/.

42. Michael Kruse, "The Executive Mr. Trump," *Politico Magazine*, July/August 2016, https://www.politico.com/magazine/story/2016/07/2016-donald-trump-boss -employer-company-hired-fired-employees-workers-management-business-214020.

43. Interview with Niall O'Dowd, December 3, 2019.

44. Michael Kruse, "How Gotham Gave Us Trump," *Politico Magazine*, June 30, 2017, www.politico.com/magazine/story/2017/06/30/donald-trump-new-york-city-crime -1970s-1980s-215316.

45. Wayne Barrett, "How a Young Donald Trump Forced His Way from Avenue Z to Manhattan," *Village Voice*, July 20, 2015, www.villagevoice.com/2015/07/20/how-a -young-donald-trump-forced-his-way-from-avenue-z-to-manhattan/.

46. Charles Kaiser, "Financing Is Set for Rebuilding of Commodore," *New York Times*, December 23, 1977, www.nytimes.com/1977/12/23/archives/financing-is-set-for -rebuilding-of-commodore-financing-arranged-for.html; and Charles V. Bagli, "A Trump Empire Built on Inside Connections and $885 Million in Tax Breaks," *New York Times*, September 17, 2016, www.nytimes.com/2016/09/18/nyregion/donald-trump-tax -breaks-real-estate.html.

47. Kruse, "How Gotham Gave Us Trump."

48. Marie Brenner, "Trumping the Town," *New York*, November 17, 1980, books .google.com/books?id=a-UCAAAAMBAJ&lpg=PP1&dq=trump&pg=PA26#v=one page&q&f=false.

49. Judy Klemesrud, "Donald Trump, Real Estate Promoter, Builds Image as He Buys Buildings," *New York Times*, November 1, 1976, www.nytimes.com/1976/11 /01/archives/donald-trump-real-estate-promoter-builds-image-as-he-buys-buildings .html.

50. Ibid.

51. According to a Mar-a-Lago member list reviewed by the authors.

52. Michael Kruse, "How Gotham Gave Us Trump."

53. Ronald Kessler, *The Season: Inside Palm Beach and America's Richest Society* (New York: HarperTough, 1999).

54. Interview with Ildikó Varga, December 6, 2019.

55. Susan Spencer-Wendel, "Crystal Designer Carving a Nice Niche in Florida," *Palm Beach Post*, June 4, 1995, www.newspapers.com/image/134412722/.

56. Ibid.

57. Leamer, *Mar-a-Lago*.

58. Les Standiford, *Palm Beach, Mar-a-Lago, and the Rise of America's Xanadu* (New York: Atlantic Monthly Press, 2019).

59. Kurt Greenbaum, "Trump Estate Offer Disputed," *South Florida Sun Sentinel*, March 30, 1988, www.sun-sentinel.com/news/fl-xpm-1988-03-30-8801200666-story.html.

60. Standiford, *Palm Beach, Mar-a-Lago, and the Rise of America's Xanadu*.

61. Leamer, *Mar-a-Lago*.

62. Russ Buettner and Susanne Craig, "Decade in the Red: Trump Tax Figures Show over $1 Billion in Business Losses," *New York Times*, May 8, 2019, www.nytimes.com/interactive/2019/05/07/us/politics/donald-trump-taxes.html.

63. Interview with Guido Lombardi, July 4, 2019.

64. *Walker v. Trump*, 549 So.2d 1098, 1102 (Fla. 4th DCA 1989).

65. Lombardi, July 4, 2019.

66. Leamer, *Mar-a-Lago*.

67. Donald Trump, *The Art of the Deal* (New York: Ballantine Books, 1987).

68. Mary Jordan and Rosalind S. Helderman, "Inside Trump's Palm Beach Castle and His 30-Year Fight to Win over the Locals," *Washington Post*, November 14, 2015, washingtonpost.com/politics/inside-trumps-palm-beach-castle-and-his-30-year-fight-to-win-over-the-locals/2015/11/14/26c49a58-88b7-11e5-be8b-1ae2e4f50f76_story.html.

69. Chase Peterson-Withorn, "Donald Trump Has Gained More Than $100 Million on Mar-a-Lago," *Forbes*, April 23, 2018, www.forbes.com/sites/chasewithorn/2018/04/23/donald-trump-has-gained-more-than-100-million-on-mar-a-lago/#31bbca1b5adc.

70. Lombardi, July 4, 2019.

71. Jacqueline Bueno, "Trump's Palm Beach Club Roils the Old Social Order," *Wall Street Journal*, April 30, 1997, www.wsj.com/articles/SB862335923489989500.

72. Sharon Churcher, "Making It by Doing Good," *New York Times*, July 3, 1988, www.nytimes.com/1988/07/03/magazine/making-it-by-doing-good.html.

73. David Corn, "Donald Trump Disses J. Lo's Butt—and More Misogynistic Comments from the GOP Leader," *Mother Jones*, March 17, 2016, www.motherjones.com/politics/2016/03/trump-women-comments-misogyny-jennifer-lopez-melania-breasts.

74. Leamer, *Mar-a-Lago*.

75. United Press International, "Trump Sues over Property Taxes," *Key West Citizen*, January 13, 1987.

76. Associated Press, "Trump Wins Tax Fight over Florida Estate," *Northwest Florida Daily News*, April 10, 1988.

77. Associated Press, "Trump Loses Tax Fight," *Panama City News Herald*, September 29, 1989.

78. Russ Buettner and Charles V. Bagli, "How Donald Trump Bankrupted His Atlantic City Casinos, but Still Earned Millions," *New York Times*, June 11, 2016, www.nytimes.com/2016/06/12/nyregion/donald-trump-atlantic-city.html.

79. Michael Crook, "Estate May Sprout Mansions," *Miami Herald*, February 19, 1991.

80. Trump and Bohner, *Trump: The Art of the Comeback*.

81. Leamer, *Mar-a-Lago*.

82. Ibid.

83. Associated Press, "Trump Making Estate a Private Social Club," *Northwest Florida Daily News*, May 15, 1993.

84. Trump and Bohner, *Trump: The Art of the Comeback*.

85. Palm Beach County Clerk's OFfice, Deed of Development Rights, 20020547996, September 13, 2002.

86. Varga, December 6, 2019.

87. Interview with Harry Hurt III, December 17, 2019.

88. Interview with Fred Weinberg, December 22, 2019.

89. Interview with Sandi Bachom, December 15, 2019.

90. Bueno, "Trump's Palm Beach Club Roils the Old Social Order."

91. Julia Ioffe, "Melania Trump on Her Rise, Her Family Secrets, and Her True Political Views: 'Nobody Will Ever Know,'" *GQ*, www.gq.com/story/melania-trump-gq -interview.

92. Steve Straehley, "U.S. Ambassador to the Dominican Republic: Who Is Robin Bernstein?" Allgov.com, November 13, 2017, www.allgov.com/news/top-stories/us-am bassador-To-the-Dominican-republic-who-is-robin-bernstein-171113?news=860362.

93. Ron Kampeas, "Robin Bernstein Talked Up Trump to Her Jewish Community. Now She's the Pick for Dominican Republic Ambassador," *Jewish Telegraphic Agency*, November 2, 2017, www.jta.org/2017/11/02/united-states/robin-bernstein-talked -up-trump-to-her-jewish-community-now-shes-the-pick-for-dominican-republic -ambassador.

94. Alex Leary, "Greetings from Mar-a-Lago: Donald Trump's Presidential Paradise," *Tampa Bay Times*, November 24, 2016, www.tampabay.com/news/politics/state roundup/greetings-from-mar-a-lago-donald-trumps-presidential-paradise/2303982/.

95. Juju Bernstein (@lajuuuju), "Thankful to spend Sunday funday with my oldest friends #since1993," November 29, 2015, www.instagram.com/p/-riVWMKhQH/.

96. "Exclusive photos: Donald Trump's Palm Beach Wedding," *Palm Beach Post*, August 13, 2018, www.palmbeachpost.com/photogallery/LK/20180813/PHOTO GALLERY/308139984/PH/1.

97. Lombardi, July 4, 2019.

98. Tim Elfrink, "Trump Names Mar-a-Lago Member with 'Basic Spanish' Dominican Republic Ambassador," *Miami New Times*, November 2, 2017, www.miami newtimes.com/news/trumps-dominican-republic-ambassador-has-only-basic-spanish -9797614.

99. *Fox 10 Phoenix*, "Donald Trump & Melania Trump Reunite in Florida for Mar-A-Lago Weekend as Crowds Cheer," YouTube, February 3, 2017, www.youtube .com/watch?v=7BoAY_m3x2I.

100. Robert Frank, "In Palm Beach, the Old Money Isn't Having a Ball," *Wall Street Journal*, May 20, 2005, www.wsj.com/articles/SB111655171289738817#CX.

CHAPTER 4. THE WINTER WHITE HOUSE

1. Emily Smith, "Trump Spent Thanksgiving Asking: Mitt or Rudy?," *New York Post*, November 26, 2016, https://nypost.com/2016/11/26/trump-spent-thanksgiving

-asking-mitt-or-rudy/?_ga=1.201777873.176864245.1480294725; and Robert Costa, "Trump Tells Visitors He's Drafting His Inaugural Speech with Reagan and Kennedy in Mind," *Washington Post*, December 28, 2016, www.washingtonpost.com/news/power post/wp/2016/12/28/trump-tells-visitors-hes-drafting-his-inaugural-speech-with-reagan -and-kennedy-in-mind/.

2. Madison Malone Kircher, "Is Donald Trump Writing His Inaugural Address from a Mar-a-Lago Receptionist's Desk? An Investigation," *New York Magazine*, January 18, 2017, www.nymag.com/intelligencer/2017/01/why-doesnt-donald-trump-have -his-own-desk-at-mar-a-lago.html.

3. Associated Press, "Fabio, Stephen Baldwin Among Few Celebrities Embracing Trump," *Columbus Dispatch*, January 8, 2017, www.dispatch.com/content/stories /national_world/2017/01/08/0108-fabio-stephen-baldwin-among-few-trump-celebrities .html.

4. Dan Scavino (@DanScavino), ".@TheSlyStallone gave this to @realDonald Trump tonight: 'To President Trump, A real champ! GREATEST KNOCKOUT IN HISTORY!' Sylvester Stallone," Twitter, December 30, 2016, https://twitter.com /DanScavino/status/815050572323753984?s=20.

5. Ted Johnson, "Sylvester Stallone Signals He Won't Take Trump Arts Post, Wants to Instead Focus on Veterans," *Variety*, December 18, 2016, www.variety.com/2016/biz /news/sylvester-stallone-donald-trump-national-endowment-for-the-arts-1201945032/.

6. Interview with Lexye Aversa, December 30, 2019.

7. Karin Brulliard, "Meet Patton the Goldendoodle. Will He Become Trump's First Dog?" *Washington Post*, December 6, 2016, www.washingtonpost.com/news/animalia /wp/2016/12/06/meet-patton-the-goldendoodle-will-he-become-trumps-first-dog/.

8. Christopher Klein, "10 Things You May Not Know About George Patton," History.com, April 26, 2019, www.history.com/news/10-things-you-may-not-know -about-george-patton.

9. Cameron Stewart, "Shark Norman Circles Trump," *The Australian*, September 16, 2017, www.theaustralian.com.au/weekend-australian-magazine/greg-norman-the-great -white-shark-circles-the-oval-office/news-story/f7d7e1891262951d2c5e6f00051d9e76.

10. Interview with Niall O'Dowd, December 3, 2019.

11. Ibid.

12. Tyler Pager, "Trump Taps Mar-a-Lago Pal with Mass. Ties for Ambassador to Ireland," *Boston Globe*, January 11, 2017, www.bostonglobe.com/news/politics/2017/01/11 /donald-trump-taps-mar-lago-pal-with-massachusetts-ties-for-irish-ambassador-brian -burns/Jt2g5aX1CeVvA3O4RbrDMN/story.html.

13. O'Dowd, December 3, 2019.

14. Shannon Donnelly, "Patrick Park May Get to Realize Dream as Austrian Ambassador," *Palm Beach Daily News*, February 13, 2017, www.palmbeachdailynews.com /lifestyles/patrick-park-may-get-realize-dream-austrian-ambassador/beWzYkOb7tf VugHw4JXqeI/.

15. Christine Stapleton, "Mar-a-Lago Member Lana Marks Returns to South Africa as U.S. Ambassador," *Palm Beach Daily News*, November 11, 2019, www.palmbeach dailynews.com/news/20191111/mar-a-lago-member-lana-marks-returns-to-south-africa -as-us-ambassador.

16. Jason Burke and Sabrina Siddiqui, "Trump Reportedly Picks Handbag Designer as Ambassador to South Africa," *Guardian*, October 2, 2018, www.theguardian.com/us-news/2018/oct/02/lana-marks-trump-us-ambassador-south-africa.

17. O'Dowd, December 3, 2019.

18. Robert S. Mueller, U.S. Department of Justice, "Report on the Investigation into Russian Interference in the 2016 Presidential Election, Volume I of II," 168–169.

19. Robert S. Mueller, U.S. Department of Justice, "Report on the Investigation into Russian Interference in the 2016 Presidential Election, Volume II of II," 24–25.

20. Mueller, Vol. 1, 170.

21. Ibid., 171.

22. Jeff Zeleny and Kevin Liptak, "Inside Mar-a-Lago for 48 Hours Critical to the Russia Investigation," CNN, December 10, 2017, www.cnn.com/2017/12/08/politics/michael-flynn-donald-trump-mar-a-lago/index.html.

23. Mueller, Vol. II, 26.

24. Ibid.

25. Michael D. Shear and Adam Goldman, "Michael Flynn Pleads Guilty to Lying to the F.B.I. and Will Cooperate with Russia Inquiry," *New York Times*, December 1, 2017, www.nytimes.com/2017/12/01/us/politics/michael-flynn-guilty-russia-investigation.html.

26. Nahal Toosi, "Inside Stephen Miller's Hostile Takeover of Immigration Policy," *Politico*, August 29, 2018, www.politico.com/story/2018/08/29/stephen-miller-immigration-policy-white-house-trump-799199.

27. Phillip Morris, "Don King Stomped a Man to Death 50 years Ago on Cedar Ave., Now Cleveland City Council Wants to Get in on the Act," *Plain Dealer*, September 16, 2016, www.cleveland.com/morris/2016/09/don_king_stomped_a_man_to_deat.html.

28. Ben Strauss, "'Mr. President, You Know What It's Like to Be a Black Man,'" *Politico Magazine*, July 14, 2017, www.politico.com/magazine/story/2017/07/14/don-king-donald-trump-black-man-215362.

29. Adam Howard, "Analysis: Why Donald Trump and Don King Make Sense Together," *NBC News*, September 22, 2016, www.nbcnews.com/politics/2016-election/analysis-why-donald-trump-don-king-make-sense-together-n652531.

30. Joseph Spinelli, "Shadow Boxing," *Sports Illustrated*, November 4, 1991, www.vault.si.com/vault/1991/11/04/shadow-boxing-while-probing-the-fight-game-for-the-fbi-in-the-early-1980s-the-author-uncovered-disquieting-links-between-the-mob-and-powerful-promoter-don-king-the-vain-quest-to-learn-more-took-an-undercover-agent-into-a-meeting.

31. Staff, "Sports People: Don King Pardoned," *New York Times*, January 5, 1983, www.nytimes.com/1983/01/05/sports/sports-people-don-king-pardoned.html.

32. Ariana Eunjung Cha, "Trump Just Met with Super-Influential Health-Care Executives You've Probably Never Heard Of," *Washington Post*, December 28, 2016, www.washingtonpost.com/news/to-your-health/wp/2016/12/28/trump-just-met-with-super-influential-health-care-executives-youve-probably-never-heard-of/.

33. David Shulkin, *It Shouldn't Be This Hard to Serve Your Country* (New York: PublicAffairs, 2019).

34. Megan Janetsky, "President Trump's Top Donors: Where Are They Now?" OpenSecrets, January 18, 2018, www.opensecrets.org/news/2018/01/trump-donors-1 -year-later/.

35. Isaac Arnsdorf, "The Shadow Rulers of the VA," *ProPublica*, August 7, 2018, www.propublica.org/article/ike-perlmutter-bruce-moskowitz-marc-sherman-shadow -rulers-of-the-va.

36. A source close to the three men said only Perlmutter was a member in an interview.

37. Dave Philipps, "Outside Influence: The Veterans Agency's Shadowy Leadership," *New York Times*, August 10, 2018, www.nytimes.com/2018/08/10/us/veterans -affairs-leadership.html.

38. Isaac Arnsdorf, "Trump Mar-a-Lago Buddy Wrote Policy Pitch. The President Sent It to VA Chief" *ProPublica*, March 6, 2019, www.propublica.org/article/trump -mar-a-lago-buddy-wrote-policy-pitch-the-president-sent-it-to-va-chief.

39. Kristina Webb, "Update: Trump Holds VA Meeting at Mar-a-Lago Saturday Night," *Palm Beach Post*, March 17, 2017, https://postonpolitics.blog.palmbeachpost .com/2017/03/17/trump-to-have-major-meeting-on-veterans-tonight-at-mar-a-lago/.

40. A crisis-management firm provided this statement to the authors on behalf of Perlmutter, Moskowitz, and Sherman on January 30, 2020.

41. Amanda Macias and Dan Mangan, "How Veteran Affairs Department Secretary David Shulkin Fell from Grace," CNBC, March 28, 2018, www.cnbc.com/2018/03/28 /how-veteran-affairs-department-secretary-david-shulkin-fell-from-grace.html.

42. Interview with Guido Lombardi, July 11, 2019.

43. Franco Ordoñez and Anita Kumar, "Secret Meeting at Mar-a-Lago Raises Questions About Colombia Peace and Trump" *Miami Herald,* April 20, 2017, www.miami herald.com/news/politics-government/article145805169.html.

44. Andrés Pastrana (@AndresPastrana), "Gracias a @POTUS @realDonald Trump por la cordial y muy franca conversación sobre problemas y perspectivas de Colombia y la región," Twitter, April 14, 2017, www. twitter.com/AndresPastrana_/status /853056886098231296.

45. Eric Lipton and Maggie Haberman, "Available to the Highest Bidder: Coffee with Ivanka Trump," *New York Times*, December 15, 2016, www.nytimes.com/2016/12/15/us /politics/ivanka-trump-charity-auction.html.

46. Interview with Harry Hurt III, December 17, 2019.

47. The authors' analysis of the number of new members at the club, as reported by the *New York Times* (52) multiplied by the lowest known membership fee ($100,000); and Nicholas Confessore, Maggie Haberman, and Eric Lipton, "Trump's 'Winter White House': A Peek at the Exclusive Members' List at Mar-a-Lago," *New York Times*, February 18, 2017, www.nytimes.com/2017/02/18/us/mar-a-lago-trump-ethics-winter -white-house.html.

48. Christine Stapleton and Carolyn DiPaolo, "Trump in Palm Beach: A Look Back at New Year's Eve Bashes at Mar-a-Lago," *Palm Beach Post*, December 30, 2019, www .palmbeachpost.com/news/20191230/trump-in-palm-beach-look-back-at-new-yearrs quos-eve-bashes-at-mar-a-lago.

49. Darren Samuelsohn, "Mar-a-Lago Hikes New Year's Eve Party Ticket Prices," *Politico*, December 20, 2017, www.politico.com/story/2017/12/20/trump-mar-a-lago-new-years-eve-party-tickets-price-307497.

50. Kevin Liptak, Jon Sarlin, and John Defterios, "Donald Trump's New Year's Eve Speech Cited Dubai Business Partner," CNN, January 3, 2017, www.cnn.com/2017/01/02/politics/donald-trump-new-years-eve-speech.

51. Interview with James Patterson, December 4, 2019.

52. Robin Fields, "Trump Gives Memberships to Celebrities," *Northwest Florida Daily News*, January 1, 1995.

53. Interview with Ronald Kessler, December 30, 2019.

54. Howie Carr (@HowieCarrShow), "Charlotte: 'Can I intern in the White House?' President Trump: 'Yes!'" Twitter, December 31, 2016, https://twitter.com/HowieCarrShow/status/815359122984095744.

55. Charlotte Carr, LinkedIn, August 2016, www.linkedin.com/in/charlottevcarr, and Howie Carr (@HowieCarrShow), "Charlotte with @GenFlynn tonight at Mar-a-Lago! She had a great night seeing Trump and his great cabinet," Twitter, December 21, 2016, https://twitter.com/HowieCarrShow/status/811779998860374016.

56. Charlotte Car, LinkedIn, August 2017, www.linkedin.com/in/charlottevcarr/.

57. Sajwani's status as a member confirmed by a Mar-a-Lago staff member.

58. Liptak, Sarlin, and Defterios, "Donald Trump's New Year's Eve Speech Cited Dubai Business Partner."

59. Interview with a Mar-a-Lago staff member.

60. Liptak, Sarlin, and Defterios, "Donald Trump's New Year's Eve Speech Cited Dubai Business Partner."

61. Ibid.

62. Drew Harwell, "Trump Says He Turned Down $2 Billion Deal in Dubai but Didn't Have To," *Washington Post*, January 11, 2017, www.washingtonpost.com/business/economy/trump-says-he-turned-down-2-billion-deal-in-dubai-but-didnt-have-to/2017/01/11/f9092f56-d82f-11e6-9f9f-5cdb4b7f8dd7_story.html.

63. Interviews with current and former Mar-a-Lago staff members.

CHAPTER 5. THE MAN IN CHARGE

1. Interviews with current and former Mar-a-Lago staff members.

2. Ibid.

3. Ibid.

4. *Graham Randall vs Mar a Lago Club*, Aaron Fuller etc., 50-2019-CA 001037-XXXX-MB (Palm Beach Cir. Fla., January 24, 2019).

5. Aaron Fuller gave this statement to the authors on March 25, 2020.

6. Ashley Parker and Josh Dawsey, "Time at Mar-a-Lago Is a Respite for Trump—and a Headache for His Staff," *Washington Post*, December 30, 2017, www.washingtonpost.com/politics/time-at-mar-a-lago-is-a-respite-for-trump--and-a-headache-for-his-staff/2017/12/29/c1c3764a-ecb1-11e7-b698-91d4e35920a3_story.html.

7. Interviews with Mar-a-Lago members and employees.

8. Josh Gerstein, "Secret Service: No Visitor Logs for Mar-a-Lago," *Politico*, October 5, 2017, www.politico.com/story/2017/10/05/mar-a-lago-visitor-logs-secret-service-trump-243478.

9. Kevin Liptak, "Trump Reunites with His Kitchen Cabinet in Mar-a-Lago," CNN, December 23, 2017, www.cnn.com/2017/12/23/politics/trump-kitchen-cabinet/index.html.

10. Interview with David Kris, November 18, 2019.

11. Interview with a Mar-a-Lago staff member.

12. Interview with a Mar-a-Lago member.

13. Interview with a former Mar-a-Lago staff member.

14. Ibid.

15. Ibid .

16. Interview with Toni Holt Kramer, November 19, 2019.

17. Interview with a source familiar with the club.

18. Interview with a Mar-a-Lago staff member.

19. Interviews with Mar-a-Lago members and staff.

20. Interview with Fred Rustmann, December 6, 2019.

21. Interview with a former Mar-a-Lago staff member.

22. Interviews with Mar-a-Lago staff members.

23. Brooke Watson, LinkedIn, February 2019, www.linkedin.com/in/watsonbrooke.

24. Michal Kranz, Pat Ralph, and Grace Panetta, "Trump's Social Media Director Dan Scavino Is the Staffer Who's Been Around the Longest—and He Started as Trump's Caddie," *Business Insider*, May 20, 2019, www.businessinsider.com/dan-scavino-bio-trump-golf-caddie-turned-social-media-director-2018-4.

25. Áine Cain, "Hope Hicks Is Taking on a Job at Fox—Here's a Look Back at the Incredible Career of the 29-Year-Old Former Model," *Business Insider*, October 9, 2018, www.businessinsider.com/hope-hicks-career-2017-12.

26. Tarini Parti, "Top Mar-A-Lago Employee Is Quietly Doing Government Work for Trump's Foreign Trip," *Buzzfeed*, May 24, 2017, www.buzzfeednews.com/article/tariniparti/a-top-mar-a-lago-employee-is-quietly-doing-government-work.

27. Tarini Parti, "The Convicted Con Artist of the Winter White House," *Buzzfeed*, April 27, 2017, www.buzzfeednews.com/article/tariniparti/the-convicted-con-artist-of-mar-a-lago.

28. Interview with a Mar-a-Lago staff member.

29. Jose Lambiet, "Undercooled Meat. Dangerous Fish. Health Inspectors Ding Trump's Mar-a-Lago Kitchen," *Miami Herald*, April 12, 2017, www.miamiherald.com/entertainment/restaurants/article144261894.html.

30. Lindsey Bever, "What Restaurant Inspectors Found Wrong in Trump's Mar-a-Lago Kitchen," *Washington Post*, April 13, 2017, www.washingtonpost.com/news/food/wp/2017/04/13/what-restaurant-inspectors-found-wrong-in-trumps-mar-a-lago-kitchen/.

CHAPTER 6. "IT'S JUST NUKES"

1. David A. Fahrenthold and Karen DeYoung, "Trump Turns Mar-a-Lago Club Terrace into Open-Air Situation Room," *Washington Post*, February 13, 2017, www

.washingtonpost.com/politics/trump-turns-mar-a-lago-club-terrace-into-open-air
-situation-room/2017/02/13/c5525096-f20d-11e6-a9b0-ecee7ce475fc_story.html.

2. Interview with a former Mar-a-Lago staff member.

3. Jason Horowitz, "A King in His Castle: How Donald Trump Lives, from His Longtime Butler," *New York Times*, March 15, 2016, www.nytimes.com/2016/03/16/us /politics/donald-trump-butler-mar-a-lago.html.

4. Interview with a Mar-a-Lago employee.

5. Interview with Guido Lombardi, July 11, 2019.

6. Ken Thomas, "Trump, Modi Exchange Hugs During Rose Garden State-ments," Associated Press, June 26, 2017, www.apnews.com/24ae2a869e404595b3684 6895d7eb67e/Trump,-Modi-exchange-hugs-during-Rose-Garden-statements.

7. Louis Nelson, "Trump Has Some Awkward Exchanges with the Japanese Prime Minister," *Politico*, February 10, 2017, www.politico.com/story/2017/02/shinzo-abe -trump-presser-golf-234905.

8. May Jeong, "You Won't Believe What Happened: The Wild Disturbing Saga of Robert Kraft's Visit to a Strip Mall Sex Spa," *Vanity Fair*, October 4, 2019, www .vanityfair.com/news/2019/10/the-disturbing-saga-of-robert-kraft.

9. "Trump Hosts Abe, Kraft at Florida Resort," *Washington Post*, February 11, 2017, www.washingtonpost.com/videonational/trump-hosts-abe-kraft-at-florida-resort /2017/02/11/003ecc5c-f038-11e6-a100-fdaaf400369a_video.html.

10. Sean Wagner-McGough, "President Trump Left his Super Bowl Party Before the Patriots' Historic Comeback," *CBS Sports*, February 5, 2017, www.cbssports.com /nfl/news/president-trump-left-his-super-bowl-party-before-the-patriots-historic -comeback/.

11. Donald Trump (@realdonaldtrump), "Golf is a game of respect and sportsman-ship, we have to respect its traditions and its rules. —Jack Nicklaus," Twitter, March 6, 2015, https://twitter.com/realdonaldtrump/status/573939334006571008?lang=en.

12. Lombardi, July 4, 2019.

13. Benjamin Haas, "Trump's Golf Diplomacy Lands in the Rough Ahead of Xi Jinping Meeting," *Guardian*, April 5, 2017, www.theguardian.com/us-news/2017/apr/05 /donald-trump-china-golf-xi-jinping.

14. Staff, "Trump, Japanese Leader Cap Visit with Golf Outing," Associated Press, April 27, 2019, www.apnews.com/e3fb6ad133ed4ded95a8f57f9e35f45c.

15. "Trump and Japan's Abe Tee Off at Florida Golf Course," *CBS News*, February 11, 2017, www.cbsnews.com/news/trump-and-japans-abe-tee-off-at-florida-golf-course/.

16. E Michael Johnson, "Donald Trump Receives $3,755 Driver from Japan's Prime Minister," *Golf Digest*, November 20, 2016, www.golfdigest.com/story/donald-trump -receives-dollar3755-driver-from-japans-prime-minister.

17. Emily Heil, "Donald Trump Gets $3,755 Gold Golf Club from Japanese Prime Minister," *Washington Post*, November 21, 2016, www.washingtonpost.com/news /reliable-source/wp/2016/11/21/donald-trump-gets-3755-gold-golf-club-from-japanese -prime-minister/.

18. Ayesha Rascoe, "Trump and Japan's Abe Take a Swing at Golf Diplomacy," Reuters, February 11, 2017, www.reuters.com/article/us-usa-trump-japan-idUSKBN15 Q0JN.

19. Paulette Martin, "President Donald J. Trump with Japan's Prime Minister Abe," Precious Moment Photography.Com Inc., February 2017, www.preciousmoment photography.com/Events/Donald-J-Trump-Events-Folder/Donald-J-Trump-Japans --Abe-Trump-National-Jupiter/i-kMZjHWD/A.

20. Horowitz, "A King in His Castle."

21. Jennifer Jacobs (@JenniferJJacobs), "Trump's press corps has been placed in a basement suite at Jupiter golf club. Black plastic over windows to give Trump privacy as he golfs," Twitter, February 11, 2017, www.twitter.com/JenniferJJacobs/status /830432228664602624.

22. Martin, "President Donald J. Trump with Japan's Prime Minister Abe."

23. Brian Costa, "Els Joins Trump Foursome, Hears About It from Pals," Wall Street Journal, February 15, 2017, www.wsj.com/articles/els-joins-trump-foursome-hears -about-it-from-pals-1487115373.

24. Mike Hayes, "This Mar-A-Lago Member Had A Great Time Photographing Trump Handling A National Security Crisis," BuzzFeed News, February 13, 2017, www .buzzfeednews.com/article/mikehayes/mar-a-lago-situation-room.

25. Chris Spargo, "'This Is Rick . . . He Carries the 'Football': Palm Beach Actor Posts Photo of Himself with Military Aide 'Carrying the Nuclear Codes' in Set of Remarkably Candid Snaps Taken at Mar-a-Lago," Daily Mail, February 13, 2017, www .dailymail.co.uk/news/article-4220530/Man-posts-photo-military-aide-nuclear-codes .html.

26. Martin, "President Donald J. Trump with Japan's Prime Minister Abe."

27. Gabriel Sherman, "'Marla Was Under Duress': Revealed in His Marla Maples Prenup, Donald Trump's Draconian Art of the Marriage Deal," Vanity Fair, June 4, 2019, www.vanityfair.com/news/2019/06/marla-maple-prenup-donald-trump-marriage.

28. Interview with Paulette Martin, November 19, 2019.

29. Ibid.

30. Martin, "President Donald J. Trump with Japan's Prime Minister Abe."

31. Interviews with Mar-a-Lago members and staff members.

32. Donald J. Trump (@realdonaldtrump), "Having a great time hosting Prime Minister Shinzo Abe in the United States!" Twitter, February 11, 2017, www.twitter.com /realDonaldTrump/status/830483672096768001.

33. Justin Elliott, "Trump's Patron-in-Chief," ProPublica, October 10, 2018, https://features.propublica.org/trump-inc-podcast/sheldon-adelson-casino-magnate -trump-macau-and-japan/.

34. Ibid.

35. Email interview with the office of Prime Minister Shinzo Abe, February 4, 2020.

36. Elliott, "Trump's Patron-in-Chief."

37. "Casino, Trump Approaching Japan 'Do You Know This Company?'" Nikkei, June 10, 2017. www.nikkei.com/article/DGXMZO17367480W7A600C1SHA000/.

38. The Original Aynsley (@acat2002), "The guy that Alec Baldwin plays on SNL made a guest appearance at #FalkLindnerWedding VC @chadblackburn1 #trump #maga #maralago #winterwhitehouse #FakeNews said he 'crashed' the wedding, but he was an honored guest. #HuffingtonPostIsFakeNews #sloppyjournalism," Instagram, February 12, 2017, www.instagram.com/p/BQa7PENl_ax/.

39. Nicholas Stein, "Yes, We Have No Profits: The Rise and Fall of Chiquita Banana. How a Great American Brand Lost Its Way," *Fortune*, November 26, 2001, https://archive.fortune.com/magazines/fortune/fortune_archive/2001/11/26/314058/index.htm.

40. Interview with a former Mar-a-Lago staff member.

41. Interview with a Palm Beacher familiar with the club.

42. The Original Aynsley (@acat2002), " When POTUS comes to the wedding. Congratulations Carl & Vanessa!! #FalkLindnerWedding #maga," Instagram, February 11, 2017, https://www.instagram.com/p/BQZhO-eF-jc/.

43. Yashar Ali, "Here's a Video of Trump Crashing a Wedding Right After Giving His North Korea Statement," *New York Magazine*, February 13, 2017, www.nymag.com/intelligencer/2017/02/watch-trump-crash-wedding-right-after-north-korea-statement.html?mid=twitter_nymag.

44. "Trump: Favorable/Unfavorable," *RealClearPolitics*, December 31, 2019, www.realclearpolitics.com/epolls/other/trump_favorableunfavorable-5493.html.

45. Interview with Toni Holt Kramer, November 19, 2019.

46. Natasha Bertrand, "A Paying Mar-a-Lago Member Took Photos of Trump Being Briefed on North Korea—and Posted Them to Facebook," *Business Insider*, February 13, 2017, www.businessinsider.com/trump-north-korea-mar-a-lago-meeting-photos-2017-2?r=US&IR=T.

47. Spargo, "'This Is Rick . . . He Carries the 'Football'.'"

48. Dawn Basham's Facebook page, accessed November 8, 2019, www.facebook.com/dawnmarie.alba.vocalist.

49. Ibid.

50. Interview with an attendee.

51. Donald J. Trump (@realdonaldtrump), "A working dinner tonight with Prime Minister Abe of Japan, and his representatives, at the Winter White House (Mar-a-Lago). Very good talks!" Twitter, February 11, 2017, www.twitter.com/realDonaldTrump/status/830558065715998726?s=20.

52. George G. Lombardi (@georgeglombardi), "Trump and Abe will deliver joint statement soon about North Korea Missile," Twitter, February 11, 2017.

53. Sean Spicer, "Press Briefing by Press Secretary Sean Spicer," The White House, February 14, 2017, www.whitehouse.gov/briefings-statements/press-briefing-press-secretary-sean-spicer-021417/.

54. Interview with Richard DeAgazio, October 28, 2019.

55. Andrew Restuccia, "White House Cellphone Ban Set to Take Effect Jan. 16," *Politico*, January 10, 2018, www.politico.com/story/2018/01/10/white-house-cell-phone-ban-333734.

56. CNN, "Trump Touts TiVo Like It's 1999," June 27, 2019, www.cnn.com/videos/politics/2019/06/27/trump-touts-tivo-jeanne-moos-pkg-ebof-vpx.cnn; and Eliana Johnson, Emily Stephenson and Daniel Lippman, "'Too Inconvenient': Trump Goes Rogue on Phone Security," *Politico*, May 21, 2018, www.politico.com/story/2018/05/21/trump-phone-security-risk-hackers-601903.

57. Shannon Donnelly, "Palm Beach Society: John Havlicek Kept His Cool at Trump's Mar-a-Lago," *Palm Beach Daily News*, April 27, 2019, www.palmbeachdaily

news.com/news/20190427/palm-beach-society-john-havlicek-kept-his-cool-at-trumps -mar-a-lago; and interview with Shannon Donnelly, December 18, 2019.

58. Fahrenthold and DeYoung, "Trump Turns Mar-a-Lago Club Terrace into Open-Air Situation Room"; and Chelsea Clinton (@ChelseaClinton, "How many of Mar-a-Lago's new members will be (already are?) members of foreign intelligence agencies & media organizations?" Twitter, February 12, 2017, www.twitter.com/Chelsea Clinton/status/830983477000540163?s=20.

CHAPTER 7. OVER HAMILTON'S DEAD BODY

1. Michael Dobbs, email to Chuck Stowell, April 11, 2017, *Property of the People*, published by *ProPublica*, www.documentcloud.org/documents/5982879-State -Department-Mar-a-Lago-Spending-Records.html.

2. Michael Dobbs, LinkedIn, www.linkedin.com/in/michael-dobbs-b4004358/.

3. Dobbs emailed a colleague at the Executive Office of the President, April 10, 2017, *Property of the People*, published by *ProPublica*.

4. Invoices for Mar-a-Lago club stays, February 10–12, 2017, *Property of the People*, published by *ProPublica*.

5. Michael Dobbs, email to John J. Stever, April 26, 2017, *Property of the People*, published by *ProPublica*.

6. Millie Pugliese, email to Michael Dobbs and Thomas Parrillo, April 6, 2017, *Property of the People*, published by *ProPublica*.

7. Ibid.

8. Thomas Parrillo, email to Michael Dobbs and Millie Pugliese, April 7, 2017, *Property of the People*, published by *ProPublica*.

9. Derek Kravitz, "How Taxpayers Covered a $1,000 Liquor Bill for Trump Staffers (and More) at Trump's Club," *ProPublica*, May 1, 2019, www.propublica.org/article /trump-inc-podcast-taxpayers-covered-liquor-bill-for-trump-staffers-and-more-mar-a -lago.

10. Beverly VanEvery, email to Thomas Parrillo, September 20, 2017, *Property of the People*, published by *ProPublica*.

11. Jennifer Sorentrue, "Chinese Leader Stay at Eau Chance for Resort, County to Stand Out," *Palm Beach Post*, March 30, 2017, www.palmbeachpost.com/business /chinese-leader-stay-eau-chance-for-resort-county-stand-out/8qBVPMkSnC4pjI7yH pobiP/.

12. Thomas Parrillo, email to Beverly VanEvery and Michael Dobbs, September 20, 2017, *Property of the People*, published by *ProPublica*.

13. Anita Kumar, "Japanese Prime Minister's Stay at Mar-a-Lago Will Be a Gift from President Trump," *McClatchy DC*, February 9, 2017, www.mcclatchydc.com/news /politics-government/white-house/article131831249.html.

14. Michael Dobbs, email to Chuck Stowell, April 11, 2017, *Property of the People*, published by *ProPublica*.

15. Alexander Hamilton, "Federalist No. 22: The Same Subject Continued (Other Defects of the Present Confederation)," in *The Federalist Papers* (Read Books Ltd., 2018).

16. Derek Kravitz and Al Shaw, "Trump Lawyer Confirms President Can Pull Money

from His Businesses Whenever He Wants," *ProPublica*, April 4, 2017, https://www.propublica.org/article/trump-pull-money-his-businesses-whenever-he-wants-without-telling-us.

17. Matt O'Brien, "Donald Trump Won't Do What Ronald Reagan, George H. W. Bush, Bill Clinton and George W. Bush Did," *Washington Post*, November 15, 2016, www.washingtonpost.com/news/wonk/wp/2016/11/15/ronald-reagan-did-it-george-h-w-bush-did-it-bill-clinton-did-it-george-w-bush-did-it-donald-trump-wont-do-it/.

18. Daniel Strauss, "Donald Trump's New Pitch: I'm So Rich I Can't Be Bought," *Politico*, July 28, 2015, www.politico.com/story/2015/07/donald-trumps-so-rich-i-cant-be-bought-120743.

19. Shelby Hanssen and Ken Dilanian, "Reps of 22 Foreign Governments Have Spent Money at Trump Properties," *NBC News*, June 12, 2019, www.nbcnews.com/politics/donald-trump/reps-22-foreign-governments-have-spent-money-trump-properties-n1015806.

20. Abbey Marshall, "Trump Claims He's the Victim of 'Phony Emoluments Clause,'" *Politico*, October 21, 2019, www.politico.com/news/2019/10/21/trump-emoluments-clause-053289.

21. Alan Zibel, "Catering to Conflicts: Influence and Self-Dealing at Trump's Businesses," *Public Citizen*, November 11, 2019, www.citizen.org/article/catering-to-conflicts-influence-and-self-dealing-at-trumps-businesses.

22. Anita Kumar, "Trump Can't Stop Bragging to Foreign Leaders About His Resorts," *Politico*, October 20, 2019, www.politico.com/news/2019/10/20/trump-resorts-emoluments-foreign-leaders-050540.

23. *Citizens for Responsibility and Ethics in Washington vs Donald J. Trump, in his official capacity as President of the United States*, emoluments complaint, 1:17-cv-00458, (U.S. Dist. Ct. S.N.Y 2017), https://s3.amazonaws.com/storage.citizensforethics.org/wp-content/uploads/2017/03/23164833/EMOLUMENTS-COMPLAINT1.pdf.

24. Ann E. Marimow and Jonathan O'Connell, "Trump Business Dealings Argued at Federal Appeals Court in Emoluments Case," *Washington Post*, December 9, 2019, www.washingtonpost.com/local/legal-issues/trump-business-dealings-argued-at-federal-appeals-court-in-emoluments-case/2019/12/09/84ee5286-1792-11ea-a659-7d69641c6ff7_story.html.

25. "TRUMP Donation of Profits from Foreign Government Patronage," https://oversight.house.gov/sites/democrats.oversight.house.gov/files/documents/Trump%20Org%20Pamphlet%20on%20Foreign%20Profits.pdf.

26. Ali Dukakis, "Critics Question Undisclosed Flow of Money from Foreign Governments to Trump Properties," *ABC News*, February 28, 2018, www.abcnews.go.com/Politics/critics-question-undisclosed-flow-money-foreign-governments-trump/story?id=53413228.

27. Kravitz, "How Taxpayers Covered a $1,000 Liquor Bill for Trump Staffers (and More) at Trump's Club."

28. Ibid.

29. Ibid.

30. David A. Fahrenthold et al., "Secret Service Has Paid Rates as High as $650 a Night for Rooms at Trump's Properties," *Washington Post*, February 7, 2020, www.washingtonpost.com/politics/secret-service-has-paid-rates-as-high-as-650-a-night

-for-rooms-at-trumps-properties/2020/02/06/7f27a7c6-3ec5-11ea-8872-5df698785a4e
_story.html.

31. Ron Fein and Brianne Gorod, "Lining Trump's Pockets," *U.S. News and World Report*, March 21, 2017, www.usnews.com/opinion/articles/2017-03-21/president -donald-trump-has-also-got-a-domestic-emoluments-clause-problem.

32. Property of the People, "Secret Service Payments to Trump Properties (Jan–June 2017)," November 21, 2019, www.propertyofthepeople.org/document-detail /?doc-id=6556375-Secret-Service-Payments-to-Trump-Properties-Jan.

33. Fahrenthold et al., "Secret Service Has Paid Rates as High as $650 a Night for Rooms at Trump's Properties."

34. Ibid.

35. Ibid.

36. Derek Kravitz, Derek Willis, Paul Cronan, Mark Schifferli, and Charlie Smart, "Paying the President," *ProPublica*, June 27, 2018, https://projects.propublica.org /paying-the-president/.

37. Fahrenthold et al., "Secret Service Has Paid Rates as High as $650 a Night for Rooms at Trump's Properties."

38. Derek Kravitz, Alex Mierjeski, and Gabriel Sandoval, "We've Found $16.1 Million in Political and Taxpayer Spending at Trump Properties," *Pro Publica*, June 27, 2018, www.propublica.org/article/political-and-taxpayer-spending-at-trump-properties -16-1-million.

39. David A. Fahrenthold, "What President Trump's Company Charges the Secret Service," *Washington Post*, March 5, 2020, www.washingtonpost.com/graphics/2020 /politics/trump-secret-service-spending/?itid=lk_interstitial_manual_16.

40. "Remarks by President Trump and Prime Minister Abe of Japan Before Bilateral Meeting | Mar-a-Lago, FL," The White House, www.whitehouse.gov/briefings -statements/remarks-president-trump-prime-minister-abe-japan-bilateral-meeting -mar-lago-fl/.

41. Donald J. Trump (@realDonaldTrump), "I will be there in two weeks, The Southern White House!" Twitter, December 12, 2019 www.twitter.com/realdonaldtrump /status/1205104256312848385?lang=en.

42. Leigh Hartman, "Mar-a-Lago: The Winter White House," *ShareAmerica*, April 4, 2017, https://web.archive.org/web/20170404194840/https://share.america.gov/mar-a -lago-winter-white-house/.

43. Sabrina Toppa, "State Department Pulls Post Gushing About Mar-a-Lago," *Mother Jones*, April 24, 2017, www.motherjones.com/politics/2017/04/trump-mar-lago -estate-state-dept-promotion-1/.

44. Share America, "Mar-a-Lago: The Winter White House," April 4, 2017, https:// share.america.gov/mar-a-lago-winter-white-house/.

45. The authors performed a monthly analysis of President Trump's public financial disclosures from 2015 to 2019. The forms do not always cover a consistent time annual period, necessitating a monthly analysis.

46. Interview with a Mar-a-Lago staff member.

47. State of Florida Department of Health, "Public Pool and Bathing Place Inspection Report," File # 2994, March 14, 2017.

48. Interview with a Mar-a-Lago staff member.

49. Ibid.

50. Interview with a frequent Mar-a-Lago guest.

51. Ibid.

52. Interview with Virginia Canter, March 31, 2020.

53. Christine Stapleton, "Not Just Cindy Yang: Royals, Felon, Pop Stars, Others Got Access to Trump's Mar-a-Lago," *Palm Beach Post*, March 20, 2019, www.palm beachpost.com/news/20190320/not-just-cindy-yang-royals-felon-pop-stars-others-got -access-to-trumps-mar-a-lago.

54. The authors' analysis of Federal Election Commission data, retrieved December 22, 2019.

55. Zach Everson, "Trump Endorsements Follow in the Wake of Candidates Spending Money at His Properties," *Fast Company*, October 17, 2018, www.fastcompany .com/90252235/trump-endorsements-follow-in-the-wake-of-candidates-spending -money-at-his-properties.

56. The authors' analysis of Federal Elections Commission Data, retrieved December 22, 2019.

57. George Bennett, "Trump Jr. Pops in on Mar-a-Lago GOP Dinner; Mixed Reaction for Palin," *Palm Beach Post*, March 17, 2018, www.palmbeachpost.com/news /national-govt--politics/trump-pops-mar-lago-gop-dinner-mixed-reaction-for-palin/fX 05i694heIteAVdCXY48J/; and "Trump Addresses Guests at Mar-a-Lago Hours After Mueller Report Delivered," *Washington Post*, March 23, 3019, www.washingtonpost .com/video/politics/trump-addresses-guests-at-mar-a-lago-hours-after-mueller-report -delivered/2019/03/23/0cf96882-8023-47c7-aa63-a22ab9328505_video.html.

58. Arron Banks, *The Bad Boys of Brexit: Tales of Mischief, Mayhem & Guerilla Warfare in the EU Referendum Campaign* (London: Biteback Publishing, 2017).

59. Interview with Fred Wertheimer, October 28, 2019.

60. Nicholas Nehamas, "Trump Org: Extremist Group Will 'Absolutely Not' Hold Event at Mar-a-Lago," *Miami Herald*, October 6, 2019, www.miamiherald.com/news /politics-government/article235855202.html.

61. Nicholas Nehamas and Tara Copp, "U.S. Marine Unit Wants to Hold Annual Ball at Presidential Venue: Trump's Mar-a-Lago Club," *Miami Herald*, September 19, 2020, www.miamiherald.com/news/politics-government/article235279797.html.

62. Nicholas Nehamas and Tara Copp, "After Dreaming of Mar-a-Lago, Marine Unit Scrambles to Find New Venue for Annual Ball," *Miami Herald*, September 24, 2020, www.miamiherald.com/news/politics-government/article235403277.html.

63. Sarah Blaskey, Nicholas Nehamas, and Caitlin Ostroff, "Trump Tourism: How Charlottesville Enabled Cindy Yang to Market Mar-a-Lago in China," *Miami Herald*, March 29, 2019, www.miamiherald.com/news/politics-government/article228456974 .html.

CHAPTER 8. THE GATEKEEPERS

1. Interview with David S. Goodboy, December 30, 2019.

2. William Kelly and Darrell Hofheinz, "More than 30 Palm Beachers on Forbes' Billionaires List," *Palm Beach Post*, October 11, 2019, www.palmbeachpost.com/news /20191011/more-than-30-palm-beachers-on-forbesrsquo-billionaires-list.

3. Alexandra Stevenson, "A Brand Name for a Hedge Fund Happy Hour: Trump's Mar-a-Lago," *New York Times,* March 9, 2017, www.nytimes.com/2017/03/09/business /dealbook/trump-mar-a-lago-for-hedge-fund-happy-hour.html.

4. Palm Beach Hedge Fund Association, "Summer Newsletter," https://myemail .constantcontact.com/PBHFA-Summer-Newsletter.html?soid=1119630609109&aid =rMUFcku-DEY.

5. Interview with Lexye Aversa, December 30, 2019.

6. CBS *Face the Nation*, "Trump: 'Hedge Fund Guys Are Getting Away with Murder'," YouTube, August 23, 2015, www.youtube.com/watch?v=Z4I5QUGRf-Q.

7. Chris Isidore, "Whatever Happened to Trump's Crackdown on 'the Hedge Fund Guys?'" CNN, November 27, 2017, www.money.cnn.com/2017/11/27/pf/taxes /trump-carried-interest-tax-break/index.html.

8. Stevenson, "A Brand Name for a Hedge Fund Happy Hour."

9. Goodboy, December 31, 2019.

10. Drew Harwell and David A. Fahrenthold, "At Mar-a-Lago, the Star Power of the Presidency Helps Charities—and Trump—Make More Money," *Washington Post*, May 13, 2017, www.washingtonpost.com/politics/at-mar-a-lago-the-star-power-of-the -presidency-helps-charities--and-trump--make-more-money/2017/05/13/e6bf6782-34ca -11e7-b412-62beef8121f7_story.html.

11. Interview with Wayne Allyn Root, October 30, 2019.

12. Terry Krepel, "Self-Proclaimed Non-Birther Hannity Promotes Another Birther-Related Conspiracy," *Media Matters for America*, August 7, 2012, www.media matters.org/sean-hannity/self-proclaimed-non-birther-hannity-promotes-another -birther-related-conspiracy.

13. According to Root's memory of the note. Root said he lost the original email in his files when he moved.

14. Ibid.

15. Ibid.

16. Wayne Allyn Root, "Commentary: My Dinner with President Donald Trump," *Las Vegas Review-Journal*, February 21, 2018, www.reviewjournal.com/opinion/opinion -columns/wayne-allyn-root/commentary-my-dinner-with-president-donald-trump/.

17. Trumpettes USA, "Trumpettes USA: About," www.trumpettesusa.com /trumpettes/about/.

18. Interview with Toni Holt Kramer, November 19, 2019.

19. Interview with a former Mar-a-Lago staff member.

20. Toni Holt Kramer, *Unstoppable Me* (Indiana: Unstoppable Me, LLC, 2018), Ebook, location 5066.

21. Kramer, November 11, 2019.

22. "Palm Springs Walk of Stars," www.palmsprings.com/walk-of-stars/.

23. Kramer, *Unstoppable Me*, location 105.

24. Ibid.

25. Kramer, November 19, 2019.

26. Kramer, *Unstoppable Me*, location 3598.

27. Ibid., location 3299.

28. Kramer, November 19, 2019.

29. Ibid.

30. Ibid.

31. Kramer, *Unstoppable Me*, location 121.

32. Ibid.

33. Kramer, *Unstoppable Me*, location 115.

34. Ibid.

35. Kramer, November 19, 2019.

36. Trumpettes USA, "Celebrate Trump Trumpettes 2020 Recap Event," YouTube, February 20, 2020, www.youtube.com/watch?v=YqmfCwFGERA&feature.

CHAPTER 9. A PROBLEM IN FLORIDA

1. Interview with Annie Marie Delgado, July 14, 2019.

2. Ashley Parker and Josh Dawey, "Time at Mar-a-Lago Is a Respite for Trump—and a Headache for His Staff," *Washington Post*, December 30, 2017, www.washington post.com/politics/time-at-mar-a-lago-is-a-respite-for-trump--and-a-headache-for-his -staff/2017/12/29/c1c3764a-ecb1-11e7-b698-91d4e35920a3_story.html.

3. Delgado, July 14, 2019.

4. Delgado, October 10, 2019.

5. Delgado, October 19, 2019.

6. Maggie Severns, "Trump Campaign Plagued by Groups Raising Tens of Millions in His Name," *Politico*, December 23, 2019, www.politico.com/news/2019/12/23/trump -campaign-compete-against-groups-money-089454.

7. Delgado, October 19, 2019.

8. Delgado, October 20, 2019.

9. Delgado, July 14, 2019.

10. Delgado, December 27, 2019.

11. David A. Fahrenthold, "'These Are Our True Friends': Trump Fans Flock to a Mar-a-Lago Celebration," *Washington Post*, January 19, 2018, www.washingtonpost .com/politics/these-are-our-true-friends-trump-fans-flock-to-a-mar-a-lago-celebration /2018/01/19/ba0b7678-fcd3-11e7-a46b-a3614530bd87_story.html.

12. Delgado, July 14, 2019.

13. Trumpettes USA, "Excited to share our next #promo #video for our upcoming event at #Mar-a-Lago Celebrating #President #Trump. We are well on our way to be SOLD OUT!! Don't miss out! https://youtu.be/uZ1cjubNrtE. #Trump2020 #MAGA #GOP #FoxNews #Christian #Jew #PresidentTrump #SeanHannity," Facebook, October 29, 2019, www.facebook.com/trumpettesusa/photos/a.167694043645129 /827456154335578/?type=3&theater.

14. David A. Fahrenthold, Lori Rozsa, and Drew Harwell, "Mar-a-Lago's New Winter Season: The Red Cross Ball Is Out, the Trumpettes Are In," *Washington Post*, November 18, 2017, www.washingtonpost.com/politics/mar-a-lagos-new-winter-season -the-red-cross-ball-is-out-the-trumpettes-are-in/2017/11/18/c965eb18-c956-11e7-aa96 -54417592cf72_story.html.

15. Fahrenthold, "'These Are Our True Friends'."

16. Mar-a-Lago membership list, reviewed by the authors (2008).

17. Fahrenthold, "'These Are Our True Friends'."

18. Josh Dawsey, "Trump Derides Protections for Immigrants from 'Shithole' Countries," *Washington Post*, January 12, 2018, www.washingtonpost.com/politics/trump-attacks-protections-for-immigrants-from-shithole-countries-in-oval-office-meeting/2018/01/11/bfc0725c-f711-11e7-91af-31ac729add94_story.html.

19. Delgado, July 14, 2019.

20. Delgado, October 20, 2019.

21. Electronic Articles of Incorporation for Trumpettes USA, Inc., Florida Department of State, February 9, 2017, http://search.sunbiz.org/Inquiry/CorporationSearch/ConvertTiffToPDF?storagePath=COR%5C2017%5C0209%5C10362491.tif&documentNumber=N17000001482.

22. The authors consulted the Internal Revenue Service on January 28, 2020.

23. Interview with Toni Holt Kramer, November 19, 2019.

24. Fiona Watson, "Bolsonaro's Election Is Catastrophic News for Brazil's Indigenous Tribes," *Guardian*, October 31, 2018, www.theguardian.com/commentisfree/2018/oct/31/jair-bolsonaro-brazil-indigenous-tribes-mining-logging.

25. SHALOMshow on TV, "Celebrating the USA and Making History!" YouTube, March 24, 2019, www.youtube.com/watch?v=VtCYZKNeZ4E&feature=youtu.be&fbclid=IwAR0MwWz0p3NKg96pw1GGYiukJw28AeDc4QjTCJ2cGuIdhvB7xnyzwG1Q84s.

26. "Bolsonaro Says Trump Approved His Son as Ambassador to Washington" *AFP*, August 9, 2019, www.timesofisrael.com/bolsonaro-says-trump-approved-his-son-as-ambassador-to-us.

27. Katharine Murphy, "Morrison Visits an Australian Box Factory in Ohio—and the Trump Crowd Goes Wild," *Guardian*, September 22, 2019, www.theguardian.com/australia-news/2019/sep/23/morrison-visits-an-australian-box-factory-in-ohio-and-the-trump-crowd-goes-wild.

28. Colin Kruger, "Trump Factor Keeps Pratt on Top of Australia's Rich List," *Sydney Morning Herald*, May 30, 2019, www.smh.com.au/business/companies/trump-factor-keeps-pratt-on-top-of-australia-s-rich-list-while-murdoch-children-re-emerge-20190530-p51s0g.html.

29. Trumpettes USA, "What an exciting weekend at Mar a Lago (The Winter White House), and a warm welcome to my newest Trumpette Gina Rinehart from Australia who has been visiting MAL. Coming up at the end of this week, we will post Gina's bio and her fabulous photos. What fun it is also, to have our first Princess Camilla Di Borbone Due Sicilie and from Belgium and Palm Beach, Erin van Poecke … ," Facebook, March 26, 2018, www.facebook.com/trumpettesusa/posts/dear-trumpettes-and-trumpsters-what-an-exciting-weekend-at-mar-a-lago-the-winter/471288649952332.

30. Kramer, November 19, 2019.

CHAPTER 10. "THE GIRL WHO OTHERS WOULD ENVY"

1. Profile of Cindy Yang posted on the Chinese social media site WeChat, May 14, 2017, https://freewechat.com/a/MzAxMjYyODEwMQ==/2649461795/1.

2. Cynthia McFadden et al., "Ex-Spa Owner Denies Selling Access to Trump, Says Dems Target Her Because She's a Chinese Republican," *NBC News*, March 20, 2019,

www.nbcnews.com/politics/donald-trump/ex-spa-owner-denies-selling-access-trump
-says-dems-target-n98538.

3. Nicholas Nehamas and Lily Dobrovolskaya, "Wanted in Russia, He Partied at
Mar-a-Lago—and Invested in Cheap South Florida Homes," *Miami Herald*, March
12, 2019, www.miamiherald.com/news/local/community/miami-dade/article222746560
.html.

4. "Charlottesville: Race and Terror," *Vice*, August 14, 2017, www.youtube.com
/watch?v=RIrcB1sAN8I.

5. Angie Drobnic Holan, "In Context: Donald Trump's 'Very Fine People on
Both Sides' Remarks (Transcript)," *PolitiFact*, April 26, 2019, www.politifact.com
/article/2019/apr/26/context-trumps-very-fine-people-both-sides-remarks/.

6. David A. Fahrenthold, "Most Charities That Deserted Trump's Florida Club
After Charlottesville Haven't Come Back," *Washington Post*, November 20, 2018,
www.washingtonpost.com/politics/most-charities-that-deserted-trumps-florida
-club-after-charlottesville-havent-come-back/2018/11/19/a4c9967e-e903-11e8-b8dc
-66cca409c180_story.html.

7. Sam Dangremond, "17 Charities Have Canceled Their Mar-a-Lago Galas in the
Past Week," *Town & Country*, August 23, 2017, www.townandcountrymag.com/society
/politics/a12033310/mar-a-lago-charity-fundraisers-canceled/.

8. Shannon Donnelly, "UPDATED: Keeping Track at Home? Here's a List of 25
Charities Leaving Mar-a-Lago," *Palm Beach Daily News*, October 23, 2018, www.palm
beachdailynews.com/news/20171204/updated-keeping-track-at-home-heres-list-of-25
-charities-leaving-mar-a-lago.

9. Sarah Blaskey, Nicholas Nehamas, and Caitlin Ostroff, "Trump Tourism: How
Charlottesville Enabled Cindy Yang to Market Mar-a-Lago in China," *Miami Herald*,
March 29, 2019, www.miamiherald.com/news/politics-government/article228456974
.html.

10. The authors' analysis of Donald Trump's public financial disclosures.

11. Andrew Rice, "How to Throw a Party at Mar-a-Lago," *New York Magazine*, June
24, 2019, http://nymag.com/intelligencer/2019/06/cindy-yang-mar-a-lago.html.

12. Interview with Guiying Zhang, March 19, 2019.

13. Tokyo Day Spa received its first license from the Florida Department of Health
in 2008.

14. Interview with Woody McLane, March 12, 2019.

15. Ibid.

16. Sarah Blaskey, Nicholas Nehamas, and Caitlin Ostroff, "Trump Cheered Patriots
to Super Bowl Victory with Founder of Spa Where Kraft Was Busted," *Miami Herald*, March 8, 2019, www.miamiherald.com/news/politics-government/article227186429
.html; and McLane, 2019.

17. Yang WeChat profile, 2017.

18. Sarah Blaskey, Nicholas Nehamas, Caitlin Ostroff, and David Smiley, "How
Did Li Yang Go from Spa Owner to Trump Selfie Queen? 'She Likes to Show Off,'
Mom Says," *Miami Herald*, March 12, 2019, www.miamiherald.com/news/politics
-government/article227438119.html.

19. Interviews with four people who knew Yang professionally and personally.

20. Yang WeChat profile, 2017.

21. Ibid.

22. Alexander Bowe, "China's Overseas United Front Work: Background and Implications for the United States," *US-China Economic and Security Review Commission*, August 24, 2018, www.uscc.gov/sites/default/files/Research/China's%20Overseas%20United%20Front%20Work%20-%20Background%20and%20Implications%20for%20US_final_0.pdf.

23. Chinese Association of Science, Education and Culture of South Florida, "About Us," http://floridachinese.org/about-us/.

24. Interview with James Xuefeng Zhang, March 15, 2020.

25. BBC Monitoring, "His Own Words: The 14 Principles of 'Xi Jinping Thought,'" BBC, October 24, 2017, https://monitoring.bbc.co.uk/product/c1dmwn4r.

26. Andrew Chatzky and James McBride, "China's Massive Belt and Road Initiative," *Council on Foreign Relations*, January 28, 2020, www.cfr.org/backgrounder/chinas-massive-belt-and-road-initiative.

27. "Full Text of President Xi's Speech at Opening of Belt and Road Forum," *Xinhua*, May 14, 2017, www.xinhuanet.com/english/2017-05/14/c_136282982.htm.

28. Zhou Xin, "Official Encourages Overseas Chinese to Become Part of Local Community," *Xinhua*, February 23, 2018, www.xinhuanet.com/english/2018-02/23/c_136994147.htm.

29. China Association for Science and Technology, "About Us," http://english.cast.org.cn/col/col473/index.html.

30. James Zhang, March 15, 2020; and "Program for the 26th Annual Convention of Chinese Association for Science & Technology USA," October 10, 2018, http://castct.org/en/wp-content/uploads/2018/10/CAST-USA-26th-Convention-Program-book.pdf.

31. Interview with Wan Le, president-elect of the China Association of Science and Technology, US chapter, March 15, 2020.

32. Qu Xianqin is a board member of Chinese Overseas Exchange.

33. Incorporation documents for Overseas International Female Organization, Florida Division of Corporations, August 10, 2015, http://search.sunbiz.org/Inquiry/CorporationSearch/ConvertTiffToPDF?storagePath=COR%5C2015%5C0813%5C10926991.tif&documentNumber=N15000007847.

34. Andres Viglucci, "The China Vanguard: State-Owned Developer Seeks to Build Big in Miami and Beach," *Miami Herald*, February 22, 2016, www.miamiherald.com/news/local/community/miami-dade/article61852957.html.

35. "Chun Wo Establishes Strategic Relationship with AECOM and CCCC to Tap US Market," *ACN Newswire,* November 16, 2015, http://en.acnnewswire.com/press-release/english/26478/chun-wo-establishes-strategic-relationship-with-aecom-and-cccc-to-tap-us-market.

36. Cindy Yang, WeChat post, April 12, 2018, https://posts.careerengine.us/p/5acf5c9a8145e154fac25e66.

37. Yang WeChat profile, 2017.

38. Bowe, "China's Overseas United Front Work: Background and Implications for the United States."

39. Jin Danhong, "The Consul General Went to Florida to Spend Thanksgiving with Overseas Chinese," *Voice of the Chinese in America*, November 26, 2015, https://mp.weixin.qq.com/s/2J9ETKd-Or_BlovGADn1OA.

40. Li Yang, "Bush Is Inviting Chinese People to Share an Expensive Breakfast," *Voice of the Chinese in America*, December 30, 2015, https://mp.weixin.qq.com/s?__biz=MzAx MjYyODEwMQ==&mid=400876341&idx=1&sn=8dc637f62572694b91465a226 b23fbf9&exportkey=A%2Bph5hn%2Fn3rAzpFD2UlUGz0%3D&pass_ticket=TbQd%2 FyaZzBTu039N24DzVkz3hxhTeo2yf6sELa2dBhy2QJGeewmy2lhOmXDzmp2x.

41. Guo Jinping, "Jeb Declared His Candidacy in the Election," *Voice of the Chinese in America*, June 17, 2015, www.asianamericanforjeb.com/articles/%E8%BF%88 %E5%9F%8E%E6%9D%B0%E5%B8%83%E5%AE%A3%E5%8F%82%E9%80%89 _%E5%8D%8E%E8%A3%94%E5%90%8C%E5%BF%83%E8%AE%AE%E6%94 %BF%E5%BF%99.

42. Cindy Yang, "The new life need to learn more, into the culture of the United States," Facebook, June 19, 2016, screenshot.

43. Blaskey et al., "How Did Li Yang Go from Spa Owner to Trump Selfie Queen?"

44. Interviews with two people who interacted with Yang in South Florida Republican circles.

45. Guiying Zhang, March 19, 2019.

46. Ibid.

47. Interview with Cliff Li, March 12, 2019.

48. Nicholas Nehamas, Caitlin Ostroff, and Sarah Blaskey, "Massage Parlor Magnate Helped Steer Chinese to Trump NYC Fundraiser, Attendee Says," *Miami Herald*, March 9, 2019.

49. Sing Tao, "Trump Breakfast Party Asian.GOP convenes local chapters," December 6, 2017, www.pavatar.us/forum_topic/5111/%E7%89%B9%E6%9C%97%E6%99 %AE%E6%97%A9%E9%A4%90%E4%BC%9A++asian.gop+%E5%8F%AC%E9%9B %86%E5%90%84%E5%9C%B0%E5%88%86%E4%BC%9A%E5%85%B1%E8%A5% 84%E7%9B%9B%E4%B8%BE.

50. Interview with an attendee at the Cipriani event.

51. China Daily USA, "Across America," December 8, 2017, https://usa.china daily.com.cn/epaper/2017-12/08/content_35258779.htm.

52. Li, March 12, 2019.

53. 11 CFR § 110.20, www.law.cornell.edu/cfr/text/11/110.20.

54. 52 U.S. Code § 30122, https://www.law.cornell.edu/uscode/text/52/30122.

55. Sarah Blaskey, Nicholas Nehamas, and Caitlin Ostroff, "Cindy Yang Helped Chinese Tech Stars Get $50K Photos with Trump. Who Paid?" *Miami Herald*, March 21, 2019, www.miamiherald.com/latest-news/article227941749.html.

56. The authors' analysis of Federal Election Commission records, retrieved November 29, 2019.

57. Li, March 12, 2019.

58. Interview with Shannon Donnelly, December 18, 2019.

59. Archived webpage for GY US Investments, https://web.archive.org/web/2018 0827153942/https://gyusinvest.com/.

60. Electronic Articles of Organization for Florida Limited Liability Company, GY US Investments LLC, Florida Department of State, http://search.sunbiz.org /Inquiry/CorporationSearch/ConvertTiffToPDF?storagePath=COR%5C2017%5C121 2%5C60620706.tif&documentNumber=L17000253608.

61. Interview with Terry Bomar, March 25, 2019.

62. Wenli Cummings, "Great event! Please let me know if you want to go! I am going!," Facebook, December 6, 2017.

63. Ibid.

64. Ibid.

65. Group photos of the event posted on Facebook.

66. Cindy Yang WeChat profile, https://freewechat.com/a/MzAxMjYyODEwMQ ==/2649461795/1.

67. Interview with Xinyue "Daniel" Lou, November 4, 2019.

68. Interview with a model who worked at the event.

69. Interview with a person familiar with Yang's political and social activities.

CHAPTER 11. "PRINCE" CHARLES

1. Sarah Blaskey, Nicholas Nehamas, and Caitlin Ostroff, "Trump Tourism: How Charlottesville Enabled Cindy Yang to Market Mar-a-Lago in China," *Miami Herald*, March 29, 2019, www.miamiherald.com/news/politics-government/article228456974.html.

2. Interview with June Teufel Dreyer, China expert at University of Miami, March 27, 2019.

3. UNWTV, "New Year's gift! You Are Invited to Visit the United Nations, the United States Congress, President Trump's Private Estate," December 25, 2017, www .un-wtv.org/Chinese/NewsContent.aspx?id=1008.

4. Patrick Boehler and Echo Hui, "Did a Golden Triangle Leader Fall for a UN Peace Prize Hoax?" *The Irrawaddy*, January 4, 2013, www.irrawaddy.com/news/burma /did-a-golden-triangle-leader-fall-for-a-un-peace-prize-hoax.html.

5. Wang Jiangsheng, "2013 U.S. Presidential Inauguration Ceremony and UN Secretary-General's High-level Round Table," January 5, 2013, http://blog.sina.com.cn/s /blog_5dd1d28c01019jsn.html.

6. UNWTV, "New Year's gift! You Are Invited to Visit the United Nations, the United States Congress, President Trump's Private Estate."

7. Interview with a person familiar with Yang.

8. United Nations Friendship Pictorial Foundation, "Warm congratulations to Dr. Charles, Secretary-General of the United Nations Chinese Friendship Association, for leading an elite Chinese delegation to the US-China Friendship and Peaceful Exchange Dinner attended by US President Trump's sister Elizabeth Trump!" January 28, 2018, www.un-fpf.org/Chinese/NewsContent.aspx?id=1068.

9. Huaqing Henchuang, "Invitation Letter to Visit the United Nations, the US Congress, President Trump's Private Estate, etc," December 28, 2017, www.web.archive .org/web/20190321182027/http://www.sohu.com/a/213351520_100084567/.

10. Interview with Xiaoqi Wang, March 25, 2019.

11. GY US Investments LLC, "Homepage," www.web.archive.org/web/201808 27153942/https://gyusinvest.com/.

12. Ibid.

13. Ibid.

14. Interview with a former GOP political operative.

15. Interview with Terry Bomar, March 25, 2019.

16. Ibid.

17. Interview with a person familiar with Yang's business and political activities.

18. Marc Caputo, "New Racial Controversy Batters DeSantis," *Politico*, September 20, 2018, www.politico.com/story/2018/09/20/ron-desantis-florida-racial-issues-830726.

19. Kenzie Bryant, "Mar-a-Lago and the Curious Case of the Six-Foot-Tall Portrait of President Trump That No One Seems to Want," *Vanity Fair*, March 29, 2018, www.vanityfair.com/style/2018/03/donald-trump-portrait-dispute-mar-a-lago-truth-about-israel-gala.

20. Charles Elmore, "Others Fled Trump's Mar-a-Lago; This Group Wanted In," *Palm Beach Daily News*, August 25, 2017, www.palmbeachdailynews.com/news/others-fled-trump-mar-lago-this-group-wanted/TER2VpWS3MeLT1cMVmIPGK.

21. Lori Rozsa, "Israel-Focused Charity Praises Trump—and Pays Him—at Mar-a-Lago Gala," *Washington Post*, February 26, 2018, www.washingtonpost.com/news/post-politics/wp/2018/02/26/israel-focused-charity-praises-trump-and-pays-him-at-mar-a-lago-gala.

22. Interviews with two people familiar with the event.

23. United Nations Friendship Pictorial Foundation, "Warm congratulations to Dr. Charles, Secretary-General of the United Nations Chinese Friendship Association, for leading an elite Chinese delegation to the US-China Friendship and Peaceful Exchange Dinner attended by US President Trump's sister Elizabeth Trump!"

24. "Meet with President Trump at Sea-Lake Manor," January 25, 2018, www.ccvalue.cn/article/74906.html.

25. Yue Yuan, "Invitation Letter to the Presidential Dinner Party," January 26, 2018, www.read01.com/zh-hk/3GPGAj2.html#.XpHlwshKjIX.

26. Hong He, "MiaoA invites you to meet with President Trump at Haihu Manor," January 25, 2018, www.jinse.com/blockchain/141675.html.

27. Shannon Donnelly, "Society Insider: Flap over Trump Paintings Just Part of 'Weird' Gala," *Palm Beach Daily News*, March 28, 2018, www.palmbeachdailynews.com/lifestyles/society/society-insider-flap-over-trump-paintings-just-part-weird-gala/BlI3QSTxi8Bb6w5v6dog3M/.

28. Interview with Paulette Martin, November 19, 2019.

29. Interviews with six guests and staff members who were present at the Truth About Israel gala.

30. Donnelly, "Society Insider: Flap over Trump Paintings Just Part of 'Weird' Gala."

31. Interview with a Mar-a-Lago staff member.

32. Ibid.

33. Cai Kailong, "Bribing the President of the United States," February 28, 2018, https://news.p2peye.com/article-509264-1.html.

34. Ibid.

35. MiaoA International (@miaoa_), "Announcement: Affected by the shooting incident in America, U.S president Donald Trump did not attend the dinner. But our users did attend the dinner party on time. MiaoA will confirm with organizer and give a satisfactory solution to the users concerned. @TimeNewBank," Twitter, February 27, 2018, https://twitter.com/miaoa_/status/968427636564217856.

36. "Remarks by President Trump at the Governors' Ball," The White House, February 25, 2018, www.whitehouse.gov/briefings-statements/remarks-president-trump -governors-ball.

37. Interview with a person who attended the event.

38. Voice of America International Television Network, "Warm Congratulations to Chinese Entrepreneur Mr. Zhang Kui for Being Invited to the United States to Participate in the "Peace of Israel Truth Dinner" That Was Supposed to Be Held by President Trump on February 25, 2018 at the US President Trump Private Sea-Lake Estate," February 28, 2018, www.usivwtv.org/Article/news/220.htm.

39. Ibid.

40. United Nations Asking Congress Web TV Inc., "Warm Congratulations to Chinese Entrepreneurs Mr. Xie Yong and Mr. Yu Lei Were Invited to Participate in the "Israel Truth and Peace Dinner" that President Trump Will Attend on February 25, 2018," February 28, 2018, www.un-wtv.org/Chinese/NewsContent.aspx?id=1099.

41. Interview with Annie Marie Delgado, December 26, 2019.

CHAPTER 12.
SGT. PEPPER'S LONELY HEARTS CLUB BAND

1. Christine Stapleton and George Bennett, "Mar-a-Lago Events Raise Money for Politicos, Revenues for Trump," *Palm Beach Post*, May 6, 2019, www.palmbeachpost .com/news/national-govt--politics/mar-lago-events-raise-money-for-politicos-revenues -for-trump/F0EK7JzzOeDTT6nTSe8qyO/+&cd=14&hl=en&ct=clnk&gl=uk.

2. Alex Isenstadt, "Trump Campaign Plagued by Groups Raising Tens of Millions in His Name," *Politico*, March 3, 2018, www.politico.com/story/2018/03/03/trump -2020-donors-bundling-433886.

3. George Bennett, "Mar-a-Lago Make-up: Trump to Headline March 3 Fundraiser," *Palm Beach Post*, February 3, 2018, http://postonpolitics.blog.palmbeachpost .com/2018/02/03/mar-a-lago-make-up-trump-to-headline-march-3-fundraiser/.

4. Interview with Annie Marie Delgado, July 14, 2019.

5. Interview with Kris Hager, December 23, 2019.

6. "Honor the Fallen: Army Staff Sgt. Joshua R. Hager," *Military Times*, https:// thefallen.militarytimes.com/army-staff-sgt-joshua-r-hager/2584266.

7. Vicky Ward, "Pro-Trump Super PAC Paid Thousands to Firm Owned by Trump's Campaign Manager," *CNN*, August 30, 2019, www.cnn.com/2019/08/30 /politics/pro-trump-super-pac-paid-thousands-to-firm-owned-by-brad-parscales-wife /index.html.

8. Christine Stapleton, "Trump Campaign Head Moves to Florida for Taxes, Travel—and Trump," *Palm Beach Post*, June 14, 2019, www.palmbeachpost.com /news/20190614/trump-campaign-head-moves-to-florida-for-taxes-travel—and-trump.

9. Mark Burns (@pastormarkburns), "Great meeting J. Pepe Fanjul tonight at the RNC Spring Retreat at Mar-a-Lago #MAGA," Facebook, March 3, 2018, https:// www.facebook.com/photo.php?fbid=10213864072070110&set=a.1147028450040&type =3&theater.

10. Mark Burns, "I'm not waiting to get elected to start serving the People of the 4th District of SC. Great discussing bringing Jobs to the SC 4th District, Greenville &

Spartanburg, SC with Chinese Businessmen today. President Trump is bringing Jobs back to the US. #SC04 #SCGOP #scpol," Facebook, March 3, 2018, www.facebook .com/pastormarkburns/posts/10213870867199984.

11. *New York Times* staff, "South Carolina Primary Election Results," *New York Times*, June 20, 2019, www.nytimes.com/elections/results/south-carolina-house -district-4-primary-election.

12. Philip Rucker, Ashley Parker, and Josh Dawsey, "'Pure Madness': Dark Days Inside the White House as Trump Shocks and Rages," *Washington Post*, March 3, 2018, www.washingtonpost.com/politics/pure-madness-dark-days-inside-the-white-house -as-trump-shocks-and-rages/2018/03/03/9849867c-1e72-11e8-9de1-147dd2df3829 _story.html.

13. Maggie Haberman, "Hope Hicks to Leave Post as White House Communications Director," *New York Times*, February 28, 2018, www.nytimes.com/2018/02/28 /us/politics/hope-hicks-resign-communications-director.html.

14. Michael D. Shear and Katie Rogers, "Jared Kushner's Security Clearance Downgraded," *New York Times*, February 27, 2018, www.nytimes.com/2018/02/27/us/politics /jared-kushner-security-clearance-trump.html.

15. Maggie Haberman et al., "Trump Ordered Officials to Give Jared Kushner a Security Clearance," *New York Times*, February 28, 2018, www.nytimes.com/2019/02/28 /us/politics/jared-kushner-security-clearance.html.

16. Rucker, Parker, and Dawsey, "'Pure Madness'."

17. Kate Kelly and Maggie Haberman, "Gary Cohn Says He Will Resign as Trump's Top Economic Adviser," *New York Times*, March 6, 2018, www.nytimes.com/2018/03/06 /us/politics/gary-cohn-resigns.html.

18. Maggie Haberman, Annie Karni, and Danny Hakim, "N.R.A. Gets Results on Gun Laws in One Phone Call with Trump," *New York Times*, August 22, 2019, www .nytimes.com/2019/08/20/us/politics/trump-gun-control-nra.html.

19. Matt Novak, "Putin Nukes Florida in New Animated Video Showing Russia's Futuristic Weapons," *Gizmodo*, March 1, 2018, www.gizmodo.com/putin-nukes-florida -in-new-animated-video-showing-russi-1823420164.

20. Kirk Semple, Ben Protess, and Steve Eder, "Thugs, Leeches, Shouting and Shoving at Trump Hotel in Panama," *New York Times*, March 3, 2018, www.nytimes .com/2018/03/03/world/americas/donald-trump-panama-hotel-orestes-fintiklis.html.

21. Rucker, Parker and Dawsey, "'Pure Madness'."

22. Brandon Carter, "Trump Visits Fla. Golf Club Ahead of Remarks at Mar-a-Lago Fundraiser," *The Hill*, March 3, 2018, https://thehill.com/homenews/administration /376559-trump-visits-fla-golf-club-ahead-of-remarks-at-mar-a-lago-fundraiser.

23. John Pacenti, "In the Annals of Weird Florida, Stormy and Trump Create a Vortex," *Palm Beach Post*, April 15, 2018, www.palmbeachpost.com/news/breaking -news/the-annals-weird-florida-stormy-and-trump-create-vortex/28SAK8gEXRwit NrMcumTzL.

24. Ben Protess, William K. Rashbaum, and Maggie Haberman, "How Michael Cohen Turned Against President Trump," *New York Times*, April 21, 2019, www.nytimes .com/2019/04/21/us/politics/michael-cohen-trump.html.

25. Donald J. Trump (@realDonaldTrump), "The United States has an $800 Billion Dollar Yearly Trade Deficit because of our 'very stupid' trade deals and policies. Our

jobs and wealth are being given to other countries that have taken advantage of us for years. They laugh at what fools our leaders have been. No more!" Twitter, March 3, 2018, www.twitter.com/realDonaldTrump/status/969991653393039361.

26. Kevin Liptak, "Trump on China's Xi Consolidating Power: 'Maybe We'll Give That a Shot Some Day,'" CNN, March 3, 2018, www.cnn.com/2018/03/03/politics/trump-maralago-remarks/index.html.

27. Anna Lapaeva (@annalapaeva_), "Listening to Mr. Trump with a smile... And understanding, that the more power, success, and popularity you have the more jealousy and negative comments might come your way. Unfortunately! I am not into politics but I support strong people who strive for success. I don't subscribe to either Democrats or Republicans - I believe in helping people. I don't subscribe to any religion, but I respect people's beliefs. For me GOD means GOOD ☺ And I believe in spirituality and good morals my parents instilled in me. The more GOOD you do the more you are going to feel the presence of "GOD"! I believe there are more GOOD souls than evil ones. That's why the Earth still goes around. Haters will always hate. But PLEASE try to be loving and caring! No matter what! Forgive those who did wrong! Be grateful for every day alive! #trump #donaldtrump #president #usa #palmbeach," Instagram, March 7, 2018, www.instagram.com/p/BgCNYOXnufL.

28. Julie Bykowicz, Joe Palazzolo, and Georgi Kantchev, "Indicted Florida Pair Known for Flashy Style, Claim of Trump Ties," *Wall Street Journal*, October 10, 2019, www.wsj.com/articles/indicted-florida-pair-known-for-flashy-style-claim-of-trump-ties-11570757074.

29. David Smiley and Samantha J. Gross, "Giuliani's Indicted Florida Associates Pursued a Florida Weed License, Too," *Miami Herald*, October 16, 2019, www.miami herald.com/news/politics-government/article236258388.html.

30. Ben Wieder and Kevin G. Hall, "Pot Lawsuit May Provide Clues to Russian Funds in Parnas, Fruman Straw Donor Scheme," *McClatchy DC*, October 11, 2019, www.mcclatchydc.com/news/politics-government/article236028683.html.

31. Josh Dawsey, Rosalind S. Helderman, and Paul Sonne, "New Recording Shows Access Lev Parnas and Igor Fruman Had to Trump at Mar-a-Lago Donor Event," *Washington Post*, January 30, 2020, www.washingtonpost.com/politics/new-recording-shows-access-lev-parnas-and-igor-fruman-had-to-trump-at-mar-a-lago-donor-event/2020/01/30/a11cb354-437e-11ea-abff-5ab1ba98b405_story.html.

32. Ari Melber, "Indicted: Giuliani Allies Arrested at Airport Boasted of Trump Relationship, Mar-a-Lago Stays," *MSNBC The Beat with Ari*, October 10, 2019, www.msnbc.com/the-beat-with-ari/watch/indicted-giuliani-allies-arrested-at-airport-boasted-of-trump-relationship-mar-a-lago-stays-71031365524.

33. Nicholas Nehamas and Kevin G. Hall, "'He Conned Us from Day One': Giuliani's Ukraine Ally Leaves Trail of South Florida Debts," *Miami Herald*, October 1, 2019, www.miamiherald.com/news/politics-government/article235626327.html.

34. Nicholas Nehamas, Kevin G. Hall, Tess Riski, and Ben Wieder, "Meet the Soviet-Born Businessmen Tangled in Trump's Impeachment Inquiry. They live in Florida." *Miami Herald*, September 26, 2019, www.miamiherald.com/news/politics-government/article235501772.html.

35. Ibid.

36. Joe Palazzolo and Rebecca Davis O'Brien, "Giuliani Associate Left Trail of Troubled Businesses Before Ukraine Probe Push," *Wall Street Journal*, October 31, 2019, www.wsj.com/articles/giuliani-associate-left-trail-of-troubled-businesses-before -ukraine-probe-push-11572527608.

37. Aubrey Belford and Veronika Melkozerova, "Meet the Florida Duo Helping Giuliani Investigate for Trump in Ukraine," Organized Crime and Corruption Reporting Project, July 22, 2019, www.occrp.org/en/investigations/meet-the-florida-duo-helping -giuliani-dig-dirt-for-trump-in-ukraine.

38. Smiley and Gross, "Giuliani's Indicted Florida Associates Pursued a Florida Weed License, Too."

39. Nehamas and Hall, "'He Conned Us from Day One'."

40. US House of Representatives Judiciary Committee, "Lev Parnas Document Production," January 17, 2020, https://judiciary.house.gov/uploadedfiles/document _production_lev_parnas_january_17_2020_parnas_photos_combined.pdf.

41. Joseph A. Bondy, (@josephabondy), "Here's the "I don't know him at all, don't know what he's about, don't know where he comes from, know nothing about him" guy, w Lev Parnas & Roman Nasirov, former head of Ukrainian Fiscal Service, at Mar-a-Lago 12/16. @POTUS @realDonaldTrump @Acosta #LevRemembers #LetLevSpeak," Twitter, January 16, 2019, www.twitter.com/josephabondystatus/1217932038260625410 ?s=20.

42. Dawsey et al., "New Recording Shows Access Lev Parnas and Igor Fruman Had to Trump at Mar-a-Lago Donor Event."

43. *United States of America v. Lev Parnas, Igor Fruman, David Correia, and Andrey Kukushkin*, "Sealed Indictment," October 10, 2019, US District Court, Southern District of New York.

44. Jonathan Swan, "Rudy Giuliani's Tasteless Hillary Joke," *Axios*, March 4, 2018, www.axios.com/rudy-giulianis-tasteless-hillary-joke-1520203032-856992af-1e13-4061 -90a4-8a61c37ffd8f.html.

45. Ibid.

46. Kenneth P. Vogel, Ben Protess, and Sarah Maslin Nir, "Behind the Deal That Put Giuliani Together with a Dirt-Hunting Partner," *New York Times*, November 6, 2019, www.nytimes.com/2019/11/06/us/politics/ukraine-giuliani-charles-gucciardo.html.

47. Ibid.

48. Rosalind S. Helderman, Tom Hamburger, Paul Sonne, and Josh Dawsey, "How Giuliani's Outreach to Ukrainian Gas Tycoon Wanted in U.S. Shows Lengths He Took in His Hunt for Material to Bolster Trump," *Washington Post*, January 15, 2020, www .washingtonpost.com/politics/how-giulianis-outreach-to-ukrainian-gas-tycoon-wanted -in-us-shows-lengths-he-took-in-his-hunt-for-material-to-bolster-trump/2020/01/15 /64c263ba-2e5f-11ea-bcb3-ac6482c4a92f_story.html.

49. Matt Berman, "Rudy Giuliani Was with His Now-Indicted Ukrainian Friend at President Bush's State Funeral Service. Jeb Bush Says It's 'Disappointing,'" *BuzzFeed News*, October 15, 2019, www.buzzfeednews.com/article/mattberman/rudy-giuliani-lev -parnas-bush-funeral.

50. Vogel et al., "Behind the Deal That Put Giuliani Together with a Dirt-Hunting Partner."

51. Rebecca Davis O'Brien, "Federal Prosecutors Probe Giuliani's Links to Ukrainian Energy Projects," *Wall Street Journal*, November 15, 2019, www.wsj.com/articles/federal -prosecutors-probe-giulianis-links-to-ukrainian-energy-projects-11573837576.

52. *USA v. Parnas et al.*

53. Michael Sallah, Tanya Kozyreva, and Aubrey Belford, "Two Unofficial US Operatives Reporting to Trump's Lawyer Privately Lobbied a Foreign Government in a Bid to Help the President Win in 2020," *BuzzFeed News*, July 22, 2019, www.buzzfeednews .com/article/mikesallah/rudy-giuliani-ukraine-trump-parnas-fruman.

54. Courtney Subramanian, "Explainer: Biden, Allies Pushed Out Ukrainian Prosecutor Because He Didn't Pursue Corruption Cases," *USA Today*, October 3, 2019, www .usatoday.com/story/news/politics/2019/10/03/what-really-happened-when-biden -forced-out-ukraines-top-prosecutor/3785620002/.

55. Ashley Parker, Rosalind S. Helderman, and Paul Sonne, "Giuliani Associate Points to Pence Snub as Ukraine Pressure Point," *Washington Post*, January 16, 2020, www.washingtonpost.com/politics/giuliani-associate-points-to-pence-snub-as-ukraine -pressure-point/2020/01/16/c889c0e6-3882-11ea-bf30-ad313e4ec754_story.html.

56. David Welna, "The Hold on Ukraine Aid: A Timeline Emerges from Impeachment Probe," NPR, November 27, 2019, www.npr.org/2019/11/27/783487901/the-hold -on-ukraine-aid-a-timeline-emerges-from-impeachment-probe.

57. The White House, "Memorandum of Telephone Conversation," declassified September 24, 2019, www.whitehouse.gov/wp-content/uploads/2019/09/Unclassified 09.2019.pdf.

58. Julian E. Barnes, Michael S. Schmidt, Adam Goldman, and Katie Benner, "White House Knew of Whistle-Blower's Allegations Soon After Trump's Call with Ukraine Leader," *New York Times*, September 26, 2019, www.nytimes.com/2019/09/26 /us/politics/who-is-whistleblower.html.

59. "Read the Whistleblower Complaint Regarding President Trump's Communications with Ukrainian President Volodymyr Zelensky," *Washington Post*, October 16, 2019, www.washingtonpost.com/context/read-the-whistleblower-complaint-regarding -president-trump-s-communications-with-ukrainian-president-volodymyr-zelensky /4b9e0ca5-3824-467f-b1a3-77f2d4ee16aa/.

60. *USA v. Parnas et al.*

61. Ibid.

62. Dawsey et al., "New Recording Shows Access Lev Parnas and Igor Fruman Had to Trump at Mar-a-Lago Donor Event."

63. Vicky Ward, "Exclusive: After Private White House Meeting, Giuliani Associate Lev Parnas Said He Was on a 'Secret Mission' for Trump, Sources Say," CNN, November 16, 2019, www.cnn.com/2019/11/15/politics/parnas-trump-special-mission-ukraine /index.html.

64. Yamiche Alcindor, "Second Video Demonstrates Lev Parnas' Access to Trump," *PBS Newshour*, January 30, 2020, www.pbs.org/newshour/politics/parnas-released -second-video-showing-his-access-to-trump.

65. Philip Bump, "The Unmitigated Ludicrousness of Trump Trying to Distance Himself from Giuliani's Work on Ukraine," *Washington Post*, November 27, 2019, www .washingtonpost.com/politics/2019/11/27/unmitigated-ludicrousness-trump-trying -distance-himself-giulianis-work-ukraine/.

66. Ibid.

67. Jordan Fabian, "Trump, Giuliani Spoke Briefly at Mar-a-Lago Party on Saturday," *Bloomberg*, December 22, 2019, www.bloomberg.com/news/articles/2019-12-22/trump-giuliani-spoke-briefly-at-mar-a-lago-party-on-saturday.

68. Cindy Yang, Facebook, March 22, 2018.

69. The authors' analysis of Federal Election Commission data, December 22, 2019.

70. Frances Robles, Michael Forsythe, and Alexandra Stevenson, "She Extols Trump, Guns and the Chinese Communist Party Line," *New York Times*, March 16, 2019, www.nytimes.com/2019/03/16/us/cindy-yang-trump-donations.html.

71. Yang, Facebook.

72. The authors' analysis of Florida Department of State corporate filings, available at https://dos.myflorida.com/sunbiz.

73. Cindy Yang, "Trump Said: They Are Stealing Elections!" November 2018, https://go8po.com/news/tp/archives/5beba19c581c4b1b7192003c.

74. Interviews with two people familiar with Yang's personal and professional life.

75. Cindy Yang, "Love the gift send to my house, MAGA," Facebook, September 2, 2018.

76. Ibid.

CHAPTER 13. SNOW ON THE GROUND

1. Interview with Claude Taylor, April 4, 2019.

2. Mihir Zaveri et al., "The Government Shutdown Was the Longest Ever. Here's the History," *New York Times*, January 25, 2019. www.nytimes.com/interactive/2019/01/09/us/politics/longest-government-shutdown.html.

3. Taylor, April 4, 2019.

4. Gerry Shih, "AP Exclusive: China Accuses Outspoken Tycoon in US of Rape," Associated Press, August 31, 2017, www.apnews.com/9a4b4be3f0fb4e7191a53b9368318513/AP-Exclusive:-China-accuses-outspoken-tycoon-in-US-of-rape.

5. Meenal Vamburkar, "Chinese Fugitive's Sherry-Netherland Pad Has New Brokers—and Another Price Cut," *The Real Deal*, November 14, 2018, https://therealdeal.com/2018/11/14/chinese-fugitives-sherry-netherland-pad-has-new-brokers-and-another-price-cut/; and Sarah Blaskey and Jay Weaver, "He's a Chinese Billionaire and a Member of Trump's Mar-a-Lago. Is He Also a Communist Spy?" *Miami Herald*, July 23, 2019, www.miamiherald.com/news/politics-government/article232973237.html.

6. Michael Forsythe, "As Trump Meets Xi at Mar-a-Lago, There's a 'Wild Card'," *New York Times*, April 4, 2017, www.nytimes.com/2017/04/04/world/asia/china-mar-a-lago-guo-wengui.html.

7. Kate O'Keeffe, Aruna Viswanatha, and Cezary Podkul, "China's Pursuit of Fugitive Businessman Guo Wengui Kicks Off Manhattan Caper Worthy of Spy Thriller," *Wall Street Journal*, October 22, 2017, www.wsj.com/articles/chinas-hunt-for-guo-wengui-a-fugitive-businessman-kicks-off-manhattan-caper-worthy-of-spy-thriller-1508717977.

8. Chun Han Wong and Felicia Schwartz, "China Wants Fugitive Guo Wengui Back—but He's Applied for U.S. Asylum," *Wall Street Journal*, September 7, 2017, www.wsj.com/articles/fugitive-chinese-businessman-seeks-u-s-asylum-1504805457.

9. *Pacific Alliance Asia v. Ho Wan, Kwok*, "Exhibit 5," New York Supreme Court, November 28, 2018.

10. Ibid.

11. O'Keeffe, Viswanatha, and Podkul, "China's Pursuit of Fugitive Businessman Guo Wengui Kicks Off Manhattan Caper Worthy of Spy Thriller."

12. Ibid.

13. Ibid.

14. Maggie Haberman, "Bannon's Work with Wanted Chinese Billionaire Began Shortly After He Left White House," *New York Times*, December 23, 2019, www .nytimes.com/2019/12/23/us/politics/steve-bannon-guo-wengui.html.

15. *Eastern Profit Corporation Limited v. Strategic Vision US LLC*, "Complaint," Case No. 18-cv-2185, United States District Court, Southern District of New York, August 9, 2018.

16. Blaskey and Weaver, "He's a Chinese Billionaire and a Member of Trump's Mar-a-Lago."

17. *Eastern Profit v. Strategic*, "Answer and Counterclaims to Second Amended Complaint," July 19, 2019.

18. Blaskey and Weaver, "He's a Chinese Billionaire and a Member of Trump's Mar-a-Lago."

19. *Eastern Profit v. Strategic*, "Answer and Counterclaims to Second Amended Complaint."

20. *Eastern Profit v. Strategic*, "Complaint."

21. *Eastern Profit v. Strategic*, "Answer and Counterclaims to Second Amended Complaint."

22. *Eastern Profit v. Strategic*, "Strategic Vision's consolidated memorandum of law in opposition to Eastern's motion for summary judgment and in support of its cross-motion against Eastern," April 6, 2020.

23. *Eastern Profit v. Strategic*, "Order," District Judge John Koeltl, May 13, 2019.

24. Interview with Claude Taylor, December 30, 2019.

25. Sarah Blaskey and Nicholas Nehamas, "Indiana Man Sparked Secret Service Investigation as He Shouted Outside Trump's Mar-a-Lago," *Miami Herald*, January 14, 2020, www.miamiherald.com/news/local/crime/article239243583.html.

26. Interview with a former Mar-a-Lago employee.

27. Interview with a Mar-a-Lago staff member.

28. Interview with Shannon Donnelly, December 18, 2019.

29. Interview with Fred Rustmann, December 6, 2019.

30. Donnelly, December 18, 2019.

31. Donald Trump (@realDonaldTrump), "I am all alone (poor me) in the White House waiting for the Democrats to come back and make a deal on desperately needed Border Security. At some point the Democrats not wanting to make a deal will cost our Country more money than the Border Wall we are all talking about. Crazy!," Twitter, December 24, 2018, https://twitter.com/realdonaldtrump/status/1077255770725601280 ?lang=en.

32. Department of Homeland Security Purchase Order, contract no. 70US0919 P70090047, accessed January 5, 2020, www.usaspending.gov/#/award/76478098.

33. Justin Rohrlich, "The US Government May Be Shut Down, but Taxpayers

Are Footing the Bill for Mar-a-Lago Party Tents," *Quartz*, December 24, 2018, https://qz.com/1506879/trumps-mar-a-lago-party-tents-are-costing-taxpayers-54000/.

34. Robles, Forsythe, and Stevenson, "She Extols Trump, Guns and the Chinese Communist Party Line."

35. Chinese social media blog post Etechome, accessed March 21, 2019.

36. Laurence Leamer, "'In Some Ways It's a More Pleasant Club When Trump Isn't Here': Mar-a-Lago Prepares for New Year's Eve Without Its Star Attraction," *Vanity Fair*, December 31, 2018, www.vanityfair.com/news/2018/12/mar-a-lago-new-years-eve.

37. Christine Stapleton and Carolyn DiPaolo, "Trump in Palm Beach: A Look Back at New Year's Eve Bashes at Mar-a-Lago," *Palm Beach Post*, December 30, 2019, www.palmbeachpost.com/news/20191230/trump-in-palm-beach-look-back-at-new-yearrsquos-eve-bashes-at-mar-a-lago.

38. Party on the Moon Facebook page, accessed January 5, 2020, www.facebook.com/watch/?v=1425024334306899.

CHAPTER 14. "FRIENDLY, CHEERFUL ORIENTAL LADIES"

1. May Jeong, "'You Won't Believe What Happened': The Wild, Disturbing Saga of Robert Kraft's Visit to a Strip Mall Sex Spa," *Vanity Fair*, October 4, 2019, www.vanityfair.com/news/2019/10/the-disturbing-saga-of-robert-kraft.

2. Jupiter Police Department, "Probable Cause Affidavit," Report No. 54-19-000819, February 22, 2019.

3. Bruce R., "This location is now called Orchids of Asia Day Spa. Same staff, services and pricing. A great atmosphere, and friendly, cheerful Oriental ladies. Marvelous services with authentic Asian Massage!," Yelp, January 7, 2013, www.yelp.com/not_recommended_reviews/tokyo-day-spa-and-massages-jupiter.

4. Jupiter Police Department, "Affidavit of Detective Andrew Sharp," Case Number 18-05410, February 15, 2019.

5. Jupiter Police Department, "Probable Cause Affidavit," Report No. 54-19-000820, February 22, 2019.

6. Jeong, "'You Won't Believe What Happened'."

7. Cindy Yang, "First time in Super Bowl," Facebook, February 3, 2019.

8. Katie Rogers and Annie Karni, "Trump Returns This Weekend to Mar-a-Lago, His Gilded Comfort Zone," *New York Times*, January 31, 2019, www.nytimes.com/2019/01/31/us/politics/mar-a-lago-trump.html.

9. Cindy Yang, Video Taken at Trump International Golf Club, Facebook, February 3, 2019.

10. Cindy Yang, "We love our president," Facebook, February 3, 2019.

11. Archived copy of GY US Investments website captured by the authors.

12. Charles Rabin, Sarah Blaskey, and Rob Wile, "Patriots Owner Robert Kraft Is Among the Hundreds Charged in Florida Sex Traffic Sting," *Miami Herald*, February 22, 2019, www.miamiherald.com/news/local/article226630229.html.

13. Jeong, "'You Won't Believe What Happened'."

14. Hannah Morse and Julius Whigham II, "Authorities Investigate Human-Trafficking at Area Day Spas," *Palm Beach Post*, February 19, 2019, www.palmbeachpost.com/news/20190219/Authorities-investigate-human-trafficking-at-area-day-spas.

15. Will Greenlee, "Florida Sheriff: 'Manifestly Obvious' This Is Human Trafficking, but Need Victim Cooperation for Case," *USA Today*, February 27, 2019, www.usa today.com/story/news/nation/2019/02/27/florida-human-trafficking-martin-county -sheriff-spa-massage-parlor/3006265002/; and interview with a federal law enforcement source.

16. Andrew Beaton, "Robert Kraft Apologizes as Defense Attorneys Say Investigation Was Illegally Conducted," *Wall Street Journal*, March 23, 2019, www.wsj.com /articles/robert-kraft-apologizes-as-defense-attorneys-say-investigation-was-illegally -conducted-11553374687.

17. Ken Belson, "Robert Kraft Case Hinges on Appeal of Video Evidence Decision," *New York Times*, October 2, 2019, www.nytimes.com/2019/10/02/sports/football/robert -kraft-appeal-case.html.

18. Interview with Cindy Yang, March 6, 2019.

19. Sarah Blaskey, Nicholas Nehamas, and Caitlin Ostroff, "Trump Cheered Patriots to Super Bowl Victory with Founder of Spa Where Kraft Was Busted," *Miami Herald*, March 8, 2019, www.miamiherald.com/news/politics-government/article227186429 .html.

20. Yang, March 6, 2019.

21. Dan Friedman, "White House: Trump 'Doesn't Know' the Massage Parlor Owner Peddling Access to Him," *Mother Jones*, March 12, 2019, www.motherjones .com/politics/2019/03/white-house-trump-doesnt-know-massage-parlor-owner -peddling-access-to-him-cindy-yang/.

22. Nicole Darrah, "Trump Dismisses Mar-a-Lago Breach as 'Just a Fluke,' Denies Knowing Cindy Yang," *Fox News*, April 3, 2019, www.foxnews.com/politics/trump -dismisses-mar-a-lago-breach-as-just-a-fluke-denies-knowing-cindy-yang.

23. Interview with Toni Holt Kramer, November 19, 2019.

24. Sarah Blaskey, Nicholas Nehamas, Caitlin Ostroff, and David Smiley, "How Did Li Yang Go from Spa Owner to Trump Selfie Queen? 'She Likes to Show Off,' Mom Says," *Miami Herald*, March 12, 2019, www.miamiherald.com/news/politics -government/article227438119.html.

25. Olivia Gazis, "Democrats Ask FBI for Criminal, Counterintelligence Investigations into Li 'Cindy' Yang," *CBS News*, March 18, 2019, www.cbsnews.com/news/demo crats-ask-fbi-for-criminal-counterintelligence-investigations-into-li-cindy-yang/.

26. Andrew Rice, "How to Throw a Party at Mar-a-Lago," *New York Magazine/Intelligencer*, June 24, 2019, http://nymag.com/intelligencer/2019/06/cindy-yang-mar-a-lago .html; and Jane Musgrave, "Conservative Commentator Karyn Turk Admits to Stealing Mom's Social Security," *Palm Beach Post*, September 27, 2019, www.palmbeachpost .com/news/20190927/conservative-commentator-karyn-turk-admits-to-stealing-mom rsquos-social-security.

27. Emily Tillett, "Former Owner of Spa Embroiled in Kraft Charges Denies Selling Access to Trump," *CBS News*, March 21, 2019, www.cbsnews.com/news/cindy-yang -former-spa-owner-denies-selling-access-to-trump/?ftag=CNM-00-10aab6j&linkId =65096264&fbclid=IwAR24XMKSoUPOaovoyJA9B36Kha_GZeJNschWco7MwXu 9Q7rRt1ZfcoiPtFQ.

28. Cynthia McFadden et al., "Ex-Spa Owner Denies Selling Access to Trump, Says Dems Target Her Because She's a Chinese Republican," *NBC News*, March 20,

2019, www.nbcnews.com/politics/donald-trump/ex-spa-owner-denies-selling-access-trump-says-dems-target-n985381.

29. Jay Weaver et al., "Feds Open Foreign-Money Investigation into Trump Donor Cindy Yang," *Miami Herald*, May 9, 2019, www.miamiherald.com/news/politics-government/article230217729.html.

30. Jay Weaver et al., "Federal Prosecutors Demand Cindy Yang Records from Mar-a-Lago, Trump Campaign," *Miami Herald*, May 29, 2019. www.miamiherald.com/news/politics-government/article230946518.html.

31. Interview with Kerry Kensington, January 14, 2020.

32. GY US Investments website captured by the authors.

33. Interview with Terry Bomar, March 25, 2019.

34. Sarah Blaskey, Nicholas Nehamas, and Caitlin Ostroff, "Chinese Woman Carrying 'Malware' Arrested at Mar-a-Lago Heading to a Cindy Yang Event," *Miami Herald*, April 2, 2019, www.miamiherald.com/news/local/crime/article228738969.html.

35. Interview with Li Weitian, March 27, 2019.

CHAPTER 15. A WOMAN CALLED VERONICA

1. *United States of America v. Yujing Zhang*, government trial exhibit, case no. 19-cr-80056, PACER (S.D. Florida, September 9, 2019).

2. *United States of America v. Yujing Zhang*, detention hearing transcript, case no. 19-cr-80056, PACER (S.D. Florida, April 8, 2019).

3. Ibid.

4. US Government Accountability Office, Presidential Security: Vetting of Individuals and Secure Areas at Mar-a-Lago, January 2019, www.gao.gov/assets/700/696549.pdf.

5. *United States of America v. Yujing Zhang*, trial testimony, Secret Service Agent Krystle Kerr, case no. 19-cr-80056, PACER (S.D. Florida, September 9, 2019).

6. *United States of America v. Yujing Zhang*, trial testimony, Willy Isidore, case no. 19-cr-80056, PACER (S.D. Florida, September 9, 2019); and interview with a Colony Hotel staff member.

7. *United States of America v. Yujing Zhang*, trial testimony, Willy Isidore.

8. Interviews with two people who worked at Mar-a-Lago.

9. Interview with a Mar-a-Lago staff member.

10. *United States of America v. Yujing Zhang*, trial testimony, Secret Service Agent Krystle Kerr.

11. Matt Schiavenza, "The Geographic Distribution of China's Last Names, in Maps," *The Atlantic*, October 22, 2013, www.theatlantic.com/china/archive/2013/10/the-geographic-distribution-of-chinas-last-names-in-maps/280776/.

12. *United States of America v. Yujing Zhang*, detention hearing testimony, Secret Service Agent Samuel Ivanovich, case no. 19-cr-80056, PACER (S.D. Florida, April 8, 2019).

13. Interview with a US law enforcement official.

14. Sarah Blaskey et al., "Cagey Chinese Spy or Fawning Trump Fan? Mar-a-Lago Intruder's Trial May Offer Up Clues," *Miami Herald*, September 6, 2019, https://www.miamiherald.com/news/local/article234489262.html.

15. Nicholas Nehamas, Sarah Blaskey, and Caitlin Ostroff, "'Extreme' Flight Risk: Chinese Woman Arrested at Mar-a-Lago Says She Owns $1.3M Home, BMW," *Miami Herald*, April 4, 2019, www.miamiherald.com/news/politics-government/article228850 604.html.

16. Blaskey et al., "Cagey Chinese Spy or Fawning Trump Fan? Mar-a-Lago Intruder's Trial May Offer Up Clues."

17. *United States of America v. Yujing Zhang*, government trial exhibit, contract between Charles Lee and Yujing Zhang, document 73-23, case no. 19-cr-80056, PACER (S.D. Florida, April 8, 2019).

18. On March 16 Charles Lee attached Cindy Yang's flyer to a WeChat message to Yujing Zhang, along with a signed contract to attend the event.

19. *United States of America v. Yujing Zhang*, defense trial exhibit, document 23-2, case no. 19-cr-80056, PACER (S.D. Florida, April 8, 2019).

20. *United States of America v. Yujing Zhang*, government trial exhibit, contract between Lee and Zhang.

21. *United States of America v. Yujing Zhang*, detention hearing transcript.

22. Blaskey et al., "Cagey Chinese Spy or Fawning Trump Fan? Mar-a-Lago Intruder's Trial May Offer Up Clues."

23. *United States of America v. Yujing Zhang*, government trial exhibit, voice and text messages between Lee and Zhang, document 73-21, case no. 19-cr-80056, PACER (S.D. Florida, September 10, 2019).

24. Ibid.

25. *United States of America v. Yujing Zhang*, government trial exhibit, Zhang's United Airlines ticket receipt, document 73-15, case no. 19-cr-80056, PACER (S.D. Florida, September 10, 2019).

26. *United States of America v. Yujing Zhang*, government trial exhibit, list of Zhang's electronic devices, document 73-18 , case no. 19-cr-80056, PACER (S.D. Florida, September 10, 2019).

27. *United States of America v. Yujing Zhang*, trial testimony, Secret Service Agent Paul Patenaude, case no. 19-cr-80056, PACER (S.D. Florida, September 9, 2019).

28. *United States of America v. Yujing Zhang*, trial testimony, Ariela Grumaz, case no. 19-cr-80056, PACER (S.D. Florida, September 10, 2019).

29. Ibid.

30. Ibid.

31. Ibid.

32. Ibid.

33. *United States of America v. Yujing Zhang*, detention hearing testimony, Secret Service Agent Samuel Ivanovich.

34. *United States of America v. Yujing Zhang*, trial testimony, Ariela Grumaz.

35. *United States of America v. Yujing Zhang*, criminal complaint, case no. 19-cr-80056, PACER (S.D. Florida, April 8, 2019).

36. *United States of America v. Yujing Zhang*, detention hearing testimony, Secret Service Agent Samuel Ivanovich.

37. Ibid.

38. *United States of America v. Yujing Zhang*, detention hearing transcript.

39. *United States of America v. Yujing Zhang*, sentencing memo, case no. 19-cr-80056, PACER (S.D. Florida, November 7, 2019).

40. Interview with a source familiar with information technology at several Trump properties.

41. Interview with Nicholas Eftimiades, February 8, 2020.

42. Jay Weaver, Nicholas Nehamas, Sarah Blaskey, Caitlin Ostroff, and Alex Daugherty, "Feds Are Investigating Possible Chinese Spying at Mar-a-Lago and Cindy Yang, Sources Say," *Miami Herald*, April 3, 2018, www.miamiherald.com/news/politics-government/article228783369.html.

CHAPTER 16. "SOMETHING NEFARIOUS"

1. Jay Weaver et al., "'She Lies to Everyone': Feds Say Mar-a-Lago Intruder Had Hidden-Camera Detector in Hotel," *Miami Herald*, April 8, 2019, www.miamiherald.com/news/politics-government/article228963409.html.

2. *United States v. Yujing Zhang*, detention hearing transcript, case no. 19-cr-80056, PACER (S.D. Florida, April 8, 2019); Nicholas Nehamas, Sarah Blaskey, and Caitlin Ostroff, "'Extreme' Flight Risk: Chinese Woman Arrested at Mar-a-Lago Says She Owns $1.3M Home, BMW," *Miami Herald*, April 4, 2019, www.miamiherald.com/news/politics-government/article228850604.html.

3. Jay Weaver, Nicholas Nehamas, Sarah Blaskey, Caitlin Ostroff, and Alex Daugherty, "Feds Are Investigating Possible Chinese Spying at Mar-a-Lago and Cindy Yang, Sources Say," *Miami Herald*, April 3, 2018, www.miamiherald.com/news/politics-government/article228783369.html.

4. Ibid.

5. *United States of America v. Yujing Zhang*, detention hearing transcript.

6. Ibid.

7. *United States of America v. Yujing Zhang*, Mar-a-Lago event contract, case no. 19-cr-80056, PACER (S.D. Florida, September 19, 2019).

8. *United States of America v. Yujing Zhang*, detention hearing transcript.

9. Ibid.

10. *United States of America v. Yujing Zhang*, detention hearing transcript.

11. *United States of America v. Yujing Zhang*, voice and text messages, document 73-21, case no. 19-cr-80056, PACER (S.D. Florida, September 19, 2019).

12. Sarah Blaskey et al. "'Up to Something Nefarious': Judge Orders Lockup of Chinese Woman Arrested at Mar-a-Lago," *Miami Herald*, April 15, 2019, www.miamiherald.com/news/local/crime/article229267494.html.

13. Interview with a person who answered the phone at the consulate number in Zhang's call logs.

14. Palm Beach County Sheriff's Office log of jail calls for Yujing Zhang.

15. *United States of America v. Yujing Zhang*, statement made in court hearing by Assistant Federal Public Defender Kristy Militello, case no. 19-cr-80056, PACER (S.D. Florida, June 11, 2019).

16. Sarah Blaskey, Caitlin Ostroff, and Nicholas Nehamas, "Chinese Woman Accused of Mar-a-Lago Trespass Wants to Fire Attorneys, Represent Herself," *Miami*

Herald, May 21, 2019, www.miamiherald.com/news/local/crime/article230650169 .html.

17. Ibid.

18. Alex Daugherty, "A Venezuelan-Born Miami Lawyer Becomes One of the Youngest U.S. Lifetime Judges Ever," *Miami Herald*, April 4, 2019, www.miamiherald .com/news/local/article228825299.html.

19. Interview with Clayton Davis, August 21, 2019.

20. Interview with Francine Adderley, August 21, 2019.

21. Jay Weaver and Sarah Blaskey, "With Classified Filing, Feds Eye National Security Case Against Mar-a-Lago Intruder," *Miami Herald*, June 12, 2019, www.miami herald.com/news/politics-government/article231465918.html.

22. Ibid.

23. Jay Weaver and Nicholas Nehamas, "U.S. Can Pursue Secret National Security Probe of Mar-a-Lago Intruder, Judge Rules," *Miami Herald*, July 10, 2019, www .miamiherald.com/article232490757.html.

24. Jay Weaver and Nicholas Nehamas, "'Thank You, USA': At Wild Trial Opener, Alleged Mar-a-Lago Intruder Says She Did No Wrong," *Miami Herald*, September 9, 2019, www.miamiherald.com/news/state/florida/article234882057.html.

25. Ibid.

26. Weaver and Nehamas, "'Thank You, USA'."

27. Ibid.

28. Jay Weaver and Nicholas Nehamas, "'Not a Wandering Tourist': Guilty Verdict for Woman Accused of Trespass at Trump's Mar-a-Lago," *Miami Herald*, September 11, 2019, www.miamiherald.com/news/local/article234961982.html.

29. *United States of America v. Yujing Zhang*, detention hearing transcript.

30. Sarah Blaskey, Nicholas Nehamas, and Ben Conarck, "Woman Arrested for Trespassing at Trump's Mar-a-Lago Is Another Chinese National," *Miami Herald*, December 18, 2019, www.miamiherald.com/news/local/article238508443.html.

31. Nicholas Nehamas and Sarah Blaskey, "Trial of Alleged Mar-a-Lago Intruder Offers Latest Peek into Security Protocols," *Miami Herald*, February 11, 2020, www .miamiherald.com/news/nation-world/article239234948.html.

32. Nicholas Nehamas and Sarah Blaskey, "No Signs, No Gate, Few Guards: Are Mar-a-Lago Intruders Actually Trespassing?" *Miami Herald*, February 12, 2020, www .miamiherald.com/news/local/crime/article240220822.html.

33. Jay Weaver, "Chinese Woman's Bizarre Intrusion on Mar-a-Lago Ends with Sentence of Time Served," *Miami Herald*, November 25, 2019, www.miamiherald.com /news/politics-government/article237725734.html.

34. Weaver and Nehamas, "'Not a Wandering Tourist'."

35. Weaver, "Chinese Woman's Bizarre Intrusion on Mar-a-Lago Ends with Sentence of Time Served."

36. Ibid.

37. Jay Weaver and Nicholas Nehamas, "Intruder at Trump's Palm Beach Club Leaves Jail, Faces Deportation to China," *Miami Herald*, December 4, 2019, www .miamiherald.com/news/local/article238047649.html.

38. Interview with a federal law enforcement official.

39. Interview with a Mar-a-Lago staff member.

40. Interview with a Mar-a-Lago staff member.

41. Ibid.

EPILOGUE. PANDEMIC AT THE DISCO

1. Maggie VandenBerghe (@fogcitymidge), Instagram, story, March 8, 2020.

2. Jair M. Bolsonaro (jairmessiasbolsonaro), "Jantar com Presidente @realdonald trump . - Mar-a-Lago/Florida/USA," Instagram, March 7, www.instagram.com/p/B9d NpoeHfOl/?igshid=efuv0erjostf.

3. Alice Su, "A Doctor Was Arrested for Warning China About the Coronavirus. Then He Died of It," *Los Angeles Times*, February 6, 2020, www.latimes.com/world -nation/story/2020-02-06/coronavirus-china-xi-li-wenliang.

4. Pam Belluck and Noah Weiland, "C.D.C. Officials Warn of Coronavirus Out-breaks in the U.S.," *New York Times*, February 25, 2020, www.nytimes.com/2020/02/25 /health/coronavirus-us.html.

5. Eric Lipton, David E. Sanger, Maggie Haberman, Michael D. Shear, Mark Maz-zetti, and Julian E. Barnes, "He Could Have Seen What Was Coming: Behind Trump's Failure on the Virus," *New York Times*, April 11, 2020, www.nytimes.com/2020/04/11/us /politics/coronavirus-trump-response.html/.

6. Adriana Brasileiro, Sarah Blaskey, and Nicholas Nehamas, "How a Mar-a-Lago Member Helped Set Up the Brazil Summit That Exposed Trump to Coronavirus," *Miami Herald*, March 13, 2020, www.miamiherald.com/news/politics-government /article241026546.html.

7. Ibid.

8. Ibid.

9. Pedro Portal, "'It's Safe for Healthy Americans to Travel,' Pence Says," *Miami Herald*, March 9, 2020, www.miamiherald.com/news/health-care/article241027676 .html/.

10. Taylor Dolven, "State Department Warns Against Traveling by Cruise Ship During Coronavirus Outbreak," *Miami Herald*, March 8, 2020, www.miamiherald .com/news/business/tourism-cruises/article241013416.html.

11. The White House, "Remarks by President Trump and President Bolsonaro of Brazil Before Working Dinner," March 8, 2020, www.whitehouse.gov/briefings-state ments/remarks-president-trump-president-bolsonaro-brazil-working-dinner-west -palm-beach-fl/.

12. Joe Hagan, "'Dishonesty . . . Is Always an Indicator of Weakness': Tucker Carlson on How He Brought His Coronavirus Message to Mar-a-Lago," *Vanity Fair*, March 17, 2020, www.vanityfair.com/news/2020/03/tucker-carlson-on-how-he-brought -coronavirus-message-to-mar-a-lago.

13. Ibid.

14. Peter Baker and Katie Rogers, "On a Saturday Night in Florida, a Presiden-tial Party Became a Coronavirus Hot Zone," *New York Times*, March 14, 2020, www.ny times.com/2020/03/14/us/politics/trump-coronavirus-mar-a-lago.html.

15. Joey Flechas and Aaron Leibowitz, "Miami Mayor Tests Positive for Corona-virus After Event with Bolsonaro and Staffers," *Miami Herald*, March 13, 2020, www .miamiherald.com/news/local/community/miami-dade/article241163311.html.

16. Baker and Rogers, "On a Saturday Night in Florida, a Presidential Party Became a Coronavirus Hot Zone."

17. Cristóbal Reyes, "1st Orange County Coronavirus Case Is Man Who Brunched at Mar-a-Lago; Unclear Whether Trump Attended," *Orlando Sentinel*, March 14, 2020, www.orlandosentinel.com/coronavirus/os-ne-orange-county-coronavirus-update-2020 0314-xfadnck4dnggbc52j2zy62xiou-story.html.

18. Emma Bowman, "President Trump Tests Negative for Coronavirus," NPR, March 14, 2020, www.npr.org/2020/03/14/815959169/president-trump-tests-negative -for-coronavirus.

19. Interview with a Mar-a-Lago staff member.

20. Ibid.

21. Ibid.

22. Ibid.

23. Joshua Partlow, Jonathan O'Connell, and David A. Fahrenthold, "Trump Organization Has Laid Off About 1,500 Employees as Pandemic Hits Business," *Washington Post*, April 3, 2020, www.washingtonpost.com/politics/trump-organization-has-laid -off-about-1500-employees-as-pandemic-spreads/2020/04/03/c413e42e-75d6-11ea-ae50 -7148009252e3_story.html.

24. Brian Spegele, Craig Karmin, and Jenny Strasburg, "Coronavirus Costing Trump Properties over $1 Million Daily in Lost Revenue," *Wall Street Journal*, April 2, 2020, www.wsj.com/articles/coronavirus-costing-trump-properties-over-1-million -daily-in-lost-revenue-11585823401.

25. Paul Martinka and Bruce Golding, "Another NYC Hospital Is Moving Bodies with a Forklift," *New York Post*, April 2, 2020, www.nypost.com/2020/04/02/another -nyc-hospital-is-moving-bodies-with-a-forklift/; and Ryan Young, Jake Carpenter, and Paul P. Murphy, "Photos Show Bodies Piled Up and Stored in Vacant Rooms at Detroit Hospital," *CNN*, April 14, 2020, www.cnn.com/2020/04/13/health/detroit-hospital -bodies-coronavirus-trnd/index.html.

26. Taylor Dolven, Sarah Blaskey, Nicholas Nehamas, and Alex Harris, "Cruise Ships Sailed on Despite the Coronavirus. Thousands of People Paid the Price," *Miami Herald*, April 23, 2020, https://www.miamiherald.com/news/business/tourism-cruises /article241640166.html.

27. Florida Department of Health, "Florida's COVID-19 Data and Surveillance Dashboard," accessed April 4, 2020, https://experience.arcgis.com/experience /96dd742462124fa0b38ddedb9b25e429.

ACKNOWLEDGMENTS

The Grifter's Club owes more debts and thanks than could be listed in an entire chapter, much less a page or two. Although there are four names on the byline, this book was a communal effort. Dozens of people participated in its crafting. Dozens more told us the stories that made it possible.

The staff and members of Mar-a-Lago went out on a limb when they chose to trust a group of outsiders to represent their experiences and tell their stories. They never expected to find themselves thrust into a world of top-level politics and national security. But when the man who owned their club was elected president, that's exactly where they ended up. Their trust in us is no small thing. The nation owes them a debt for the information they shared, which would otherwise have remained hidden from the public.

The authors owe a special thanks to all of our sources who stuck with us to the bitter end because they were dedicated to our mission. We called and called, and they never stopped picking up the phone. They never stopped trying to help. We are grateful for their tremendous honesty and bravery.

While we cannot possibly list all who deserve our thanks, we would be remiss not to mention the following people who went above and beyond in giving life to this project:

Cristalyne Bell flew to Miami (twice) at a moment's notice to help us meet what felt like impossible deadlines. She wrote, reported, fact checked, copy edited, compiled footnotes, and logged sleepless nights alongside the authors. She cared as if this book were her own. It is. (And a shout-out to her husband, Scot McCullough, for helping too.)

Casey Frank, our editor at the *Miami Herald*, may have been a bit surprised when Sarah called him one afternoon and said she had found a big story: a selfie of a South Florida spa owner standing with Donald Trump. But he let us run to the ends of the earth chasing leads and whims. His encouragement and his dedication to scrappy reporting brought this team together and allowed us to tell the story of Mar-a-Lago in a way that has never quite been done before. We could not be more grateful for his faith in each of us.

Benjamin Adams, our editor at PublicAffairs, and David Patterson, our agent at Stuart Krichevsky Literary Agency, conceived this book after reading our work in the *Miami Herald*. It would never have occurred to four local news reporters that our stories might merit a fuller treatment. Ben also showed incredible patience, understanding, and kindness when the COVID-19 pandemic blew our production schedule out of the water. So did our project manager, Christine Marra, and copy editor, Josephine Moore.

None of the authors would be where they are today without our experiences at the *Miami Herald*, the newsroom that raised and nurtured us. Thanks in particular to the team who reported, produced, and edited our Mar-a-Lago stories with us—Aaron Albright, Eddie Alvarez, Monika Leal, Adriana Brasileiro, Rob Wile, Taylor Dolven, David Smiley, Mary Behne, Adrian Ruhi, Kevin G. Hall, and Alex Daugherty, to name a few. This book also owes thanks to executive editor Aminda Marqués González, managing editor Rick Hirsch, senior editor Dave Wilson, and assistant city editor Curtis Morgan, who allowed four of their reporters to take on an ambitious project alongside their day jobs. In addition, we owe a huge debt to our fellow reporters who covered the news in our absence. They are our colleagues and our true friends.

Please subscribe to the *Miami Herald* and *el Nuevo Herald* to give a future to local journalism like ours.

And special thanks to One Herald Guild, our newsroom union. OHG always has our backs and fights to protect hard-hitting, watchdog journalism every day.

The other MVPs:

Shelly Ci turned around a reporting assignment that had been impossible for other journalists. It took her a week. Several chapters of this book include her essential reporting.

Keenan Chen remains the only journalist (that we know of) who ever managed to interview Charles Lee. Prince Charles was a vital voice in this story, possible only because Keenan pulled off the impossible while working with the *Herald*. Hats off to you, Keenan.

Julie Ford, our publisher's attorney, wrote many a clever turn-of-phrase in these pages (not bad for a lawyer!) and guided our reporting to exactly where it needed to go.

Owen Churchill, Meng Jing, Daniel Ren, and the team at the *South China Morning Post* partnered with *Herald* reporters to write the most complete profile to date of Yujing Zhang and her ill-fated trip to Mar-a-Lago.

Jiaying Li and the other students in Joan Chrissos's journalism classes at the University of Miami helped us with our initial reporting and translation. (We really hope Jiaying got an A+.)

The *Palm Beach Post* and *Palm Beach Daily News* have relentlessly covered day-to-day happenings at the club. In almost every case they have provided the first draft of history. No other publications are cited more in this book. Support local news.

ProPublica, Public Citizen, Citizens for Responsibility and Ethics in Washington, and Property of the People fought tirelessly for the public's right to information and the release of records, many of which are cited in this project.

South Florida Republicans welcomed us into their fundraisers and rallies. They trusted us with nuance. We strive every day to live up to that mandate.

April Hines at the University of Florida unearthed records on Mar-a-Lago from across the country.

Yemile Bucay's reporting at Columbia University laid the foundation for this book.

Benjamin Feibleman reported with us in Palm Beach. His photography inspired some of the more colorful writing in this book. (We haven't totally forgiven him for dropping Sarah's car keys down a sewage grate.)

Joe Richard transcribed audio of crucial interviews when the world looked bleak and time was running short.

Martín González Gómez, Jeremy Bowers, and Jeremy Merrill helped debug code and provided much-needed encouragement. (More code went into this book than you might expect!)

And the biggest MVPs of all—our families and friends who put up with the long hours, time away from home, and the general craziness brought on by writing a book. They choose to love us anyway, and we couldn't be more grateful. (Special thanks to Danielle and Marta, who put up with a second book project right after the first was completed.)

You all are our heroes.

ABOUT THE AUTHORS

Jose Iglesias/*Miami Herald*

L-R: Caitlin Ostroff, Nicholas Nehamas, Jay Weaver, and Sarah Blaskey

SARAH BLASKEY is an investigative reporter and data specialist at the *Miami Herald*. For their reporting on Trump tourism, she, Nehamas, and Ostroff were named finalists for the 2020 Livingston Award for Excellence in National Reporting.

NICHOLAS NEHAMAS is an investigative reporter for the *Miami Herald*. He was part of a team that won the 2017 Pulitzer Prize for Explanatory Reporting on the Panama Papers.

CAITLIN OSTROFF is a data reporter who used data analysis and computer coding to report investigative pieces for the *Miami Herald*. She is a graduate of the University of Florida and is now with the *Wall Street Journal*.

JAY WEAVER has covered courts, government, and politics for more than twenty-five years for the *Miami Herald*. A graduate of UC Berkeley, he was part of a team that won a Pulitzer Prize for Breaking News in 2001. He and Nicholas Nehamas were also 2019 Pulitzer Prize finalists for a series on international gold smuggling.

PublicAffairs is a publishing house founded in 1997. It is a tribute to the standards, values, and flair of three persons who have served as mentors to countless reporters, writers, editors, and book people of all kinds, including me.

I. F. STONE, proprietor of *I. F. Stone's Weekly*, combined a commitment to the First Amendment with entrepreneurial zeal and reporting skill and became one of the great independent journalists in American history. At the age of eighty, Izzy published *The Trial of Socrates*, which was a national bestseller. He wrote the book after he taught himself ancient Greek.

BENJAMIN C. BRADLEE was for nearly thirty years the charismatic editorial leader of *The Washington Post*. It was Ben who gave the *Post* the range and courage to pursue such historic issues as Watergate. He supported his reporters with a tenacity that made them fearless and it is no accident that so many became authors of influential, best-selling books.

ROBERT L. BERNSTEIN, the chief executive of Random House for more than a quarter century, guided one of the nation's premier publishing houses. Bob was personally responsible for many books of political dissent and argument that challenged tyranny around the globe. He is also the founder and longtime chair of Human Rights Watch, one of the most respected human rights organizations in the world.

．　　．　　．

For fifty years, the banner of Public Affairs Press was carried by its owner Morris B. Schnapper, who published Gandhi, Nasser, Toynbee, Truman, and about 1,500 other authors. In 1983, Schnapper was described by *The Washington Post* as "a redoubtable gadfly." His legacy will endure in the books to come.

Peter Osnos, *Founder*